UNIV. OF CALIFORNIA
WITHDRAWN
D1266932

JAPAN'S INFLUENCE ON AMERICAN NAVAL POWER 1897–1917

BY

OUTTEN JONES CLINARD

v. 36
1947
stack set 1

UNIVERSITY OF CALIFORNIA PUBLICATIONS IN HISTORY
Volume 36, pp. vi + 1–236

One of 30 copies printed on 100% rag paper

UNIVERSITY OF CALIFORNIA PRESS
BERKELEY AND LOS ANGELES
1947

Barry University Library
Miami, FL 33161

UNIVERSITY OF CALIFORNIA PUBLICATIONS IN HISTORY

VOLUME XXXVI
1947

EDITORS

R. J. Kerner

G. H. Guttridge

J. D. Hicks

One of 30 copies printed on 100% rag paper

JAPAN'S INFLUENCE ON AMERICAN NAVAL POWER 1897–1917

BY

OUTTEN JONES CLINARD

UNIVERSITY OF CALIFORNIA PRESS
BERKELEY AND LOS ANGELES
1947

University of California Publications in History
Editors (Berkeley): R. J. Kerner, G. H. Guttridge, J. D. Hicks

Volume 36, pp. vi + 1–236

Submitted by editors April 17, 1946

Issued December 5, 1947

Price: cloth, $3.75; paper, $3.00

University of California Press
Berkeley and Los Angeles
California

Cambridge University Press
London, England

PRINTED IN THE UNITED STATES OF AMERICA

D6
C3
v.36

PREFACE

THE GENERAL BOARD of the Navy Department, under date of October 17, 1903, after mature consideration, recommended to the Secretary of the Navy, William H. Moody, that the United States should have a fleet "equal or superior to that of any probable enemy"; and the Board estimated that this would require forty-eight battleships by 1920. From 1903 until 1915, this was the only naval policy in the national administration; yet it was never the naval policy of the United States, only of the General Board. What, then, was the naval policy of the United States? For all practical purposes she had none, and could have none until the policy-making authority, the executive and the Congress with the support of the electorate, should choose to formulate one. The General Board, or even the Navy Department itself, cannot determine naval policy because that function is a coöperative process in our government, requiring far wider sources of information than are available to any single executive agency as well as greater authority than is possessed by any one branch of the government.

A critic even went so far as to suggest that the General Board's recommendation of forty-eight battleships was based on nothing more substantial than a desire to have one battleship for each of the forty-eight states of the Union. Such a suggestion, although doing little justice to the Navy Department, does indicate that the formulation of policies for a great nation involves more than might appear at first glance. For naval policy, the problem is one of great complexity. Since no nation maintains a costly navy as a matter of choice, the problem resolves itself in the first place into a searching analysis of the national strategy in order to determine why the nation finds it necessary to assume the financial burden of a naval establishment. With the rapid expansion of American interests in the Pacific from 1897 to 1914, and with the rounding out of the national strategy of the United States between 1914 and 1917, as a result of the lessons of the World War, it finally became possible to develop a logical and consistent naval policy in the Pacific. Therefore, to analyze the national strategy of the United States in the area of the Pacific Ocean, especially as it influenced naval policy, and to trace the development of American naval policy under that influence will be the twofold problem with which this work will be concerned.

M652743

Most recent writers on the subject of American naval policy seem to be fascinated by such subjects as the number, tonnage, and speed of the ships of the various categories, the number and caliber of the guns of the fleet, the weight of the broadside which the fleet, or any part of it, can fire at any one time, and a host of other similarly technical questions. Although these matters may be of considerable interest to certain groups, especially to naval engineers who are really competent to consider such subjects, they yield little insight into those fundamental factors which ultimately determine the naval policy to be pursued by the nation. In short, the type of navy to be maintained is largely a matter for determination by the technical experts of the navy itself;[1] and this can be determined only after the wider and more basic problem of the need for a navy has been solved. The determination of the latter problem is vested by the Constitution in the policy-making body, the Congress of the United States, which can determine the naval needs of the nation in the light of those other great policies over which it exercises control and which together make up the national strategy. It is this more basic problem, therefore, which provides the central theme of this study; and it is hoped that the completed work will be devoid neither of value nor interest.

It is a pleasure to acknowledge with thanks the aid received in the writing of this study. The late Professor Eugene I. McCormac, under whose direction this research and writing was originally conducted, was most kind and patient. For his genuine interest and helpful suggestions, I am deeply grateful. Thanks are due to Professor Robert J. Kerner for suggesting the general subject of this work and for his continued interest in its progress. I wish also to express my gratitude to the Native Sons of the Golden West for their generosity in providing, through the department of history of the University of California, the funds which made possible a full year of uninterrupted research and study.

OUTTEN JONES CLINARD

Berkeley, California

[1] A naval spokesman puts it this way: "Granting all that can be said as to the impropriety of naval officers attempting to dictate the naval policy of the country—an impropriety which no American naval officer will question—they nevertheless have an obviously important function in the formulation of such policies. Their professional knowledge and advice must necessarily be utilized by statesmen if the vital interests of the country are to be safeguarded at the conference table." Dudley W. Knox, Captain, U.S.N., "The London Treaty and American Naval Policy," *United States Naval Institute Proceedings,* LVII (August, 1931), 1087.

CONTENTS

CHAPTER I

IMPERIAL AMERICA

. . . So far from being a protection, as it formerly was, the geographical distribution of the Empire has become in the last twenty years a steadily increasing source of danger. It multiplies enormously not only the occasions which give rise to wars, but also the probability of those wars being waged against us not by single Powers, but by coalitions. We cannot stand in everybody's way without expecting to be jostled. We cannot in an age of fierce land-hunger hold up for our own use territory enough for half a dozen mighty empires, and think we can always avert hostility by amiable intentions, or isolate our opponents by skilful diplomacy.—FIELD MARSHAL EARL ROBERTS.

ON JULY 17, 1916, Senator John W. Weeks of Massachusetts rose in the Senate and asserted that the "question of what is an adequate Navy for us is not one to be determined by our naval experts; it is one for the administration and Congress to outline. Many important international and far-reaching matters have a bearing on the course to be taken."[1] The occasion was the debate on the naval construction bill of 1916, involving a great expansion of the fleet. The question was whether or not the existing world situation justified such an expenditure of public funds, and Congress was about to accept the long-standing views of the Navy Department that the ships should be built.

Three years before, the Navy's General Board had pointed the way to a solution of the problem of what constituted an adequate navy for the United States. Stating that it did not believe that the nation stood "ready to abandon or modify any of its well-established national policies," the Board affirmed "its position that the naval policy of the country should be to possess a fleet powerful enough to prevent or answer any challenge to these policies." The "absolute strength necessary to accomplish this is a question that depends upon the national policies of prospective challengers and the force they can bring against us . . ."[2] Thus, the identity of the "prospective challengers" had to be revealed before a consistent naval policy could be formulated. The expansion of American inter-

[1] *Congressional Record,* LIII, July 17, 1916, p. 11180. Cited hereafter as *Cong. Rec.*

[2] Report of the General Board, in *Annual Reports of the Navy Department,* 1913, pp. 30, 31.

ests and activities in the Pacific area had made the appearance of a challenger inevitable. Therefore, the years from 1897 to 1917 were decisive in American history; for during this period, the entire national strategy of the United States in the Pacific was given a new unity and a new direction by the emergence of the "probable enemy" of the future. That "enemy" was Japan.

Even before 1897, the interests of the United States and Japan had come into momentous conflict in Hawaii at a time when European powers were rapidly absorbing the Pacific islands. Confronted on the one hand by extensions of European territorial jurisdiction and on the other by demands of the Japanese for admission to Hawaii, the United States faced the choice either of annexing the islands herself or of seeing them pass under foreign domination. Out of this dilemma came an abrupt change not only in the policy of the United States Government, but also in the attitude of the American people toward the acquisition of overseas territory. General conditions in the world had made such a change in viewpoint possible.

With the rise of industralism in the nineteenth century appeared a new type of colonialism, bearing little resemblance to the old mercantilist attitude toward settlement and development of vacant lands. The new imperialism manifested itself as a struggle for control of markets and of industrial raw materials. In some parts of the world, therefore, expansion meant the outright annexation of territories already more or less thickly populated by "backward" peoples, as in the partitioning of Africa and the absorption of the Pacific islands. In other parts, as in the Middle East and the Far East, where the populations by comparison were well advanced, the new imperialism appeared as a contest for spheres of exclusive influence, in which the dominant power would possess a virtual trade monopoly. Of the four principal reasons advanced to explain these expansions of Europe—economic, strategic, moral (the "white man's burden"), and nationalistic (*der Volksgeist*)—the economic cause has been most prominent.

The American position on the acquisition of outlying territories has been dictated with one notable exception—the Philippines—largely by consideration for the defense of the continental territory. The United States based her actions upon the well-recognized right of self-protection, described by Elihu Root as "the right of every sovereign state to protect itself by preventing a condition of affairs in which it will be too late to protect itself."[3] In insisting upon this fundamental right for herself, the United States has, throughout her existence, carefully guarded against the acquisition by any of the great powers of territories which might be used as bases of hostile action against the North American Continent.

Prompt and vigorous has been the action of the United States Government whenever such acquisitions seemed imminent. A striking demonstration was an incident in 1912, when an American group attempted to sell a large tract of land on Magdalena Bay to a Japanese syndicate. On the west coast of Lower California commanding the route from the Panama Canal to the western coast of the United States, this bay in the hands of a strong foreign power would constitute a direct threat to national security. The Senate, immediately alert to the threat, declared in the Lodge Resolution of August 2, 1912, that the United States would view with "grave concern" the possession of such harbors by any organization or group subject to the control of any foreign government.[4] In urging the adoption of the resolution, Senator Henry Cabot Lodge of Massachusetts said:

> ... this resolution rests on a generally accepted principle of the law of nations, older than the Monroe doctrine. It rests on the principle that every nation has a right to protect its own safety, and that if it feels that the possession by a foreign power, for military or naval purposes, of any given harbor or place is prejudicial to its safety, it is its duty as well as its right to interfere.[5]

[3] "The Real Monroe Doctrine," *The American Journal of International Law,* VIII (July, 1914), 432.

[4] *Cong. Rec.,* XLVIII, August 2, 1912, p. 10045. The fact should be noted that the Secretary of State, Philander C. Knox, refused to approve the transfer of the lands at Magdalena Bay, although the request for approval was presented by the American owners in several separate proposals. See *Senate Documents* (Serial 6177), 62d Cong., 2d sess., No. 694, May 23, 1912.

[5] *Cong. Rec.,* XLVIII, August 2, 1912, p. 10045. Referring to the resolution, Rear Admiral Stephen B. Luce wrote: "This is a notice, I presume, to Germany to keep out of the Danish West Indies, rather than to Japan to keep out of Magdalena Bay." See Rear Admiral Albert Gleaves, *Life and Letters of Rear Admiral Stephen B. Luce, U. S. Navy: Founder of the Naval War College* (New York: Putnam's, 1925), p. 308. (Luce to Lodge, August 5, 1912.) Senator Lodge replied: "The immediate cause of the resolution was Magdalena Bay, the attempt of the Japanese, through private individuals and the medium of corporations or syndicates, to get control of it. However, I had St. Thomas in mind also, but I thought it not wise to bring it forward as it was not necessary to do so.... you may have noticed that the German press snarled about the resolution and evidently disliked it while the London *Times* gave it cordial approval." See *ibid.,* pp. 308, 309. (Lodge to Luce, August 7, 1912.) See also the statement of Elihu Root of June 13, 1908, when, as Secretary of State, he in-

It has not always been possible to prevent the acquisition by foreign nations of strategically important territories merely by refusing to approve a transfer or by adopting resolutions. In some instances, the United States Government has been compelled to take substantive action. Thus, the United States has been forced into acquiring possessions not contiguous to her continental territories in order to prevent more aggressive nations from gaining possession of them.

Until the last decade of the nineteenth century, there seemed little likelihood that public opinion in the United States would countenance overseas expansion. But the speeding up of ocean transportation and the rapid development of American industries were working a change in American sentiment. Moreover, the impending breakup of the Spanish island empire as a result of Spain's defeat by the United States helped to create a situation in which the United States was constrained to assume theretofore unwanted responsibilities.[6] The consummation of these events finally came in the extension of United States territorial sovereignty across the Pacific to the very doors of Asia, inevitably involving the nation in foreign controversies.

Discerning Americans had long predicted the future importance of the Pacific area to the United States and to the rest of the world. As early as 1868, when Congress was debating the appropriation to pay for Alaska, Representative Nathaniel P. Banks of Massachusetts declared confidently that the Pacific Ocean would "be the theater of the triumphs of civilization in the future." He asserted that since the Alaskan Peninsula, with the Aleutian Islands, was "the key of this ocean . . . we have in our grasp the control of the Pacific ocean, and may make this great theater of action for the future whatever we may choose it shall be."[7] Even as he spoke,

---

formed the government of Ecuador that the sale of the Galapagos Islands to Germany, or to any other European power, "would give that country a strategic position from which it could dominate all the countries on the north-west coast of South America . . . and that . . . the United States would not permit the Islands to be occupied by any other than an American country." Quoted in Philip C. Jessup, *Elihu Root* (New York: Dodd Mead, 1938), I, 562, 563.

[6] James M. Callahan, *An Introduction to American Expansion Policy,* West Virginia University Studies in American History, Series I (Morgantown, W. Va.: 1908), p. 34. Professor Callahan asserted that American public opinion grew "in favor of possessing distant islands for the protection and encouragement of American interests in the Pacific and the Far East—as well as at home."

[7] *Congressional Globe,* 40th Cong., 2d sess., June 30, 1868, Appendix, p. 388.

changes were in the making which were to focus the earnest attention of the United States upon the Pacific area.

The tremendous industrial expansion of the nation was a potent factor in the evolution of policies in the Pacific not only for the United States, but for Europe's industrial nations as well. In the decade from 1889 to 1898, American industry and agriculture increased production on such a scale that the unfavorable balance of foreign trade in 1889 amounting to $2,730,277 was converted into an apparent balance in favor of the United States of $615,432,676 in the fiscal year 1897–1898. The nation's exports in the latter year reached the then staggering sum of $1,231,482,333, more than double the imports of that year.[8] Of these exports, metals and metal manufactures showed the greatest increase.

Portentous, indeed, was this reversal of America's trade situation. It involved the breaking of Great Britain's virtual monopoly as the leading producer of pig iron. By producing 34.1 per cent of the total output in 1890, the United States for the first time assumed the lead. The following table demonstrates graphically how the American iron and steel industry rose to world leadership:[9]

PRODUCTION OF PIG IRON, STEEL, AND STEEL RAILS, UNITED STATES AND GREAT BRITAIN, 1867–1899
(in long tons)

Year	Pig iron		Steel		Steel rails	
	Gr. Brit.	U. S.	Gr. Brit.	U. S.	Gr. Brit.	U. S.
1867	4,761,023	1,305,023	....	19,643	....	2,277
1870	5,963,515	1,665,179	....	68,750	....	30,357
1880	7,749,233	3,835,191	1,375,382	1,247,335	732,910	852,196
1890	7,904,214	9,202,703	3,679,043	4,277,071	1,019,606	1,867,837
1899	9,421,435	13,620,703	4,955,325	10,639,857	838,148	2,270,585

Thus, the United States became the world's greatest producer of iron and steel. At the same time, she became the greatest purveyor of heavy railroad equipment; for the rise in steel production coincided with the great era of railroad building, especially in the

[8] Bureau of Statistics, *Monthly Summary of Foreign Commerce of the United States,* 1900–1901 (July, 1900), 150.

[9] Chart compiled from the annual publication of the United States Geological Survey, *Mineral Resources of the United States.* Complete figures for Great Britain were not available. Steel rails were first produced in the United States in 1867.

United States, Canada, Siberia, and Manchuria. The demand for American steel rails and other railroad materials kept pace with the increases in steel production. More than this, it turned the attention of American industry and finance more and more toward the Pacific area, where the imperialistic nations were already contending for exclusive control.

With the expansion of the steel industry arose a demand for adequate supplies of the principal strategic metals: manganese, tungsten, antimony, tin, nickel, and chromium. These metals, because of their peculiar properties and their highly specialized uses, had assumed an importance out of all proportion to the amount of each consumed annually; and the United States was forced to look beyond her borders for an ever greater percentage of her normal requirements of each. In 1889, the United States had produced about 85 per cent of the manganese she consumed; in 1900, but 5 per cent.[10] Examples of such deficiencies could be multiplied. Significant, too, was the fact that supplies of these metals were found mainly in and about the Pacific area—Russia, Asiatic Turkey, India, Malaya, China, the East Indies, and the Pacific islands.

Even recognized deficiencies in these vital metals, however, could not diminish the enthusiasm with which American industry viewed the future. So pronounced was the optimism of industrialists in the United States that a representative publication of the iron and steel trade commented:

> The United States is now entering upon the commercial career long ago seen to be its manifest destiny. . . . No other nation on earth is so well situated to become the future workshop of the world. Nowhere else is food so abundant and cheap, with manufactures so well established and the finest raw materials so plentiful and accessible. In its ability to sustain itself the United States is unique among nations. Its independence, politically and commercially, may well excite the envy of other powers. They cannot, however, stay its progress.[11]

Despite such outbursts of optimism, the elements were already present which were to destroy the illusion of independence from the rest of the world. The other powers, excited more by fear of American competition than by envy, were even then taking steps to check the expansion of American commercial activity. In short,

[10] United States Geological Survey, *Mineral Resources of the United States, 1900*, p. 126.

[11] "The United States the Rising Nation" (editorial), *The Iron Age*, LX (August 19, 1897), 15.

the very prosperity about which the industrialists boasted was to prove the chief factor in revealing how mistaken the idea of American economic independence was.

The great powers of Europe—Great Britain, Germany, France, and even Russia—were having industrial expansions of their own; and they had no traditions of isolation and no Monroe Doctrine to hamper them in their search for foreign markets. Quite natural, then, was the convergence of their interest upon the area of the Pacific and Indian Oceans.[12] The two decades between 1880 and 1900 were marked by the rapid extension of the territorial sovereignty of the several European powers over the African Continent and the unappropriated Pacific islands. The British, reaching toward the North Pacific, completed the Canadian Pacific Railway in 1885, and thereby secured a means of direct communication across the North American Continent on their own territory. The Russians likewise were soon to look out upon the Pacific through a direct rail connection from St. Petersburg and Moscow to Vladivostok. Begun in 1891, the Trans-Siberian Railway was completed in 1902. The French had also undertaken a project to secure direct transportation facilities to the Pacific area—the Panama Canal, for the construction of which a French company had been organized in 1879. Work on the canal, which began in 1883, was destined to be completed by the United States. Thus, the prophecy of Nathaniel P. Banks in 1868 that the Pacific Ocean "will be the theater of the triumphs of civilization in the future" seemed about to be fulfilled.

In these circumstances, the outbreak of the Spanish-American War crystallized the trend toward commercial imperialism in the United States. The destruction of the Spanish fleet wherever it could be found became the immediate objective of the United States Navy. Since no warship could span the Pacific without recoaling, coaling stations and a base of operations against Spanish forces in the Far East became urgent necessities. Commodore George Dewey's victory over a Spanish squadron on May 1, 1898, provided an operating base at Manila; but a coaling station in mid-Pacific still had to be obtained. All eyes then turned to Hawaii as the only logical solution of the problem.

[12] This is pointed out by Commodore George W. Melville, Chief Engineer, United States Navy. See *Sen. Docs.* (Ser. 3600), 55th Cong., 2d sess., No. 188, March 14, 1898.

American interest in the Hawaiian Islands as a strategic point antedated the Civil War. Through depredations on American commerce by the Confederate cruiser *Shenandoah* during that war, the value of the islands was clearly demonstrated.[13] But despite the earnest recommendations of an Army investigating board in 1873 that a naval base be established at Pearl Harbor,[14] nothing was done. The American people were not yet convinced of the need for such an extension of the naval frontier. By 1875, however, in signing a commercial reciprocity treaty with Hawaii, the United States Government did take the precaution of exacting a pledge from King Kalakaua that he would "not lease or otherwise dispose of or create any lien upon any port, harbor, or other territory in his dominions, or grant any special privilege or rights of use therein to any other power, state, or government..."

Involved in the treaty was merely a recognition of American interests in the islands. But the activities of the European powers in the Pacific were to transform that recognition into a concession of specific rights to the United States when the treaty came up for renewal in 1884. Then alive to the importance of the Pacific area, the Senate held up the treaty for three years—it was finally approved in 1887—until the United States was granted exclusive control over Pearl Harbor, including the privilege of establishing coaling and repair facilities for the United States Navy. The United States thereby secured her interest in Pearl Harbor for the seven-year term of the treaty; but obviously this security would continue only so long as Hawaii remained independent.

A combination of events soon produced a crisis in Hawaiian affairs. First came the McKinley Tariff of 1890, which deprived the Hawaiian sugar growers of their position of equality with domestic growers in the American market. Then the Republicans, who were known to favor annexation of Hawaii, lost the election of 1892 to the Democrats under Grover Cleveland, whose views were not definitely known. When Queen Liliuokalani chose this occasion to proclaim a new and illegal constitution for Hawaii, the sugar planters

[13] For an account of this and other Confederate naval activities in the Pacific during the Civil War, see Brainerd Dyer, "Confederate Naval and Privateering Activities in the Pacific," *The Pacific Historical Review,* III (December, 1934), 433–443.

[14] The Schofield-Alexander Report, May 8, 1873. See *Senate Executive Documents* (Ser. 3062), 52d Cong., 2d sess., No. 77, February 17, 1893, pp. 151–154 *passim.*

speedily overthrew the monarchy and sought annexation to the United States.[15]

A treaty of annexation was negotiated in 1893 and submitted to the Senate by President Benjamin Harrison shortly before he left office. But this treaty was not approved before the Congress expired because Democratic Senators wished to await the action of the incoming administration. Shortly after his inauguration, President Cleveland withdrew the treaty from the Senate, his chief public objection being the circumstances in which it had been negotiated. He also asserted significantly that added "importance attached to this particular treaty on annexation because it contemplated a departure from unbroken American tradition in providing for the addition to our territory of islands of the sea more than 2,000 miles removed from our nearest coast."[16] After this, there was little for the annexationists to do but await a Republican return to power, which came in 1897.

By 1897, the Hawaiian Government[17] had become involved in serious difficulty with Japan over the immigration problem. In order to get a steady labor supply for the sugar planters, Hawaii had entered into an agreement with the Japanese Government in 1886, stipulating that the Japanese Immigration Company was to send over Japanese laborers when authorized to do so by the Hawaiian Government. The influx increased year by year, and the Japanese began to demand for these immigrant laborers the same rights as were possessed by native Hawaiians. The demands were based on the Japanese-Hawaiian commercial treaty of 1871, in which the citizens of either country had been granted reciprocal rights to enter, acquire property, and carry on trade in the other country on the same terms granted to citizens of the most-favored nation.

In order to make the most of this provision, the Japanese Government seized upon a phrase in the Spanish-Hawaiian commercial

[15] For a detailed account of these events and of the part played by John L. Stevens, the American Minister in Honolulu, see Julius W. Pratt, *Expansionists of 1898: The Acquisition of Hawaii and the Spanish Islands* (Baltimore: Johns Hopkins Press, 1936), chaps. ii–iv.

[16] In a special message to Congress, December 18, 1893. See James D. Richardson, ed., *A Compilation of the Messages and Papers of the Presidents, 1789–1917* (New York: 1917), XIII, 5893. Cited hereafter as *Messages and Papers*.

[17] Hawaii was then a republic under a constitution proclaimed on July 4, 1894.

treaty of 1863, which provided that Spanish traders should "enjoy the same rights and privileges which are granted to natives." The fact that this phrase referred only to commercial rights and that the Spanish had never used it to claim political rights, did not deter the Japanese. They demanded for their nationals, traders and laborers alike, all the rights enjoyed by native Hawaiians, including the right to vote.

Moreover, they shipped in laborers far in excess of the number authorized by the Hawaiian Government until the islands appeared to be in danger of being dominated by the Japanese. When the Hawaiian Government sought to avert the threat by restricting immigration to those Japanese holding valid permits under the treaty of 1886, Japan retaliated by sending a warship to the islands and demanding unrestricted admission of her subjects and an end to the practice of requiring permits.[18] These demands, of course, could not be granted if Hawaii hoped to maintain her independent existence; in fact, annexation to the United States seemed to be the only solution for the tiny republic. "It is the white race against the yellow . . ." commented the the Honolulu *Star*. "Nothing but annexation can save the islands."[19]

This, then, was the situation when the Republican party returned to power under William McKinley on March 4, 1897. That the United States Government was fully informed of the Japanese threat to Hawaii is evident from the remarks of Theodore Roosevelt, Assistant Secretary of the Navy in the new administration and an advocate of naval preparedness.

> If I had my way, we would annex those islands to-morrow. If that is impossible, I would establish a protectorate. . . . I have been getting matters in shape on the Pacific Coast just as fast as I have been allowed. My own belief is that we should act instantly before the two new Japanese warships leave England. I would . . . *hoist our flag over the islands leaving all details for after action.* . . . I believe we should build the Nicaraguan Canal at once, and . . . should build a dozen new battleships, half of them on the Pacific Coast. . . . I am fully alive to the danger from Japan.[20]

The State Department acted promptly to check the threatened

[18] *Cong. Rec.*, XXXI, June 11, 1898, pp. 5773, 5774.

[19] Quoted in *The Literary Digest*, XIV (April 24, 1897), 771.

[20] Quoted in Henry F. Pringle, *Theodore Roosevelt: A Biography* (New York: Harcourt, Brace, 1931), p. 171. (Roosevelt to Captain Alfred T. Mahan, May 3, 1897.) Italics by Pringle.

danger by negotiating a treaty of annexation with Hawaii; and it was signed and submitted to the Senate on June 16, 1897.[21]

The ever-watchful Japanese were aware of the negotiations between the United States and Hawaii, and they had no intention of yielding their gains in the islands without protest. Consequently, Toru Hoshi, Japanese Minister in Washington, on the day before the treaty was actually signed, inquired of the State Department what provisions had been made in the proposed treaty to protect the interests of Japanese subjects in Hawaii. He declared that Japan could not "view without concern the prospect of a sudden and complete change in the status of Hawaii whereby the rights of Japan and of Japanese subjects may be imperilled."[22] He was informed by Secretary of State John Sherman on the day the treaty was signed that, although the United States assumed none of the obligations of treaties or agreements between Hawaii and other governments, there was nothing in the treaty derogatory to the legitimate rights of Japan.[23]

After the signing of the treaty and its submission to the Senate, however, the Japanese Government entered a formal protest against the annexation of Hawaii. This protest of June 19, 1897, was based on three principal grounds:

> First. The maintenance of the status quo of Hawaii is essential to the good understanding of the Powers which have interests in the Pacific.
>
> Second. The annexation of Hawaii would tend to endanger the residential, commercial and industrial rights of Japanese subjects in Hawaii secured to them by Treaty and by the constitution and laws of that country.
>
> Third. Such annexation might lead to the postponement by Hawaii of the settlement of claims and liabilities already existing in favor of Japan under treaty stipulations.[24]

Secretary Sherman, in his reply, reminded Hoshi that Japan had long been aware of the special interest which the United States had manifested in Hawaii's destiny. And he recalled to the Japa-

---

[21] See President McKinley's annual message to Congress, December 6, 1897, in *Messages and Papers*, XIV, 6263. See also W. Stull Holt, *Treaties Defeated by the Senate: A Study of the Struggle between President and Senate over the Conduct of Foreign Relations* (Baltimore: Johns Hopkins Press, 1933), pp. 163, 164.

[22] Quoted in Thomas A. Bailey, "Japan's Protest against the Annexation of Hawaii," *The Journal of Modern History*, III (March, 1931), 51. (Hoshi to Sherman, June 15, 1897.)

[23] *Ibid.* (Sherman to Hoshi, June 16, 1897.)

[24] *Ibid.*, p. 52. (Hoshi to Sherman, June 19, 1897.)

nese Minister that no protest of any kind had been received in 1893 when a similar treaty was under consideration. Finally, he asserted that the legitimate interests of Japan and of Japanese subjects in Hawaii would, as a matter of course, be fully respected.[25]

When the Japanese Government continued to protest despite the repeated assurances of the State Department, the administration began to fear that, added to a serious situation in Cuba, it might have to face a conflict in the Pacific. President McKinley himself, striving to avoid a quarrel with Spain or Japan, became somewhat pessimistic about the outcome.[26] Fully credited was a belief that should the United States become involved with Spain over Cuba, Japan would seize the opportunity to enforce her demands upon the Hawaiian Government.[27]

On July 10, 1897, Japan boldly reasserted her opposition to the annexation of Hawaii. The time for action had come. As a first step on the same day, the following instructions were sent to the American Minister in Honolulu:

> Watch situation carefully. If Japanese should openly resort to force, such as military occupation or seizure of public property, you will confer with local authorities and Admiral, land suitable force, and announce provisional assumption of protectorate by United States over Hawaii pending consummation of annexation treaty, declaring at same time that all rights established in favor of third parties will be respected. This contingency is, however, not expected and you will be exceedingly cautious to do nothing that might tend to precipitate it, nor act except in face of overt act of hostility by Japan.[28]

Thus, the United States prepared to resist Japanese aggression in Hawaii even to the use of armed force if necessary.

Further steps followed, disclosing the sterner character of the American attitude. Feeling that the honor of the nation was being questioned by the repeated Japanese protests, Secretary Sherman,

---

[25] John Bassett Moore, *A Digest of International Law as Embodied ... Especially in Documents ... Issued by Presidents and Secretaries of State of the United States* (Washington: 1906), V, 348, 349. (Sherman to Hoshi, June 25, 1897.) See also *ibid.*, I, 504, 505; and Bailey, *loc. cit.*, p. 52.

[26] Henry Cabot Lodge, ed., *Selections from the Correspondence of Theodore Roosevelt and Henry Cabot Lodge, 1884–1918* (New York: Scribner's, 1925), I, 277. (Roosevelt to Lodge, September 15, 1897.)

[27] *Ibid.*, pp. 278, 279. (Roosevelt to Lodge, September 21, 1897.) Roosevelt had just urged the President to take prompt precautionary measures at the first sign of trouble with Spain in order to meet the Spanish threat and to prevent Japanese participation against the United States.

[28] Quoted in Bailey, *loc. cit.*, p. 50. (Telegram, Sherman to H. M. Sewall, July 10, 1897.)

in a note to Hoshi on August 14, 1897, flatly rejected the protest of July 10 in language so blunt as to leave no doubt of the American attitude. Sherman pointed out that most of the Japanese interest in Hawaii had been built up under the Hawaiian Republic, a government which had announced from the outset its intention to seek annexation to the United States and had made provision for it in its constitution. The Japanese Government had thereafter "permitted and encouraged the immigration of its subjects and the growth of its commerce under these conditions, and with a full knowledge of the policy of the United States" so that there could be "no well-founded cause of complaint if only the usual and legitimate results flow from the proposed annexation."[29] With this the Japanese Government had to be content, and its formal withdrawal of opposition to annexation followed in December.[30] But the attitude of the Japanese was not to be forgotten. The suspicion aroused in the mind of Theodore Roosevelt was to have an extremely important influence upon his subsequent policies as President of the United States.

Germany, too, had found the annexation of Hawaii objectionable. The nullification of all Hawaiian treaties as a consequence of annexation constituted in her view a threat to German interests. From this attitude came one of those political proposals so typical of the period. The Imperial Government sought to enlist the cooperation of Great Britain, the other great power most interested in Hawaii, in a scheme to secure counterbalancing gains for themselves. Suggested were two solutions, either of which would be acceptable to Germany. The first proposal contemplated the transfer of American claims in Samoa to Germany and Great Britain as compensation for American annexation of Hawaii. If this proposal were accepted by the United States, Germany and Great Britain would then enter an agreement whereby Germany would get all of Samoa, and Great Britain would receive the Tonga (Friendly) Islands as her share.

Should these measures prove unacceptable to the United States, the German Government proposed the neutralization of the Hawaiian Islands under a joint control similar to that exercised in

[29] Moore, *op. cit.*, I, 505, 506. (Sherman to Hoshi, August 14, 1897.)

[30] For Secretary Sherman's response to Hoshi's note in which the withdrawal of opposition was announced, see *ibid.*, p. 507. (Sherman to Hoshi, January 8, 1898.)

Samoa, this in "recognition of the equivalence of German and English interests in Hawaii with those of the United States in Samoa."[31] Lord Salisbury, the British Prime Minister, gave the German Ambassador an inconclusive answer; and it soon became evident, through introduction of other matters into the discussion, that the British Government had no intention of interfering in American-Hawaiian affairs.[32] So Germany's scheme failed, and she was compelled to await another opportunity to seek the compensation she so strongly desired.

In the United States, meanwhile, Congress had adjourned on July 24, 1897, without Senate action on the annexation treaty. The Hawaiian Government, however, went ahead and ratified the treaty on September 10, 1897. President McKinley, in his annual message to Congress on the following December 6, urged the Senate to take similar action.[33] But this recommendation produced no response until events made action necessary. The battleship *Maine,* which had arrived in Havana Harbor on January 25, 1898, to protect American lives and property during the Cuban revolt then in progress, was destroyed on the night of February 15 by what the United States Government maintained was an external explosion. War with Spain loomed closer.

Confronted with this ominous situation, the Senate initiated a move on March 16 to annex the Hawaiian Islands by joint resolution. The report on the resolution by the Committee on Foreign Relations reviewed the steps by which the relations of the United States and Hawaii had become progressively more intimate until,

---

[31] These instructions were sent to Count Paul von Hatzfeldt, German Ambassador in London, by the Imperial Chancellor, Prince Chlodwig von Hohenlohe, July 18, 1897. See *Die Grosse Politik der Europäischen Kabinette, 1871–1914: Sammlung der Diplomatischen Akten des Auswärtigen Amtes,* edited by Johannes Lepsius and others (Berlin: Deutsche Verlagsgesellschaft für Politik und Geschichte, 1922–1926), XIII, 28, 29. Cited hereafter as *Die Grosse Politik.*

[32] See the reports of Count Hatzfeldt in *ibid.*, pp. 29–45 *passim.* Such matters as British commercial and naval facilities in Samoa, the reaction of Australia to the cession of Britain's Samoan rights to Germany, and the possession of the Manua Islands and German New Guinea were among the new elements introduced by Lord Salisbury. Perhaps the most serious obstacle to Anglo-German coöperation, however, was the notice served by Great Britain on July 30, 1897, of the abrogation of the existing commercial treaty with Germany. When informed of this, the Kaiser exploded angrily: "Hätten wir eine starke, achtunggebietende Flotte gehabt, wäre Kündigung nicht erfolgt; als Antwort muss eine schleunige bedeutende Vermehrung unserer Neubauten ins Auge gefasst werden." See *ibid.*, p. 35. (William II to Prince Hohenlohe, August 1, 1897.)

[33] *Messages and Papers,* XIV, 6263, 6264.

in effect, Hawaii was independent in name only. So great, in fact, was American authority by treaty that the Hawaiian Government could not so much as grant a cable concession to Great Britain or send its own vessels into Pearl Harbor without the consent of the United States. American missionaries and other emigrants to the islands had depended upon the continuance of American predominance in making homes and investments in Hawaii. To these transplanted Americans, the government owed "all the friendly care that a father can owe to his sons who have with his consent left their home to seek their fortunes in other lands."[34]

The principal argument advanced in favor of annexation, of course, was the menace of Japanese infiltration. The committee pointed to the fact that Japan had "OPENLY PROTESTED against the annexation of Hawaii to the United States upon grounds that indicate an unjust suspicion of our national honor in our future dealing with her subjects in those islands."[35] Japan's protest had been withdrawn, but her demands on the Hawaiian Government had not been. Should the United States refuse to annex the islands, the committee was convinced that Japan would renew her aggressive attitude toward Hawaii.

Appended to the report were a number of supporting documents, in one of which appeared this significant statement:

> *The present Hawaiian-Japanese controversy is the preliminary skirmish in the great coming struggle between the civilization and the awakening forces of the East and the civilization of the West.*
>
> The issue is whether, in that inevitable struggle, Asia or America shall have the vantage ground of the control of the naval "Key of the Pacific," the commercial "Cross-roads of the Pacific."[36]

Thus, although the impending struggle with Spain accounted in large measure for the introduction of the resolution, the situation in the Pacific was the committee's primary concern. And when war actually came to the Pacific, Congress was easily induced to adopt the resolution.

The United States declared war against Spain on April 25, 1898. Already prepared for hostilities through the foresight of Theodore Roosevelt, the United States Navy's Asiatic Squadron under the

[34] *Senate Reports* (Ser. 3622), 55th Cong., 2d sess., No. 681, March 16, 1898, p. 6.
[35] *Ibid.*, p. 8.
[36] *Ibid.*, p. 31.

command of Commodore George Dewey immediately moved upon the Spanish squadron at Manila, where, on May 1, Dewey won a complete victory. An expeditionary force to carry through the conquest of the Philippine Islands was indispensable, and Dewey requested that such a force be sent. Convoys of troopships, which were soon steaming across the Pacific, turned inevitably to the now important harbor of Honolulu to replenish their almost exhausted supplies of coal, water, and other necessities.

If Dewey had been defeated at Manila, the importance of Hawaii would not have been lessened. He would have been faced with the appalling prospect of retiring across the Pacific, probably in a crippled condition, because he would then have lacked even a harbor of refuge in Asiatic waters. Since none of his ships could have crossed the Pacific without recoaling, the utmost for which he could have hoped would have been to reach Honolulu in safety. Hawaii, therefore, assumed a position of tremendous strategic importance.

The Navy Department had prepared for the coming war by accumulating a large supply of coal at Honolulu, not in the American concession of Pearl Harbor, which was still undeveloped.[37] Military necessity had compelled the United States to violate the neutrality of the Hawaiian Republic by using one of her ports as a base of naval and transport supply. The Hawaiian Government, far from objecting, actually offered to assist the United States even to the extent of entering into a formal alliance against Spain.[38] But President McKinley declined the offer in the hope that Congress would end his responsibility for illegal use of the islands by annexing them.

Another joint resolution to accomplish this purpose had been introduced in the House on May 4, 1898, three days after Dewey's victory at Manila. Once again a committee of Congress reviewed

[37] As pointed out above, the United States had been granted the right in 1887 to establish a naval station and supply base in Pearl River Harbor. When war was declared in 1898, nothing had been done to remove the coral reef which blocked the entrance to the harbor or to improve the harbor itself. Thus, it became necessary for the navy to establish its coal dump in Honolulu. See *Sen. Docs.* (Ser. 3732), 55th Cong., 3d sess. No. 62, Part 2, January 13, 1899, p. 474. (Statement of Commander R. B. Bradford, Chief of the Bureau of Equipment, United States Navy, to the Peace Commission in Paris, October 14, 1898.)

[38] Thomas A. Bailey, "The United States and Hawaii during the Spanish-American War," *The American Historical Review*, XXXVI (April, 1931), 555. (Instructions from Henry E. Cooper, Hawaiian Minister of Foreign Affairs, to F. M. Hatch, Hawaiian Minister in Washington, May 10, 1898.)

the reasons for the annexation of the Hawaiian Islands, now more than ever imperative. The only group of islands in mid-Pacific with a landlocked harbor, Hawaii in the hands of the United States "would secure both our fleet and our coast," and at the same time deprive the enemy of all facilities for operations in the eastern Pacific.[39] Again a committee warned against the danger of losing this strategic position through Japanese infiltration, which threatened to continue if the United States failed to annex the islands promptly. Such a failure, the committee pointed out, would jeopardize not only the security, but the commercial interests of the United States as well. For, by 1898, some three thousand American citizens had come into possession of about three-fourths of all the landed property in Hawaii. Almost all of the islands' exports went to the United States, and three-fourths of their imports came from there.[40] The whole commercial life of the islands was based on their ties with the United States.

The chief argument, of course, and the most effective one used in favor of annexation at this time, was that of military necessity. The United States chose to conduct an offensive war in the Pacific, a war in which she expected the great European powers to remain neutral, whereas at the same time she failed herself to respect Hawaiian neutrality. Representative Robert R. Hitt of Illinois summed up the anomalous situation succinctly: "While we are demanding the observance of neutrality by other nations, we disregard it ourselves. We are compelled to it by military necessity. That is the fact. What is the honorable solution? Annex them and end it all."[41]

Even the stanchest opponents of annexation were ready to admit that the element of military necessity was the motivating force behind President McKinley's advocacy of the acquisition of Hawaii. Senator Benjamin R. Tillman of South Carolina, while roundly denouncing the sugar planters and their intrigues, affirmed his belief "in the honesty, the patriotism, the integrity, and the purity of William McKinley." He said, "I believe the President is honestly desirous of having the islands annexed solely to relieve him of the responsibility and criticism in connection with their use

[39] *House Reports* (Ser. 3721), 55th Cong., 2d sess., No. 1355, May 17, 1898, p. 2.

[40] *Ibid.*, pp. 4, 5.

[41] *Cong. Rec.*, XXXI, June 11, 1898, p. 5773.

for our Army and Navy."[42] Exigencies of the war had made the annexation of Hawaii inevitable.

Congressional decision for annexation came at last. The House passed the joint resolution on June 15, 1898, followed by the Senate on July 6. Formal transfer of sovereignty took place on August 12, the very day on which the Secretary of State, William R. Day, and the French Ambassador, Jules Cambon, acting for the Spanish Government, signed a preliminary peace protocol officially ending hostilities between the United States and Spain. On the following day, the Spanish garrison in Manila capitulated; and the United States Government was confronted with a new and far more serious problem—the problem of what to do with the Philippine Islands.

Unlike other territorial acquisitions of the United States, annexation of the Philippines could not be justified on grounds of the military defense of continental United States. But defense of America's expanding economic interests was becoming equally as important as territorial defense. And competent American observers had long recognized the future importance of the Far East as a market for American manufactured products. They were also convinced that the United States would have to contend with the European powers for access to those markets. Respecting Great Britain, there seemed little reason for concern, since American products had been admitted freely into British dominions with the result that the British Empire was absorbing about 60 per cent of the exports of American domestic merchandise.[43] Other European powers, however, sought exclusive markets for their own products so that when they gained political control of territory, they hindered trade therein with other nations or excluded it altogether.[44]

Americans had looked with growing apprehension upon the rapid absorption by European powers of all unappropriated islands in the Pacific "of possible value commercially or strategically." In fact, the United States had been urged to seize the opportunity to annex Hawaii "not in feeding the land hunger of

[42] *Ibid.*, June 30, 1898, p. 6530.

[43] John R. Procter, "Hawaii and the Changing Front of the World," *The Forum*, XXIV (September, 1897), 40. The actual figures for the fiscal year ending June 30, 1897, were: total exports of domestic merchandise, $1,032,007,603; total exports to the British Empire, $590,438,562. Bureau of Statistics, *The Foreign Commerce and Navigation of the United States*, 1896–1897, pp. 419, 420.

[44] Procter, *loc. cit.*, p. 40.

mere territorial aggrandisement, but in following a noble pathway of commercial expansion."[45] Senator Albert J. Beveridge of Indiana, a firm believer in the beneficent mission of the United States in the world, not only agreed that American commercial expansion was "noble," but he believed it was necessary as well. He said:

> American factories are making more than the American people can use; American soil is producing more than they can consume. Fate has written our policy for us; the trade of the world must and shall be ours. And we will get it as our mother [England] has told us how. We will establish trading-posts throughout the world as distributing-points for American products. We will cover the ocean with our merchant marine. We will build a navy to the measure of our greatness. Great colonies governing themselves, flying our flag and trading with us, will grow about our posts of trade. Our institutions will follow our flag on the wings of our commerce. And American law, American order, American civilization, and the American flag will plant themselves on shores hitherto bloody and benighted, but by those agencies of God henceforth to be made beautiful and bright.[46]

There were, of course, many advocates of an aggressive world policy for the United States who agreed heartily with Senator Beveridge; but the great mass of the American people, steeped in a tradition of isolation, looked upon Senator Beveridge and other expansionists as grasping imperialists or irresponsible visionaries.

Thus, when news of Dewey's victory at Manila reached the United States, its full significance could not at once be realized. The reaction of Secretary of State Day, when he was informed of Dewey's feat, demonstrates the advance of events over public opinion. "Unfortunately," he said, "there is nothing we can do but give those islands back to Spain."[47] This statement seemed to represent the general sentiment of most of the people, and the prospect of mere commercial advantage would have had little influence in changing their opinion.[48] Indeed, the commercial world itself did not realize immediately that a prize of inestimable value had fallen

[45] *Sen. Docs.* (Ser. 3600), 55th Cong., 2d sess., No. 188, March 14, 1898, p. 29. Views of Commodore Melville.

[46] In a speech at the Middlesex Club in Boston on April 27, 1898, two days after the declaration of war on Spain. See Claude G. Bowers, *Beveridge and the Progressive Era* (Boston: Houghton Mifflin, 1932), p. 69.

[47] In a conversation with Myron T. Herrick, in whose house Secretary Day was staying when the news reached him. See T. Bentley Mott, *Myron T. Herrick, Friend of France: An Autobiographical Biography* (New York: Doubleday, Doran, 1929), p. 325. (Myron T. Herrick, American Ambassador to France, to President Warren G. Harding, May 9, 1923.)

[48] *Ibid.*

to the United States. The authoritative trade journal, *The Commercial and Financial Chronicle* of New York, in an editorial on May 7, 1898, pointed out that the Philippines had proved to be "Spain's most vulnerable point," and warned that, were the United States in Spain's place, she would be no less vulnerable. The continental United States, the editor argued, was invulnerable; and he concluded that if "this war shall teach no other useful lesson to the United States, it will at least have pointed out unmistakably our existing source of strength and our conceivable future source of weakness."[49]

A week later, however, the same editor returned to the subject and, forgetting his previous concern over possible weakening of American military power, presented a logical statement of the three principal arguments later used to justify retention of the islands by the United States. These were: first, the political advantage to be gained by possession of territory in the Far East; second, the commercial advantages of a trading center and a colony rich in her own right; and third, and most effective of all, the moral obligation of the United States to protect the Filipinos after she destroyed Spanish authority in the islands. And the editor gloated:

> ... By a combination of diplomatic chances the United States has grasped this rich commercial prize at the very moment when every powerful European State has been reaching after such possessions and in the very waters where the struggle for colonial acquisition has been in progress.[50]

The "struggle for colonial acquisition" by the European powers had appeared in the Far East with its center in the Chinese Empire. Watchful of their own interests, the Germans had found both the excuse and the conditions for pursuing their aims in China. In 1895, Germany had joined with France and Russia to force Japanese return of the Liaotung Peninsula to China after Japan, victorious in the Sino-Japanese War, had obtained it in the Treaty of Shimonoseki.[51] Clearly, some reward for this act of intercession on

[49] "The Battle of Manila" (editorial), *The Commercial and Financial Chronicle,* LXVI (May 7, 1898), 878.

[50] "The United States and the Philippines" (editorial), *ibid.* (May 14, 1898), 922, 923.

[51] *Die Grosse Politik,* IX, 256–258. (Hohenlohe to William II, March 19, 1895.) See also *ibid.,* XIV:1, 5–7. (Marschall von Bieberstein, Foreign Secretary, to Vice-Admiral Friedrich von Hollmann, Minister of Marine, March 11, 1895); and the Journal of the Imperial Chancellor for September 11, 1895, in *Denkwürdigkeiten des Fürsten Chlodwig zu Hohenlohe-Schillingsfürst,* edited by Friedrich Curtius (Stuttgart and Leipzig: 1906), II, 520, 521.

behalf of China was expected. But not until November, 1897, when two German missionaries were murdered in Shantung Province, were the Germans to take steps to collect that reward by occupying Chinese territory. When China consented to a ninety-nine-year lease of Kiaochow Bay with its port of Tsingtao to Germany on March 6, 1898, the way was opened to the other powers. Russia demanded and received a twenty-five-year lease of the Liaotung Peninsula with the valuable ports of Talienwan (Dairen) and Port Arthur. In the following month, France claimed her share, receiving a ninety-nine-year lease on Kwangchow Bay. These three agreements also included valuable railway construction concessions. Great Britain, although not a member of the intervening group, proceeded to acquire from the Chinese Government a lease of the port of Weihaiwei on the northern coast of Shantung "for so long a period as Port Arthur shall remain in the occupation of Russia."[52]

The United States had looked upon these developments with some concern, but the impending war with Spain had prevented any action. Occupation of the Philippines thus came as an almost unbelievable stroke of good fortune. As *Iron Age* expressed it, suddenly "and without premeditation, we seem to have placed in our hands an opportunity to gain a footing at the gateway of Asiatic trade such as the strongest European powers have been able to acquire only by prolonged and costly effort."[53]

But interest in what the United States would do with the Philippines was not confined to the United States. *The Spectator* (London) observed that the chancelleries of Europe were "already twittering with excitement and putting out little feelers, and looking at Manila like children at a cake which they want badly but think it decorous not to ask for or see." Reasons were presented to

[52] The British Government had negotiated for an agreement with Russia that neither power would acquire territorial possessions on the Gulf of Pechili, but without success. See *Die Grosse Politik,* XIV:1, 161. (German Foreign Office Memorandum of an oral communication from Sir Frank Lascelles, British Ambassador in Berlin, April 4, 1898.) The Russian Government had anticipated that Great Britain would attempt to check Russian expansion southward through Manchuria; and Czar Nicholas II had foreseen the British reaction as early as 1895, when he said to Prince von Hohenlohe, German Imperial Chancellor, "Ja, die [the English] wollen immer alles für sich haben. Wo jemand etwas nimmt, wollen die Engländer sich gleich viel mehr nehmen." See *Denkwürdigkeiten des Fürsten Chlodwig zu Hohenlohe-Schillingsfürst,* II, 521. (Journal, St. Petersburg, September 11, 1895.)

[53] "The War and an Opportunity" (editorial), *The Iron Age,* LXI (June 23, 1898), 15.

show why the possession of the Philippines by any of the great powers except the United States would be considered undesirable. England already had too much territory. Possession of the islands by Germany would promote the already aggressive designs of that power upon China. Russian occupation would bring that nation too close to Australia; and France, the ally of Russia, would be just as great a threat to the British Empire. Finally, the deliverance of a Christian population into the hands of pagan Japan would be impossible. That the United States should keep the islands, therefore, was inevitable, "chiefly because they [the United States] are determined that China, which is their biggest natural foreign market, shall not be closed to their trade."[54]

In the international drama which ensued, the United States was to find both friends and opponents among the powers of Europe; but the leading roles were to be played by England and Germany. England, in a difficult diplomatic situation,[55] was unusually friendly toward the United States. This friendliness was manifested in many ways and on many occasions during the Spanish-American War. Colonial Secretary Joseph Chamberlain, in a celebrated speech at Birmingham, openly advocated an alliance with the United States: "And I even go so far as to say that, terrible as war may be, even war itself would be cheaply purchased if in a great and noble cause the Stars and Stripes and the Union Jack should wave together over an Anglo-Saxon alliance."[56] And in a more concrete way, Great Britain demonstrated her friendliness. After Dewey's victory in Manila Bay, Captain Edward Chichester, of the Royal Navy, was careful not only to observe American belligerent rights, but also to convince the German Vice-Admiral, Otto von Diederichs, that if the aggressive and insolent attitude of the

---

[54] This article from the *Spectator*, as quoted in the *Singapore Free Press*, June 7, 1898, was forwarded to the Secretary of State by the American Consul General in Singapore. See *Sen. Docs.* (Ser. 3732), 55th Cong., 3d sess., No. 62, Part 2, January 13, 1899, p. 348. (E. Spencer Pratt to Day, June 8, 1898.)

[55] For a good summary of the situation in which Great Britain found herself in 1898, see Sidney B. Fay, *The Origins of the World War* (2d ed.; New York: Macmillan, 1939), I, 128, 129.

[56] *The Times* (London), May 14, 1898, p. 12. See also Chamberlain's letter to Arthur James Balfour, then First Lord of the Treasury, in which the Colonial Secretary advocated seeking American support for Britain's policy in China. The British Government was attempting to force the Russians to open Port Arthur and Talienwan as treaty ports "to all on precisely similar conditions." Blanche E. C. Dugdale, *Arthur James Balfour: First Earl of Balfour* (London: Hutchinson, 1936), I, 252, 253. (Chamberlain to Balfour, February 3, 1898.)

latter led to conflict with Dewey, the British ships would be found on the side of the Americans.[57]

Germany, on the other hand, pursuing her policy of expansion in the Far East and the Pacific, looked jealously upon American success in the Philippines. At first, the German Government had been largely concerned with the protection of German interests in the islands. When the press of France and Russia showed a keen interest in the future disposition of the Philippines, Bernhard von Bülow, the German Foreign Secretary, suggested to the Kaiser that Germany might have to come to an agreement with Great Britain and the United States in order to protect German interests in the islands against the French and Russians.[58] As their hope for a kingdom in the Philippines under a German prince faded and their alternative plan—neutralization of the islands—was coldly received,[59] the German Government became more and more convinced that the war offered an ideal opportunity to extend German possessions in the Pacific. The German Ambassador in Washington, Theodor von Holleben, was accordingly notified that the Kaiser wished to take advantage of every occasion provided by the war to secure "maritime fulcra in East Asia." He was also instructed to report fully on public opinion in the United States on the question of whether all of the territory or only coaling stations would be kept. Desired, too, was information on whether or not prominent

---

[57] For the report of Captain Chichester, see *British Documents on the Origins of the War, 1898–1914,* edited by George P. Gooch and Harold W. V. Temperley (London: H. M. Stationery Office, 1926–1938), I, 105–107. Cited hereafter as *British Documents.* The account of the Manila incident by Admiral Dewey was published in 1913 in his *Autobiography of George Dewey: Admiral of the Navy* (New York: 1913), pp. 252–267, 277. For the German view, see the reply of Admiral Diederichs, "A Statement of Events in Manila, May–October, 1898," *Journal of the Royal United Service Institution,* LIX (November, 1914), 421–446. See also *Die Grosse Politik,* XV, 62–64, and note **. (Memorandum of Oswald von Richthofen, German Acting Foreign Secretary, July 25, 1898.)

[58] *Die Grosse Politik,* XV, 35, 36. (Bülow to William II, May 14, 1898.) Bülow suggested the agreement with England and the United States, or with England alone, because he thought it would offer greater security for Germany than would such an agreement with Russia and France against the naval powers; and the Kaiser agreed with him. For a detailed account of German-American relations during the Spanish-American War, based on the dispatches published in *Die Grosse Politik,* see Lester B. Shippee, "Germany and the Spanish-American War," *The American Historical Review,* XXX (July, 1925), 754–777.

[59] *Die Grosse Politik,* XV, 39, and note **. (Bülow to Hatzfeldt, May 18, 1898.) In this dispatch, the Foreign Secretary made it clear that Germany could not agree to the transfer of the Philippines, in whole or in part, to any foreign power without suitable compensation for Germany.

American politicians realized the advantages of diplomatic coöperation with Germany, which could be achieved "only on the basis of mutual considerations in questions such as coaling stations, maritime fulcra, and the like."[60]

Without waiting for a complete report from Washington, the Foreign Office expressed its views to the American Ambassador in Berlin, Andrew D. White, whose friendship for Germany had only recently been publicly avowed.[61] White was told that Germany wanted Samoa and the Caroline Islands, the former as compensation for American annexation of Hawaii and the latter to soften German resentment aroused when the powers handed the Congo over to Belgium in 1885. In addition, Germany wanted one or two bases in the Philippines and in the Sulu Archipelago. To White these proposals seemed "altogether fair," and he promised to urge them upon the State Department.[62] Similar approaches were made to John Hay, American Ambassador in London, with similar results; but Hatzfeldt doubted that Hay would "warmly" espouse German interests.[63] Hatzfeldt was right. Hay was convinced that Germany was trying to get something for nothing; but he informed President McKinley that the Germans were in no position to force the issue. The hostility of France and Russia on one side and of England on the other would obviate any real danger for the United States in politely ignoring the desires of the German Government.[64]

[60] *Ibid.*, pp. 44, 45. (Bülow to Holleben, July 1, 1898.)

[61] Upon the occasion of a celebration of America's Independence Day, July 4, 1898, at Leipzig, when he said: ". . . in this German policy of fairness and justice toward our country, I recognize the best guarantee for that legitimate territorial and commercial expansion which Germany so eagerly and rightly desires, and for the continuance and increase of the good will which is so important for both countries." See *Die Grosse Politik*, XV, 55, note. See also *Autobiography of Andrew Dickson White* (New York: 1904–1905), II, 168–170.

[62] *Die Grosse Politik*, XV, 53. (Richthofen to Hatzfeldt, July 10, 1898.) Germany's price a month earlier had been higher; for, in addition to concessions elsewhere, she had asked in the Pacific area for Portuguese Timor, the whole of the Sulu Archipelago, at least one of the Philippine Islands (Mindanao), the Caroline Islands, and Samoa. See *ibid.*, XIV:1, 261. (Bülow to Hatzfeldt, June 8, 1898.)

[63] *Ibid.*, XV, 61. (Hatzfeldt to the Foreign Office, July 13, 1898.)

[64] Charles S. Olcott, *The Life of William McKinley* (Boston: 1916), II, 133, 134. (Hay to McKinley, July 14, 1898.) Hay, in reporting his conversation with Hatzfeldt to the State Department, told Secretary Day that the German Ambassador had said: "The Emperor, and his Ministers as well, have no disposition to interfere with, or deprive us, of our rights of conquest in any direction. It is out of the question that Germany should entertain any such intentions; Germany stands between two groups of powers, independent of

These German importunities coincided with the threatened clash between Dewey and Diederichs in Manila Bay, which gave the United States Government an opportunity to evade a direct reply to Germany's expressed desires. Ambassador White informed the German Foreign Office merely that negotiations for the disposition of territory not yet in American possession would be somewhat "premature."[65] Before Germany's territorial objectives could again be impressed upon the United States Government, Secretary Day and Jules Cambon, representing Spanish interests in Washington, had agreed on the preliminary peace terms. The fate of the Philippines was to be decided by the United States and Spain; so the Germans were compelled to seek support elsewhere to achieve their aims in the Pacific.[66] Ironically, Germany's efforts to secure concessions from the United States had helped convince American leaders that, in order to avoid a great war, the United States must hold the Philippines.[67]

each. On one side is England, on the other Russia and France in alliance. It is impossible that Germany should go far abroad seeking adventures; she needs all her power at home." Quoted in Alfred L. P. Dennis, *Adventures in American Diplomacy, 1896–1906* (New York: Dutton, 1928), p. 93. (Hay to Day, July 14, 1898.) Hay, however, had been warned by Cecil Spring-Rice, then a Secretary of the British Embassy in Berlin, that Germany would seek compensation for the American annexation of Hawaii if the United States did not act promptly after the war began. See Stephen Gywnn, ed., *The Letters and Friendships of Sir Cecil Spring Rice: A Record* (Boston: Houghton Mifflin, 1929), I, 246, 247. (Spring-Rice to Hay, April 30, 1898.)

[65] *Die Grosse Politik,* XV, 62. (Memorandum by Freiherr von Richthofen, Acting Foreign Secretary, July 25, 1898.) During the course of this conversation, White broached the subject of the presence of such a large German squadron in Manila Bay, which had caused some "uneasiness" in the United States, and suggested that the situation would be improved if the German ships were to remain stationary instead of moving about so much. This was interpreted as a request by the United States that the German vessels be withdrawn, and drew a sharp reply later from the Foreign Secretary. See *ibid.,* p. 64. (Bülow to the Foreign Office, July 27, 1898.) See also Gwynn, *op. cit.,* I, 251, 252. (Spring-Rice to Hay, July 16, 1898.)

[66] Germany renewed her attempts to gain British support for the neutralization of the Philippines, but the British Government would have nothing to do with it. See *Die Grosse Politik,* XV, 71, 72. (Hatzfeldt to the Foreign Office, August 9, 1898.) The German Government thereupon decided to drop the question of the Philippines. See *ibid.,* p. 74, note †. (Richthofen to Joseph von Radowitz, German Ambassador in Madrid, August 13, 1898.)

[67] Others, too, were convinced that this was true. Senator Beveridge, visiting in Japan, had an interview with Marquis Ito, Japan's Premier, who told the Senator: "First you must keep the islands. . . . because if you do not, another Power will immediately take them, involving the world in war in all probability, for which you will be responsible." See Bowers, *op. cit.,* p. 110. (Interview of July 26, 1899.) There is reason to believe that this view was also held in some circles in Germany. The assertion was made that the Americans "are the only

But first the American people had to be convinced that no other course was possible. The initial reaction in the United States to the naval victory at Manila was that the islands must be returned to Spain. By June 3, 1898, the President, in announcing acceptable peace terms, asserted that the Philippines were "to be allowed to remain with Spain except a port and necessary appurtenances, to be selected by the United States, shall be ceded to the United States."[68] The first breach had been made, and within two weeks, the situation changed radically. Powerfully advocated by the Filipinos' gallant struggle for freedom, the idea of the moral responsibility of the United States had been interposed. Secretary Day, although originally of the opinion that the islands must be returned, admitted that the insurgents "must have just consideration in any terms of settlement"; and he also acknowledged that it "is most difficult without fuller knowledge to determine as to [the] disposition of [the] Philippine Islands."[69] It was only a short step to the view that the United States must accept her destiny there."[70]

The administration did not yet share the opinion of Senator Lodge that the "feeling of the country . . . [was] overwhelming against giving the Philippines back to Spain."[71] The obvious course was to await the outcome of the war and the development of American public opinion. With the signing of the protocol that ended hostilities on August 12, 1898, the government was in a position to consider the Philippine question. In the first place, the United States had been assured of British support for American retention of the islands and against their acquisition by any other power.[72]

---

ones who can, through annexation, quickly solve the Philippine question and to the universal satisfaction of the foreigners residing in the Philippines without making of the group an eternal bone of contention, which the colony otherwise without doubt would be." See "Die Lage auf den Philippinen," (unsigned article), *Export: Organ des "Centralvereins für Handelsgeographie und Förderung Deutscher Interessen im Auslande,"* XX (November 24, 1898), 593.

[68] This statement, sent confidentially to Hay in London, was the result of an inquiry from Joseph Chamberlain as to the conditions upon which the United States would be willing to make peace. See Tyler Dennett, *John Hay: From Poetry to Politics* (New York: Dodd Mead, 1933), p. 190. (Day to Hay, June 3, 1898.)

[69] *Ibid.*, p. 191. (Day to Hay, June 14, 1898.)

[70] Senator Lodge tells how he and Captain Mahan secured this admission from Judge Day after a two-hour discussion of the Philippine question. See Lodge, *op. cit.*, I, 313. (Lodge to Roosevelt, June 24, 1898.)

[71] *Ibid.*

[72] The dispatch in which Hay informed the State Department of the views of the British Government is quoted in part in Dennett, *op. cit.*, p. 191. (Hay to Day, July 28, 1898.)

Second, the defeated Spanish Government had agreed to leave the disposition of the Philippines to the peace conference. The United States Government therefore sought the "fuller knowledge" mentioned by Secretary Day before deciding what to do with the islands. Indicative of the inquiries made were the following instructions to Admiral Dewey of August 13, 1898:

> The President desires to receive from you any important information you may have of the Philippines; the desirability of the several islands; the character of their population; coal and other mineral deposits; their harbor and commercial advantages, and in a naval and commercial sense which would be the most advantageous.[73]

Dewey replied: "Luzon is in almost all respects the most desirable of these islands, and therefore the one to retain. In it is situated Manila, the most important commercial as well as the most populous port of all the islands—a port that in our hands would soon become one of the first ports of the world." Luzon possessed the finest harbor in all the Philippine Islands in Subig Bay, only sixty miles north of Manila. The bay, in Dewey's opinion, was ideal for a naval station; for it was landlocked, provided ample anchorage in deep water, and commanded the shipping lanes from Manila to the trade centers of East Asia. Dewey concluded "that Luzon . . . [is] by far the most valuable island in the group, whether considered from a commercial or military standpoint."[74]

President McKinley accepted Dewey's judgment. In his instructions to the Peace Commission on September 16, 1898, he set forth the principles which were to govern the negotiations respecting the Philippines. A strange mixture, indeed, were these principles, including pure altruism, manifest destiny, international politics, and practical business considerations. According to the President, our "aim in the adjustment of peace should be directed to lasting results and to the achievement of the common good under the demands of civilization rather than to ambitious designs." Turning to the Philippine question, he asserted that, "without any original thought

[73] *Annual Reports of the Navy Department*, 1898:2, pp. 122, 123. (Acting Secretary of the Navy to Dewey, August 13, 1898.)

[74] *Sen. Docs.* (Ser. 3732), 55th Cong. 3d sess., No. 62, Part 2, January 13, 1899, pp. 383, 384. (Dewey to John D. Long, Secretary of the Navy, August 29, 1898.) Dewey's opinion thus coincided with that of Senator Lodge who, just two weeks earlier, had expressed the hope that the administration would "at least keep Manila, which is the great prize, and the thing which will give us the Eastern trade." See Lodge, *op. cit.*, I, 337. (Lodge to Roosevelt, August 15, 1898.)

of complete or even partial acquisition, the presence and success of our arms at Manila imposes upon us obligations which we cannot disregard." These obligations, the United States "must meet and discharge as becomes a great nation on whose growth and career from the beginning the Ruler of Nations has plainly written the high command and pledge of civilization." After sounding this call of manifest destiny, he passed to more practical matters. "Incidental to our tenure in the Philippines is the commercial opportunity to which American statesmanship can not be indifferent." Taking notice of the activity of the powers in the Far East and foreshadowing the policy soon to be formally announced in the "Hay Doctrine," McKinley said: "It is just to use every legitimate means for the enlargement of American trade; but we seek no advantages in the Orient which are not common to all. Asking only the open door for ourselves, we are ready to accord the open door to others." The President finally concluded that the United States could "not accept less than the cession in full right and sovereignty of the island of Luzon."[75]

The transition to the view that the entire archipelago should be retained was easily made. Convinced by a tour of the Midwest that the American people wanted to keep the islands, the President, on October 26, 1898, instructed the Peace Commission in Paris to demand the entire Philippine Archipelago. The reason given was that "information which has come to the President since your departure convinces him that the acceptance of the cession of Luzon alone, leaving the rest of the islands subject to Spanish rule, or to be the subject of future contention, can not be justified on political, commercial, or humanitarian grounds."[76] Only after the United States promised to pay to Spain $20,000,000 "for the sake of immediate peace" did the Spanish Government consent to the cession.

Although President McKinley still insisted that the United States was concerned solely with the welfare of the natives,[77] many believed that the acquisition of the Philippines opened the door of glittering opportunity for Americans. Among the first to realize

[75] *Sen. Docs.* (Ser. 4039), 56th Cong., 2d sess., No. 148, February 27, 1901, pp. 6, 7.

[76] *Ibid.*, p. 35. (Secretary of State Hay to Judge Day, Chairman of the American Peace Commission, October 26, 1898.)

[77] In a speech at Boston, February 16, 1899. See *Speeches and Addresses of William McKinley from March 1, 1897, to May 30, 1900* (New York: 1900), pp. 188, 189.

this were the manufacturers. As early as June 23, 1898, *Iron Age* commented that the "manufacturers of the United States do not need to be told that their home markets are overcrowded, or of the desirability of an outlet for surplus products. But the point to be made is that our acquisition of new territory involves opportunities for entering aggressively some fields of trade where Americans have been practically without prestige hitherto."[78] Such an aggressive trade campaign in China would inevitably bring the United States into conflict with the European powers who had attempted to monopolize the field. Particularly resentful would be Russia and Germany, for their claims to spheres of influence lay in North China, where American trade was already large and likely to expand still more.

American exports to China had increased by 126 per cent in ten years, rising from $7,926,560 in 1888 to $17,969,068 in 1897. In the same decade, however, American imports from China increased by only 11 per cent.[79] After citing the fact that nearly one-half the total value of American exports to China consisted of cotton goods, a British trade journal observed acutely that

> . . . two points of interest may be noted. One is that the demand for American cotton goods comes especially from Manchuria and the North of China generally, where Russia is striving to obtain a predominant position, and the other that the value of the exports from the United States to China are at present 50 per cent. greater than those from Germany. Obviously, therefore, *the States have good reason to support our policy of the open door.*[80]

The same journal later asserted that the European powers, concerned at the tremendous industrial expansion and the great increase in wealth and power of the United States, were trying "to hem America in and prevent the expansion of her influence and of her commercial interests . . ."[81]

That the United States Government was fully prepared to support the open-door policy from whatever source it might be pro-

[78] "The War and an Opportunity" (editorial), *The Iron Age,* LXI (June 23, 1898), 15.

[79] Bureau of Statistics, *The Foreign Commerce and Navigation of the United States,* 1887–1888, p. xl; *ibid.,* 1896–1897, p. 419. The figures cited include those for Hong Kong and for China proper.

[80] *The Economist, Weekly Commercial Times, Banker's Gazette and Railway Monitor* (London), LVI (May 14, 1898), 730. Italics mine.

[81] "America and the Philippines" (editorial), *ibid.* (November 5, 1898), 1587. The writer concluded: "We do not believe that all the Powers of Europe combined can prevent the inevitable coming greatness of the United States . . ."

posed, President McKinley had already indicated to the Peace Commission. In his annual message to Congress on December 5, 1898, he reiterated America's desire only for equality of opportunity in the markets of China, declaring that the United States had "not been an indifferent spectator of the extraordinary events transpiring in the Chinese Empire, whereby portions of its maritime provinces . . . [were] passing under the control of various European powers . . ." The United States Government, he said, was willing to accept the assurances of the powers that the ports which they had seized would remain open to the commerce of all nations on equal terms; but the United States considered her new position in the Far East sufficiently important to establish an "equitable claim to consideration and friendly treatment in this regard . . ."[82] He intimated that the United States would be on guard against any discrimination, and that the government would protect by all proper means the interests of the United States and of her citizens in the Far East.

The President's mild remonstrance, however, did not deter the powers, who, despite their noble assurances, were busily consolidating control of their spheres of influence to the exclusion of other powers. Germany, for example, disturbed at the British lease of Weihaiwei, secured from the British Government the following formal agreement:

> England formally declares that, in establishing herself at Wei-hai Wei, she has no intention of injuring or contesting the interests of Germany in the Province of Shantung, or of creating difficulties for her in that province. *It is especially understood that England will not construct any railroad communication from Wei-hai Wei, and the district leased therewith, into the interior of the provinces.*[83]

The British Government thereby recognized Germany's right to build railways in Shantung to the exclusion of British interests, and at the same time virtually renounced Britain's right even to compete with Germans in Shantung.[84] Obviously, such an agreement was not in accord with the principle of equal opportunity;

[82] *Messages and Papers*, XIV, 6327, 6328.

[83] *British Documents*, I, 33, 34. (Sir Frank Lascelles, British Ambassador in Berlin, to Bülow, April 20, 1898.) The italicized portion of this agreement was apparently added at the insistence of the German Government. See *Die Grosse Politik*, XIV:1, 162, 163.

[84] The German Government held this view. See *Die Grosse Politik*, XIV:1, 171. (Bülow to William II, April 21, 1898.)

but it was not to be the last of its kind. Even after President McKinley's remarks in his annual message, motivated in part at least by the Anglo-German agreement, other such agreements were negotiated.[85]

The United States watched these developments with growing anxiety, strongly opposed to the dismemberment of the Chinese Empire, and yet, lacking public support at home, unable to act aggressively in Far Eastern politics to protect American interests.[86] Nonetheless, what could not be attained by active participation in the politics of the Far East[87] could possibly be attained by other means. The result was the open-door notes of September 6, 1899.[88] Assured of the support of the British Government, Secretary Hay secured from all the great powers pledges to observe and to support the principle of equal opportunity in the trade, navigation, and commerce of China.[89] Thus, the advent of the United States into the Orient led to the formulation of one of the permanent policies in American foreign relations. In the years that followed, American diplomacy in the Far East directed every effort toward the maintenance of the open-door policy. And just as assiduously, Japan and Russia turned their efforts toward the nullification of the same principle, especially after Russia's continued encroachment upon Manchuria led to war between those two powers.

Another important outcome of American territorial expansion across the Pacific was the building of the Panama Canal under American ownership and control. Here, too, Britain showed her

[85] The Scott-Mouravieff correspondence is a good example. By this exchange of notes on April 28 [29], 1899, between Sir Charles S. Scott, British Ambassador to Russia, and Count Michael Mouravieff, Russian Foreign Minister, Great Britain and Russia agreed to respect the exclusive right of each other to seek railway concessions south and north of the Great Wall of China respectively. See *British Documents,* I, 40, 41. (Marquess of Salisbury to Henry G. O. Bax-Ironside, British Chargé d'Affaires in Peking, April 30, 1899.)

[86] William R. Thayer, *The Life and Letters of John Hay* (Boston: 1915), II, 241. (Hay to Paul Dana, editor of *The New York Sun,* March 16, 1899.)

[87] Secretary of State John Hay described the position of the United States as follows: " 'Give and take'—the axiom of diplomacy to the rest of the world—is positively forbidden to us, by both the Senate and public opinion. We must take what we can and give nothing—which greatly narrows our possibilities." See *ibid.,* p. 247.

[88] The first notes were sent to Germany, Great Britain, and Russia on this date. Similar notes were later sent to France, Italy, and Japan. See *Papers Relating to the Foreign Relations of the United States,* 1899, pp. 128–143. Cited hereafter as *Foreign Relations.*

[89] For an excellent account of Hay's diplomacy, see Dennett, *op. cit.,* chap. xxiv. See also Dennis, *op. cit.,* chap. viii.

friendliness; for, without her consent, the United States would have been bound by treaty to admit her to joint ownership and control.[90] Existing conditions, however, accentuated by the war with Spain and overseas expansion, made inevitable the negotiation of a new agreement with Great Britain freeing the United States to construct the canal as a national enterprise, but open to the commerce of all nations on a basis of equality.

President McKinley, in his annual message to Congress on December 6, 1897, had referred to the proposed canal as "the great highway of trade between the Atlantic and Pacific" whose "utility and value to American commerce is universally admitted."[91] A year later the war with Spain had been fought and won, and the impact of new conditions upon the President's mind was evident in his annual message to Congress:

> ... That the construction of such a maritime highway is now more than ever indispensable to that intimate and ready intercommunication between our eastern and western seaboards demanded by the annexation of the Hawaiian Islands and the prospective expansion of our influence and commerce in the Pacific, and that our national policy now more imperatively than ever calls for its control by this Government, are propositions which I doubt not the Congress will duly appreciate and wisely act upon.[92]

That the government should take immediate steps to secure the abrogation of the Clayton-Bulwer Treaty was to be expected. After long negotiation and the failure of one treaty, the British Government yielded its principal claims; and a treaty was signed at Washington on November 18, 1901, which cleared the way for construction of an isthmian canal under the control of the United States alone.

Throughout the negotiations, the British Government showed every desire to comply with the wishes of the United States. Although it is true that it was reluctant to yield on some points, the Marquess of Lansdowne, Britain's Foreign Secretary, did not exaggerate when he said: "His Majesty's Government have approached the consideration of this important question with a sincere desire to facilitate the progress of the great enterprise in

[90] Under the terms of the Clayton-Bulwer Treaty of April 19, 1850, which also prohibited the fortification of the Canal Zone.

[91] *Messages and Papers,* XIV, 6265.

[92] December 5, 1898. The President was urging Congress to authorize a canal commission to carry on the work of surveying possible routes across the Isthmus of Panama. See *ibid.,* p. 6327.

which both Governments take such interest."[93] Great Britain's friendliness toward the United States is explained only in part by her political isolation in Europe and the hard and costly war she was waging against the Boers in South Africa.

Not altogether unwelcome to the British was the advent of the United States as a colonial and commercial rival in the Far East. The chief aim of the United States in China was the maintenance of the open door, a policy which the British Government had long advocated and practiced so that no conflict between the interests of the two powers seemed likely. Annexation of Hawaii had thwarted Japanese ambitions in those islands, and the Japanese had not forgotten it.[94] The same effect had been produced with respect to Germany when the United States acquired the Philippine Islands. Enunciation of the open-door policy meant that the United States would compete actively for the trade of North China, where Russia and Japan were already engaged in the rivalry that led them to war. Thus, the United States and Great Britain not only found their respective aims and interests akin, but they also found themselves confronted by the same rivals, two of whom—Germany and Russia—were intense political enemies of Great Britain.

American territorial expansion across the Pacific had in this devious way inextricably involved the United States in Far Eastern politics; and the futility of a policy of isolation had been demonstrated. American admission to the markets of China was sure to be resisted. To back her diplomacy in the Far East, therefore, the United States required a fleet in the Pacific. Great Britain realized that an American fleet could serve her purposes as well as a British fleet and readily consented to the construction of the Panama Canal. Thus was formed the Anglo-Saxon "alliance" which was China's bulwark until 1914. The United States had become an imperial power in the Pacific. But, as she discovered after the Russo-Japanese War of 1904–1905, imperialism involved not only great advantages but also grave national responsibilities. Diplomacy in imperialistic competition ceases to be self-executing; and to be effective, sufficient force must be available. The United States was to learn this through bitter experience.

[93] *Parliamentary Papers*, 1902, CXXX (Cmd. 905), January, 1902, p. 3. (Marquess of Lansdowne to Gerard A. Lowther, First Secretary of the British Embassy in Washington, August 3, 1901.)

[94] Gwynn, *op. cit.*, I, 444, note. (Roosevelt to Spring-Rice, December 27, 1904.)

Barry University Library
Miami, FL 33161

CHAPTER II

NAVAL POLICY IN TRANSITION

Formerly America lived more or less in isolation. To-day she has become the greatest export nation of the world and is exciting the jealousy of other great nations in threatening their supremacy in commerce, industry, and finance. In addition recent events have thrown us into the political vortex of the world, and the dangers of being unprepared are becoming greater and greater with each succeeding year.—RICHMOND PEARSON HOBSON, 1908.

FOR THE FIRST hundred years of her independent existence, the United States normally maintained only such sea forces as were deemed necessary to protect American shipping in both coastal and foreign trade. As late as 1890 Mahan considered this the chief function of a navy possessed by a nation without aggressive tendencies.[1] To this fact he attributed the low estate to which the American fleet had fallen—the United States no longer had a thriving merchant marine. Only after the Russo-Japanese War of 1904–1905 did Mahan admit that navies could have a legitimate military function even though the nation had no merchant marine and no aggressive intentions.[2]

In 1881, however, President Arthur apparently recognized this function of naval power; at least he realized that the United States needed an efficient navy despite the doldrums into which American merchant shipping had slipped. He accordingly urged upon Congress his "conviction that every consideration of national safety, economy, and honor imperatively demands a thorough rehabilitation of our Navy."[3] The President's recommendation resulted in the building of the "New Navy" under succeeding administrations. Under the able leadership of William C. Whitney, Secretary of the Navy in Grover Cleveland's first cabinet, the Navy Department was reorganized on an efficient basis; and construction was begun on the vessels that were to make an American victory over Spain speedy and certain.[4] After the war the United States, still dazzled

[1] Alfred T. Mahan, *The Influence of Sea Power upon History, 1660–1783* (Boston: 1890), p. 26.

[2] *Idem, Naval Strategy, Compared and Contrasted with the Principles and Practice of Military Operations on Land* (Boston: 1911), pp. 446, 447.

[3] See his annual message to Congress, December 6, 1881, in *Messages and Papers,* X, 4638. See also George F. Howe, *Chester A. Arthur: A Quarter-Century of Machine Politics* (New York: Dodd Mead, 1934), chap. xxi.

[4] Allan Nevins, *Grover Cleveland: A Study in Courage* (New York: Dodd Mead, 1932), pp. 217–223.

by the ease of her triumph, began to neglect the very weapon which had made the victory possible. The fact that the adversary had been only a second-rate naval power was overlooked, and President Arthur's advice to "be prepared" was apparently forgotten.

This reaction unfortunately came at the very time when the United States had increased her world responsibilities beyond anything she had ever before assumed, responsibilities which were certain to plunge her into conflict with other powers. Theodore Roosevelt recognized this; but he was determined to maintain the national policies of the United States, saying with typical forthrightness: "We do not shrink from the struggle before us."[5] The President knew that these policies could be supported only by sea power. He later expressed his opinion clearly when he said: "The United States Navy is the surest guarantor of peace which this country possesses."[6] To be expected, therefore, was a frequent urging upon Congress of the necessity of building up the fleet.

The Navy Department, recognizing after the Spanish-American War the tremendous task confronting it in two oceans, had already attacked the problem. In March, 1900, the General Board, headed by Admiral George Dewey, was established for the express purpose of considering "questions relating to the efficient preparation of the fleet in case of war and for the naval defense of the coast."[7] By 1903 "a fixed and definite 'policy'" was formulated and

> . . . adopted by the board for its guidance, after mature and deliberate consideration of all the elements involved and after a careful estimate and forecast of the future as to what would be the naval development of those foreign countries with which conflict might be probable, and what should be our own development to insure peace if possible, or superiority of force if war should be forced upon us. Expressed in concrete words, the "*policy*" of the board has been to provide the Nation with a fleet equal or superior to that of any probable enemy, as a guarantor of peace; and its forecast was that a fleet of 48 battleships, with the attendant lesser units and auxiliaries, ready for action by 1920 would accomplish this result.[8]

As the Board had strongly emphasized, this was a program for its own guidance: "*This policy—as a policy—has remained a General Board policy only,* without adoption by the Government or

[5] December 2, 1902. See *Messages and Papers,* XV, 6750.

[6] December 3, 1906; see *ibid.,* XVI, 7446.

[7] Report of John D. Long, Secretary of the Navy, November 17, 1900, in *Annual Reports of the Navy Department,* 1900, p. 19.

[8] Report of the General Board, in *ibid.,* 1913, p. 32.

even by the Navy Department, and without being understood by the people or Congress."[9] Consequently, not until 1916 did the Board succeed in persuading the President and Congress to adopt in full any of its annually recommended construction programs.[10] But, in 1916, the President and Congress not only accepted the General Board's recommendations, but adopted a program exceeding anything the Board had ever recommended. The story of this reversal of roles is the story of the development of a sound naval policy as in integral part of the national strategy.

After the Spanish-American War, Germany was the naval power which loomed as the "probable enemy" to which the General Board had referred. Japan was still faithfully following the advice of Baron Tadasu Hayashi "to keep perfectly quiet, to lull the suspicions that have arisen against her . . ."[11] Only a few Americans recognized the growing strength of Japan's land and sea power; and fewer still considered her as the "probable enemy," even after her show of hostility preceding our annexation of Hawaii.

Great Britain, the world's greatest sea power, was not considered a "probable enemy" for several reasons. In the first place, her interests coincided with those of the United States in areas where the United States came into conflict with other powers. For example, the British Government tacitly accepted the Monroe Doctrine because it meant continued security and prosperity for British commerce and investments in the South American Republics. In the Far East, Britain supported the Hay Doctrine of the open door because that, too, accorded with her own commercial and financial interests.[12] Second, Great Britain was exempted from the role of a

[9] *Ibid.*, p. 30.

[10] See below, Appendix II, pp. 176–179.

[11] A. M. Pooley, ed., *The Secret Memoirs of Count Tadasu Hayashi, G. C. V. O.* (New York: 1915), p. 113. The quoted material is from a summary of articles written by Count Hayashi, which appeared in *Jiji Shimpo* in June and July, 1895, after Japan had been robbed of the fruits of her victory over China by the intervention of the powers in April.

[12] In a letter to King Edward VII of England, President Roosevelt said: "In matters outside our borders, we are chiefly concerned, first with what goes on south of us, second with affairs in the Orient; and in both cases our interests are identical with yours." See Joseph B. Bishop, *Theodore Roosevelt and His Time, Shown in His Own Letters* (New York: 1920), II, 263. (Roosevelt to King Edward VII, March 9, 1905.) See also Allan Nevins, *Henry White: Thirty Years of American Diplomacy* (New York: Harper, 1930), p. 241. (White to Roosevelt, February 25, 1905.) In this letter, Henry White quotes a conversation with King Edward in which the latter had expressed sentiments almost identical with those of President Roosevelt.

"probable enemy" because of the weakness of the British Army. Without a powerful army to occupy and to hold American territory, Britain could not hope to defeat the United States even if the Royal Navy should succeed in its mission. Third, the British had yielded a hostage to peace in the possession of the Dominion of Canada, their greatest as well as their most vulnerable dominion. It was popularly believed in the United States that, if for no other reason, fear of losing Canada would effectually prevent Great Britain's ever going to war against the United States.[13]

Finally, Anglo-American relations, seriously threatened by the Venezuela–British Guiana boundary dispute in 1895, had materially improved after the settlement in the following year. To Richard Olney, Secretary of State under President Cleveland, had fallen the task of delivering several sharp notes to Great Britain in the Venezuela dispute, as well as the pleasure of expressing the real bond of kinship which existed between the two great Anglo-Saxon nations:

> . . . There is a patriotism of race as well as of country—and the Anglo-American is as little likely to be indifferent to the one as to the other. Family quarrels there have been heretofore and doubtless will be again, and the two peoples, at the safe distance which the broad Atlantic interposes, take with each other liberties of speech which only the fondest and dearest relatives indulge in. Nevertheless, that they would be found standing together against any alien foe by whom either was menaced with destruction or irreparable calamity, it is not permissible to doubt. Nothing less could be expected of the close community between them in origin, speech, thought, literature, institutions, ideals—in the kind and degree of the civilization enjoyed by both. . . .[14]

Delivered almost on the eve of the outbreak of war with Spain, this address approached prophecy. Great Britain did come to the support of the United States against the menace of German aggression in the Philippines, as she had a year earlier when Germany sought British support against American annexation of Hawaii. Britain's

[13] It is not to be inferred from this discussion that Japan and Great Britain were not considered as possible future foes at this time. Every nation which possessed a measurable strength at sea was considered as such a possibility. Especially was this true of Great Britain and Japan after the conclusion of their alliance in 1902. Germany, however, seemed to be the only power with which the United States was likely to come into serious conflict; Germany, therefore, assumed for the moment in the public mind the role of the "probable enemy."

[14] "International Isolation of the United States," *The Atlantic Monthly*, LXXXI (May, 1898), 588. The substance of this article was originally delivered as an address by Secretary Olney at Harvard College, March 2, 1898.

friendly action in making possible American ownership and control of the Panama Canal needs no recounting here.

Germany, on the other hand, under the aggressive leadership of Bismarck and William II, had disputed American policies and interests on numerous occasions, and showed little disposition to yield any of her pretensions. An example was the partitioning of the Samoan Islands. The United States, pursuing her policy of recognizing the sovereignty of local rulers, concluded a treaty of commerce with the Samoan envoy in Washington on January 17, 1878, which granted to the United States the use of Pago Pago Harbor for naval purposes. Thereafter, the United States Government made every effort to maintain Samoan independence against Germany's constant and mounting pressure for the right to "protect" her nationals and their commercial enterprises in the islands. So great had become the pressure by 1885 that Secretary of State Thomas F. Bayard, although still asserting that the United States would view with concern any attempt to bring the islands "under the domination of a foreign sovereign," yielded so far as to suggest that the islands should be neutralized.[15]

But Germany's insistence on political control continued, and only the great hurricane of March 16, 1889, prevented open naval hostilities at Apia. Thereupon, the three interested powers—Germany, Great Britain, and the United States—reached a temporary settlement of the problem by placing the native government under the protection and supervision of all three powers. The agreement did not prove satisfactory because the Germans continued to stir up internal political strife in the islands. Finally, to end a situation which she found extremely distasteful, the United States consented to partitioning of the Samoan Islands. By the terms of the treaty, signed December 2, 1899, the islands were divided between the United States and Germany, Great Britain receiving compensation elsewhere.[16]

Although the United States profited most by the treaty, securing the island of Tutuila with its splendid harbor of Pago Pago, the methods used by the German Government and the German agents in Samoa to gain their ends had created a bad impression in the

[15] *House Executive Documents* (Ser. 2560), 50th Cong., 1st sess., No. 238, April 2, 1888, pp. 10, 11. (Bayard to Berthold Greenebaum, American Consul at Apia, June 19, 1885.)

[16] See Dennis, *Adventures in American Diplomacy, 1896–1906*, pp. 106 ff.

United States. This impression was confirmed by Germany's attitude toward the proposed American annexation of Hawaii in 1897. Theodore Roosevelt, at that time Assistant Secretary of the Navy, wrote to Captain B. H. McCalla, United States Navy: "I entirely agree with you that Germany is the power with which we may very possibly have ultimately to come into hostile contact. How I wish our people would wake up to the need for a big navy."[17] Germany's activities during the Spanish-American War confirmed anew and strengthened these views. Thus, when Germany was about to send a part of her fleet to enforce her demands upon Venezuela in 1902, President Roosevelt again affirmed his faith in the efficacy of a powerful American fleet in maintaining peace.

> We are glad indeed that we are on good terms with all the other peoples of mankind, and no effort on our part shall be spared to secure a continuance of these relations. . . . we shall be a potent factor for peace largely in proportion to the way in which we make it evident that our attitude is due, not to weakness, not to inability to defend ourselves, but to a genuine repugnance to wrongdoing, a genuine desire for self-respecting friendship with our neighbors. The voice of the weakling or the craven counts for nothing when he clamors for peace; but the voice of the just man armed is potent. We need to keep in a condition of preparedness, especially as regards our navy, not because we want war, but because we desire to stand with those whose plea for peace is listened to with respectful attention.[18]

According to President Roosevelt's account of the denouement of the Venezuela episode, Germany was compelled to listen "with respectful attention."[19]

Thus, to Henry Adams' truism that "the sudden appearance of Germany as the grizzly terror . . . in twenty years effected what Adamses had tried for two hundred in vain,—frightened England into America's arms,"[20] could be added a sequel: many Americans became convinced not only that Germany was the "probable enemy" of the United States, but also that the war would be fought in the Pacific.[21] When war came, it was freely predicted, the first

[17] Bishop, *op. cit.*, I, 78. (Roosevelt to McCalla, August 2, 1897.)

[18] *Ibid.*, pp. 230, 231. Speech at ceremonies dedicating the new building of the New York City Chamber of Commerce, November 11, 1902.

[19] *Ibid.*, chap. xx.

[20] Quoted in Thayer, *The Life and Letters of John Hay*, II, 172.

[21] Major General Arthur MacArthur, for example, was quoted "as predicting a war in the immediate future between the United States and Germany, and that the principal scene of the fighting would be in the Pacific Ocean, with the Hawaiian Islands as an objective point." *The New York Times*, December 11, 1903, p. 1.

attack would be directed at the Philippines as America's most vulnerable point.[22] The islands were almost as far from the United States as from Western Europe. Moreover, Germany had a well-equipped base at Tsingtao; and she owned the great chain of islands which lay across the American line of communication between Hawaii and the Philippines. To the Marshall Islands, annexed in 1885, she had added by purchase from Spain in 1899 the Carolines and the Marianas, except Guam, which fell to the United States in the Treaty of Paris. Obviously Germany could best wage war against the United States in the Far East, where she possessed distinct strategic advantages.

The course pursued by the United States Government added proof that Germany was considered as the "probable enemy." An obvious counterbalance to Germany's position in the Far East was a well-equipped, strongly fortified American naval base in the Philippines, which the government quickly took steps to procure. Congress, in the Naval Appropriation Act of March 3, 1901, directed the Navy Department to investigate and report on the best possible site for a naval base in the Philippines.[23] The commission appointed by the Secretary of the Navy unanimously chose Olongapo on Subig Bay as the ideal site. In his annual report for 1901, Secretary Long recommended that the necessary appropriations be made at once, since American "interests in that part of the world necessitate the presence of a large fleet in Asiatic waters at all times."[24] Also urged by Long was an increase in the fleet, which he termed "a far greater factor in our relations with the world than it was before the recent national expansion." He then added: "If we are to have a Navy at all it must be commensurate with these great extensions—greater in international even than in territorial importance."[25]

Although Congress failed to act upon the recommendations, the

---

[22] In the Senate debate on the naval appropriation bill for 1905, Senators Augustus O. Bacon of Georgia and Edward W. Carmack of Tennessee both predicted that the first attack upon the United States would be in the Philippines as the weakest point, in *Cong. Rec.*, XXXVIII, March 3, 1904, p. 2733. Senator Chauncey M. Depew of New York agreed that the first attack would come in the Philippines, not because of their weakness, but because they were the most valuable American possession; and their capture would enable the enemy to drive the United States out of the Far Eastern trade. See *ibid.*, p. 2732.

[23] *U. S. Statutes at Large*, XXXI (1901), 1120.

[24] Report of the Secretary of the Navy, November 4, 1901, in *Annual Reports of the Navy Department*, 1901, p. 17.

[25] *Ibid.*, p. 28.

Roosevelt administration continued its efforts to strengthen the American position in the Pacific.[26] President Roosevelt took advantage of a revolution on the Isthmus of Panama in November, 1903, to recognize Panamanian independence and to conclude a treaty with the new government, which granted the strip of land across the isthmus on which the United States was to build the Panama Canal. The President denied that he or any other official of the United States Government had instigated the revolt, and asserted that the recognition of Panama was

> . . . justified by the highest considerations of our national interests and safety. In all the range of our international relations, I do not hesitate to affirm that there is nothing of greater or more pressing importance than the construction of an interoceanic canal. Long acknowledged to be essential to our commercial development, it has become, as the result of the recent extension of our territorial dominion, more than ever essential to our national self-defense. . . . Reasons of convenience have been superseded by reasons of vital necessity, which do not admit of indefinite delays.[27]

These views received stanch support from the Navy's General Board, which chose this time to formulate its policy of a fleet of forty-eight battleships with the attendant smaller craft by 1920. To attain its goal, the Board estimated that it would be necessary to lay down two battleships every year; but Secretary Moody would recommend but one to Congress, and only one was authorized in the act of 1904.[28]

The General Board's program thus fell behind just at the time when American relations with Germany were manifestly improving, and the United States was for a short time in danger of being lulled into a false sense of security. President Roosevelt, in a letter to Sir Cecil Spring-Rice, described succinctly the course which

[26] William H. Moody, successor to John D. Long as Secretary of the Navy, declared in his report for 1903 that, although "it is almost five years since we acquired the Philippine Islands, no steps have been taken to establish a naval base there." He, too, urged that Congress should take action, but without success. See Report of the Secretary of the Navy, November 23, 1903, in *ibid.*, 1903, p. 13.

[27] In a special message to the Senate, January 4, 1904, in *Messages and Papers*, XV, 6921, 6922. For a competent study of the events leading to the establishment of the Republic of Panama, see William D. McCain, *The United States and the Republic of Panama* (Durham, N. C.: Duke University Press, 1937).

[28] Appendix II, below, pp. 176–179, is a table showing the annual recommendations (1903–1914) of the General Board and the Secretary of the Navy for additions to the fleet and those additions authorized by acts of Congress.

American relations with Germany had pursued for some years:

> . . . I have more than once been greatly exasperated with the Kaiser myself. When I first came into the Presidency [1901] I was inclined to think that the Germans had serious designs upon South America. But I think I succeeded in impressing on the Kaiser, quietly and unofficially, and with equal courtesy and emphasis, that the violation of the Monroe Doctrine by territorial aggrandisement on his part around the Caribbean meant war, not ultimately, but immediately, and without any delay. He has always been as nice as possible to me since and has helped me in every way, and my relations with him and the relations of the two countries have been, I am happy to say, growing more close and more friendly.[29]

The general European situation, of course, accounted for the "more friendly" attitude of Germany toward the United States. In 1904 England and France settled their outstanding colonial differences, and entered into an *entente cordiale* which meant that the ring of encircling powers was being drawn evermore tightly around Germany. As a result, the German Government challenged the Anglo-French Entente in Morocco and succeeded in forcing the French Government to agree to an international conference to settle the Moroccan question. The Kaiser hoped for the support of President Roosevelt just as he had supported the President in successfully concluding the peace negotiations between Russia and Japan at Portsmouth.[30] Thus, the growing cordiality between the United States and Germany was closely bound up with the international situation in Europe. The Kaiser's motive in seeking better relations with the United States, however, was undoubtedly influenced equally by the startling rise of Japan as a new specter on the Eastern horizon, which also caused the United States to reconsider her entire strategy in the Pacific.

War between Russia and Japan began on February 8, 1904; and Japan upset all expectations by her uniform success. In the United

[29] Gwynn, *The Letters and Friendships of Sir Cecil Spring Rice: A Record,* II, 10. (Roosevelt to Spring-Rice, British Chargé d'Affaires in St. Petersburg, November 1, 1905.)

[30] See Fay, *The Origins of the World War,* I, 152–192; Bishop, *op. cit.,* I, 374–424, 467–505. The Kaiser himself expressed great satisfaction at being able to lend his support to the President of the United States in his successful efforts to bring about peace between Japan and Russia. *Stenographische Berichte über die Verhandlungen des Reichstags,* XI Legislaturperiode, II Session, 1905–1906, I, 2. (Thronrede, Eröffnungssitzung, November 28, 1905.) The Kaiser took the same occasion, significantly, to direct honeyed words at Tokyo: "I accompany the entry of Japan into the ranks of the great powers with sincere wishes for a peaceful mission of civilization for this highly gifted people."

States, Russia had been considered the more powerful and also the more dangerous because of her steady and determined penetration of Manchuria. The concern of Americans had been voiced by Senator Lodge, who asserted that there "is more interest in this matter of trade than is generally realized." American trade in Manchuria was "assuming very large proportions," and he recommended that the United States "take very strong grounds" in order to check the Russian advance.[31] This resentment of Russia's politico-commercial activity largely accounted for American sympathy for Japan.

So strong was this sympathy that President Roosevelt, convinced that the United States could maintain the balance of power in the Far East, felt secure in giving Japan the diplomatic support of the United States. He warned France and Germany "in the most polite and discreet fashion that in the event of a combination against Japan to try to do what Russia, Germany and France" had done to her in 1895, the United States would assist Japan.[32] On July 27, 1905, General Count Taro Katsura, the Japanese Premier, stated categorically to Secretary of War William Howard Taft, then touring the Far East as the personal representative of President Roosevelt, that Japan had no "aggressive designs whatever on the Philippines." In return, Taft assured him that Japan and Great Britain could depend upon "appropriate action by the United States" to maintain the peace of the Far East "quite as confidently as if the United States were under treaty obligations to take" such action.[33] In addition, the Japanese Premier was informed that the President would approve, as promoting the peace of the Far East, Japanese control of the foreign relations of Korea. Six months earlier Roosevelt had concluded that permanent peace in Asia

[31] Lodge, *Selections from the Correspondence of Theodore Roosevelt and Henry Cabot Lodge, 1884–1918*, II, 15. (Lodge to Roosevelt, May 21, 1903.) Senator Lodge asserted that some of his correspondents were even demanding that a fleet be sent to the Far East.

[32] The President tells of this warning in a letter to Cecil Spring-Rice, First Secretary of the British Embassy in St. Petersburg. See Gwynn, *op. cit.*, I, 478. (Roosevelt to Spring-Rice, July 24, 1905.)

[33] Tyler Dennett, "President Roosevelt's Secret Pact with Japan," *Current History*, XXI (October, 1924), 15–21. See also Jessup, *Elihu Root*, II, 5; and Henry F. Pringle, *The Life and Times of William Howard Taft: A Biography* (New York: Farrar and Rinehart, 1939), I, 298, 299. President Roosevelt's views, expressed by Secretary Taft in this conversation on July 27, 1905, were confirmed by the President on July 31 by cable in the following words: "Your conversation with Count Katsura absolutely correct in every respect. Wish you would state to Katsura that I confirm every word you have said." See Pringle, *Theodore Roosevelt: A Biography*, p. 384.

could be secured only through such control, and he had expressed himself accordingly.[34] This assurance, therefore, cannot be regarded as a concession on the part of the United States except, perhaps, in form.

Japan, on the other hand, was committed, first, to a policy of nonaggression toward the Philippine Islands. This represented a definite gain for the United States, because many competent authorities believed that Japan coveted the islands. President Roosevelt on March 16, 1905, expressed the view that, although Japan might not "have designs on the Philippines," the United States should strengthen her military and naval forces so that she could "hold the Philippines against *any* foe."[35] In the second place, Japan had pledged to President Roosevelt a month before the battle of Tsushima that she would adhere to the "position of maintaining the Open Door in Manchuria and of restoring that province to China."[36] And, on February 23, 1904, just two weeks after the outbreak of hostilities with Russia, Japan had signed a protocol with Korea which, although it made Korea a virtual protectorate of Japan, contained the following clause:

> III. The Imperial Government of Japan definitely guarantees the independence and territorial integrity of the Corean Empire.[37]

President Roosevelt was undoubtedly relying on this pledge when he consented to Japan's control of Korea's foreign relations. A Japanese writer and former member of the Imperial Diet asserted, however, that Japan had been compelled "to make such an illogical declaration in order to justify her cause in the eyes of the leading powers."[38] This was soon to be revealed as the official attitude of the Japanese Government.

When the peace negotiations with Russia were opened at Ports-

---

[34] Tyler Dennett, *Roosevelt and the Russo-Japanese War: A Critical Study of American Policy in Eastern Asia in 1902–5* (New York: Doubleday, Page, 1925), p. 161. (Roosevelt to George von Lengerke Meyer, American Ambassador in Rome, February 6, 1905.)

[35] In a letter to the Chairman of the House Committee on Military Affairs, Representative John A. T. Hull of Iowa. This letter, dated March 16, 1905, is quoted in Dennett, *Roosevelt and the Russo-Japanese War*, p. 162.

[36] In a telegram quoted in *ibid.*, pp. 179, 180. (Baron Jutaro Komura, Japanese Minister for Foreign Affairs, to President Roosevelt, April 25, 1905.)

[37] *British and Foreign State Papers*, XCVIII (1904–1905), 842. Tyler Dennett gives the date of this protocol as February 25, 1904. See his *Roosevelt and the Russo-Japanese War*, p. 109.

[38] Kungoro Shigeoka, "What Japan Should Do for Korea," excerpts in *The American Review of Reviews*, XXX (September, 1904), 349.

mouth, New Hampshire, on August 9, 1905, Japan stood before the world as the defender of China and Korea; and she enjoyed widespread confidence and popularity in the United States. Less than one month later, the situation was reversed. Japan's demands for a money indemnity in addition to the cession of territory by Russia turned American public opinion against Japan. The change was so marked that American newspaper reporters at the conference informed Baron Roman Rosen, Russian Ambassador to the United States and a member of the Russian delegation at Portsmouth, that whereas 90 per cent of the newsmen had been pro-Japanese at the opening of the conference, the proportions had been almost exactly reversed as a result of the Japanese demands.[39] This growing dislike of the Japanese encouraged the carrying out of the restrictive measures affecting the Japanese in California, which were to cause serious difficulty and real concern for the United States Government.

Although President Roosevelt had lent his diplomatic support to the Japanese throughout the war, he was realist enough to distrust both sides. On December 27, 1904, just six days before the fall of Port Arthur, the President, in a long letter to Spring-Rice, unburdened himself of his private opinions of the two belligerents and on the probable effects of the war upon the United States and Great Britain. Russia, according to the President, had treated the United States and Great Britain badly, her diplomats unscrupulously promoting Russian ambitions in China without regard for the rights and interests of other powers. Japan, on the other hand, had conformed to Western civilized practices in seeking to enlarge her influence in China; but, said the President,

> . . . I wish I were certain that the Japanese down at bottom did not lump Russians, English, Americans, Germans, all of us, simply as white devils inferior to themselves not only in what they regard as the essentials of civilisation, but in courage and forethought, and to be treated politely only so long as would enable the Japanese to take advantage of our various national jealousies, and beat us in turn.

The President, doubting Japan and certain of Russia's attitude, declared that whether "Russia wins or Japan wins, the victor will

[39] Baron Roman R. Rosen, *Forty Years of Diplomacy* (London: 1902), I, 267. President Roosevelt himself was convinced that continued demands by the Japanese for a money indemnity would mean "a considerable shifting of public opinion" against Japan, and he so informed the Japanese. See Gwynn, *op. cit.*, I, 487. (Roosevelt to Baron Kentaro Kaneko, August 22, 1905.)

in the long run only yield either to England or to the United States substantially the respect which England or the United States is enabled to exact by power actual or potential." With a note of cynicism he added that "no nation can depend upon the mere friendship of any other, even though that friendship is genuine, unless it has itself such strength as to make its own friendship of value in return." Thus, if the interests of the United States and Great Britain had been sacrificed in the peace between Russia and Japan, or if they had combined against the United States and Great Britain, it would have occasioned no great surprise. The President reached the inescapable conclusion that

> ... we must trust in the Lord and keep our powder dry and our eyes open. What turn military or diplomatic affairs will take, I have no idea but so far as possible I intend, as your people should intend, to be vigilant and reasonably ready to adopt whatever course is called for.[40]

On January 31, 1905, President Roosevelt created by executive order a new board on fortifications and coastal defenses with instructions "to revise the Report of the Endicott Board,"[41] and "with further instructions to extend its examinations so as to include estimates and recommendations relative to defenses of the insular possessions."[42] The board, headed by Secretary of War Taft, in its report of February 1, 1906, stressed the importance of two insular bases the protection of which by land fortifications was essential for the successful operation of the fleet. Guantanamo, on the southern coast of Cuba, was vital for the naval protection of the Caribbean approaches to the Panama Canal. Subig Bay stood in the same relation to the defense of the Philippine Islands; "and its protection by fixed defenses is of the gravest importance, not only in order that the fleet may protect Manila, but that it may have facilities for docking, repairing, and provisioning in those distant waters."[43]

[40] The text of this letter is in Gwynn, *op. cit.*, I, 441–446. (Roosevelt to Spring-Rice, December 27, 1904.)

[41] The Endicott Board, headed by Secretary of War William C. Endicott, had been appointed pursuant to an act of Congress of March 3, 1885, to survey the coastal defenses of the United States; and it had submitted its report on January 16, 1886. The report, of course, had dealt only with the continental United States. See *Annual Report of the Secretary of War*, 1886, II: 1, Appendix No. 3.

[42] The text of the Executive Order is printed in *Annual Reports of the War Department*, 1905, I, 21, 22.

[43] The report of the Taft Board may be found in *Sen. Docs.* (Ser. 4913), 59th Cong., 1st sess., No. 248, March 5, 1906.

Subig Bay had thus been chosen as the Pacific insular naval base to be developed and fortified even ahead of Pearl Harbor.[44]

Congress, however, was not so easily convinced, especially in view of the capture of Port Arthur the fortifications of which had been considered impregnable. Senator Henry M. Teller of Colorado informed the Senate that the fall of Port Arthur demonstrated that modern guns could destroy any fortifications; therefore, the Philippine Islands would have to be defended in their entirety by the American fleet. Should the fleet fail, then all the fortifications which might reasonably be constructed would be ineffectual against any real naval power. Since the islands were indefensible without a superior fleet and since they entailed only heavy expenditures without compensating advantages, Senator Teller declared: "I hope the time will come when we shall be rid of the Philippine Islands. I hope the time is not far distant when the American people will conclude that it is not the province of a nation like ours to attempt the civilization of any other country perforce."[45] In contrast Senator Stephen B. Elkins of West Virginia declared that "the Philippine Islands, as we have them, will prove of great advantage to the United States. I think they furnish a base for operations in the East, where we must extend our commerce and protect American interests. Relatively, our trade and commerce with the Orient is destined to be more important than with Europe."[46] But Congress, influenced by the capture of Port Arthur by the Japanese, adopted a "wait and see" attitude; and the appropriation bill which was enacted provided funds only for the normal needs of the insular defenses, the Philippine Islands not even being mentioned.[47]

In other quarters, too, the outcome of the Russo-Japanese War had a tremendous effect. Few expert observers had foreseen a Japanese victory, Great Britain being most skeptical of Japan's ability to defeat the Russians. In fact, Admiral Sir John Fisher was said to have pointed out on the map to Lord Lansdowne, the British

[44] Despite strong opposition by some naval officers, the Navy Department, in 1904, had selected Subig Bay as "the primary naval base of the Philippines." See MS Letter, President of the General Board to the Secretary of the Navy, December 30, 1904.

[45] In the Senate debate on the fortifications appropriation bill for the fiscal year 1907. *Cong. Rec.*, XL, March 20, 1906, pp. 4020, 4021. For the earlier views of Senator Teller on the same subject, see *ibid.*, XXXI, June 25, 1898, p. 6347.

[46] *Ibid.*, XL, March 20, 1906, p. 4021.

[47] The clauses of the act of June 25, 1906, pertaining to the insular defenses are in *U. S. Statutes at Large,* XXXIV (1907), 464, 465.

Foreign Secretary, "the exact spot where the Japanese fleet would be annihilated."[48] Although Prime Minister Balfour did not believe that Russia could crush Japan, neither did he believe that Japan could defeat Russia.[49] Such an inconclusive war, he believed, "would not be an unmixed curse" because it would make it easier for England to deal with Russia in the Near East, Persia, and elsewhere.[50] But as the war progressed and it became apparent that Russia was no match for the aggressive Japanese, both the British and the United States Governments began to sense the danger of Russian defeat and, perhaps, elimination as a Far Eastern power.[51] Accordingly, shortly after the fall of Port Arthur in January, 1905, President Roosevelt began the negotiations which were to result in the conclusion of the hostilities. The President admitted afterward that although humanitarian motives had played an important part in his action, "he had also been influenced by the desirability of keeping Russia in the Far East to preserve the balance of power."[52]

---

[48] Thomas W. L. [Lord] Newton, *Lord Lansdowne: A Biography* (London: Macmillan, 1929), p. 307.

[49] See his Cabinet Memorandum for Lord Lansdowne of December 22, 1903, in Dugdale, *Arthur James Balfour, First Earl of Balfour*, I, 376, 377.

[50] *Ibid.*, p. 378. (Balfour to King Edward VII, December 28, 1903.) The German Ambassador in Washington, Baron Hermann Speck von Sternburg, reported to the German Foreign Office that President Roosevelt had expressed similar views in the following words: "Es liege in unserem Interesse, dass der Krieg zwischen Russland und Japan sich in die Länge ziehe, dass beide Mächte sich nach Möglichkeit aufreiben und dass nach Friedensschluss ihre geographischen Reibungsflächen nicht beseitigt werden, dass sie sich mit Bezug auf die Grenzen ihrer Interessensphären in ähnlicher Weise gegenüberstehen als vor dem Krieg. Das wird sie auf dem Kriegsfuss erhalten und ihre Gelüste nach anderen Gebieten mindern. Japan wird Deutschland dann nicht in Kiautschou und uns nicht in den Philippinen bedrohen. Russlands Aufmerksamkeit wird von seinen Westgrenzen abgelenkt und bleibt im Osten konzentriert." *Die Grosse Politik*, XIX:1, 112, 113. (Speck von Sternburg to the Foreign Office, March 21, 1904.)

[51] In a report of a later conversation with President Roosevelt, the German Ambassador in Washington reported the President as saying: "Die militärische Erfolge Japans hätten die hiesigen Erwartungen mehr als übertroffen, es sei zu hoffen, dass in den bevorstehenden militärischen Konflikten die Verluste auf beiden Seiten möglichst gleich verteilt würden; eine starke Schwächung Russlands im fernen Osten wünsche er nicht." The President still hoped for a peace which would leave Russia and Japan facing each other in the Far East as before the war, each still powerful enough to keep the other occupied. See *Die Grosse Politik*, XIX:1, 114. (Speck von Sternburg to Chancellor Bülow, May 9, 1904.) For the views of the British Prime Minister, see Dugdale, *op. cit.*, I, 387.

[52] Summary of part of a letter to Senator Eugene Hale of Maine, in Thomas A. Bailey, *Theodore Roosevelt and the Japanese-American Crises: An Account of the International Complications Arising from the Race Problem on the Pacific Coast* (Stanford University, California: Stanford University Press, 1934), p. 82. (Roosevelt to Hale, October 27, 1906.)

The destruction of the Russian fleet by the Japanese under Admiral Heihachiro Togo in the battle of Tsushima Strait late in May, 1905, struck a heavy blow to the President's expectations. He had anticipated a hard and even battle which, even though the Japanese should emerge victorious, would take a heavy toll of their fleet.[53] With the Russian fleet completely annihilated, his worst fears seemed about to be realized. He could not foresee the effects upon the interests of the European powers and the United States in the Far East, which would flow from the rise of Japan to the stature of a world power. Nonetheless, he had no doubts about the policy to be pursued by the United States—to treat the Japanese with the utmost courtesy and justice, but at the same time to keep the United States Navy at a peak of strength and efficiency. He wrote:

> ... If we follow this course we shall have no trouble with the Japanese or any one else. But if we bluster; if we behave rather badly to other nations; if we show that we regard the Japanese as an inferior and alien race, and try to treat them as we have treated the Chinese; and if at the same time we fail to keep our navy at the highest point of efficiency and size—then we shall invite disaster.[54]

Even as the President wrote, events were in progress which were to emphasize the truth of his statements.

For several years Japanese immigration into the United States had caused smoldering resentment along the Pacific Coast. In 1900 the Japanese Government had voluntarily attempted to prohibit the emigration of Japanese laborers to the United States; but its efforts had been ineffectual. The Russo-Japanese War had aroused fears along the Pacific Coast that a new flood of Japanese immigration would begin with the peace. Anti-Japanese agitation began early in 1905, led by San Francisco newspapers. The State Legislature of California, on March 2, 1905, adopted a resolution vigorously opposing immigration of Japanese and demanding the protection of the federal government. A campaign to combat the admission of more Japanese to the United States was organized by California labor groups, and boycotts of Japanese business houses were openly advocated.[55] The San Francisco School Board announced on May 6, its decision to segregate all school children of

[53] Lodge, *op. cit.*, II, 130. (Roosevelt to Lodge, June 5, 1905.)

[54] Gwynn, *op. cit.*, I, 473. (Roosevelt to Spring-Rice, June 16, 1905.)

[55] For a detailed account of these events, see Raymond L. Buell, "The Development of the Anti-Japanese Agitation in the United States," *Political Science Quarterly*, XXXVII (December, 1922), 605–622.

"the Mongolian race" from the white children. At the height of the excitement, President Roosevelt privately expressed his displeasure not so much at the agitation itself as at the shortsightedness of the Senators and Representatives of the Pacific states, who had refused to support an increase in the United States Navy only the year before. The President said:

> ... It gives me a feeling of disgust to see them challenge Japanese hostility and justify by their actions any feeling the Japanese might have against us, while at the same time refusing to take steps to defend themselves against the formidable foe whom they are ready with such careless insolence to antagonize. How people can act in this way with the Russo-Japanese war going on before their eyes I cannot understand. I do all I can to counteract the effects, but I cannot accomplish everything.[56]

Despite the President's disapprobation, the attempts of California Congressmen to secure the passage of legislation to exclude Japanese just as Chinese were excluded, continued and kept the campaign alive through the winter of 1905–1906.[57]

In the meantime, the Japanese emerged victorious from their war with Russia and were feeling far from friendly toward the United States. From Japanese officers become insolent in their overweening pride of victory, American military attachés with the Japanese armies gained the impression that the United States was regarded as having thwarted Japan's ambitions in both the Hawaiian and the Philippine Islands.[58] The United States was also blamed for the failure of the Japanese plenipotentiaries at Portsmouth to secure better terms from the Russians.[59] The arrogance and boastfulness of the triumphant Japanese Army, moreover,

---

[56] Lodge, *op. cit.*, II, 122. (Roosevelt to Lodge, May 15, 1905.)

[57] *Cong. Rec.*, XL, December 5, 1905, p. 115. (H. R. 3160 introduced by Representative Duncan E. McKinlay of Santa Rosa, California.) *Ibid.*, December 18, 1905, p. 568. (H. R. 8975 introduced by Representative Everis A. Hayes of San Jose, California.) No action was taken on either of these bills.

[58] Gwynn, *op. cit.*, I, 444, note. (Roosevelt to Spring-Rice, December 27, 1904.)

[59] President Roosevelt himself said that both sides felt they should have received better terms; but the Japanese, as the victors, were more bitter about it. There was rioting and some damage to American property in Japan; and Roosevelt became an object of general dislike by Japanese. He said he had expected this and "did not resent it in the least." *Theodore Roosevelt: An Autobiography* (New York: 1913), p. 586. For a contrary view, see Tatsuji Takeuchi, *War and Diplomacy in the Japanese Empire* (New York: Doubleday, Doran, 1935), p. 159, note 133. Takeuchi maintains that no direct criticism against President Roosevelt was voiced in the Japanese press throughout the whole period of the negotiation and ratification of the treaty. "The attacks were directed against the [Japanese] government."

had been responsible for unwarranted acts of aggression and discourtesy in Manchuria. Even one of Japan's own leaders, Count Tadasu Hayashi, later Foreign Minister, admitted that the indiscretion of the military forces had not only turned the Chinese against Japan, but also "won the adverse criticism of Europeans and Americans."[60] Thus, increasingly tart recriminations were being exchanged across the Pacific.

In these circumstances, the San Francisco School Board decided to carry out its segregation ruling of May 6, 1905, and on October 11, 1906, ordered all Chinese and Japanese pupils transferred to the Oriental Public School. To the Japanese, this appeared to place them in a position inferior to that of other racial groups in the city. Coupled with this was the stigma of the state law which authorized such segregation. The pertinent section authorized school trustees "to exclude children of filthy or vicious habits, or children suffering from contagious or infectious diseases, and also to establish separate schools for Indian children and for children of Mongolian or Chinese descent."[61]

The furor which ensued far surpassed any earlier reaction. So violent became the controversy that war seemed imminent.[62] The President thought it advisable to be prepared for the worst. He urged upon Senator Hale, Chairman of the Senate Committee on Naval Affairs, the necessity "of keeping our navy in such shape as to make it a risky thing for Japan to go to war with us." The President said:

> If these troubles merely affected our internal arrangements, I should not bother you with them; but of course they may possibly bring about war with Japan. I do not think they will bring it about at this moment, but even as to this I am not certain, for the Japanese are proud, sensitive, war-like, are flushed with the glory of their recent triumph, and are in my opinion bent upon establishing themselves as the leading power in the Pacific.[63]

In view of the greatly weakened condition of Russia and the internal upheaval which had resulted, President Roosevelt was convinced that the balance of power in the Far East had been

---

[60] Pooley, *op. cit.*, p. 265. At the close of the Russo-Japanese War, Count Hayashi was still in London as Japanese Ambassador.

[61] Section 1662 of the Political Code of the State of California, as amended March 5, 1903. *Statutes of California and Amendments to the Codes*, 35th Session, 1903, p. 86.

[62] For a detailed account of the course of the controversy, see Bailey, *Theodore Roosevelt and the Japanese-American Crises*, chaps. ii–viii.

[63] *Ibid.*, p. 82. (Roosevelt to Hale, October 27, 1906.)

destroyed. Even though Japan did not go to war over the treatment of her nationals in the United States, the President feared that continued friction would result in Japan's acceptance of the United States "instead of Russia as the national enemy whom she will ultimately have to fight . . ."[64]

In his annual message to Congress of December 3, 1906, Roosevelt pleaded for tolerance and fair play for all immigrants; but he succeeded only in inflaming anti-Japanese feeling still more by referring to the San Francisco school order as "a wicked absurdity." He alluded to the anti-Japanese riots and boycotts as a "sure mark of a low civilization," warning that such demonstrations were "fraught with the gravest consequences to the nation."[65] He asserted the right of the federal government, under existing treaties, to protect alien residents against discrimination,[66] and promised "that the Nation would at once, and in efficient and satisfactory manner, take action that would meet the needs of California." By assuring San Francisco officials that illegal immigration of Japanese laborers would be stopped, the President persuaded them to rescind the school order and even to admit some nonadult Japanese to white schools.[67] But the fight for the total exclusion of Japanese immigrants from the United States continued unabated both in Congress and in California.

Meanwhile, the Japanese wasted little time in confirming the impression created by their demands on Russia at Portsmouth. They proceeded methodically to clear the way for the unrestricted exploitation of their newly acquired sphere of influence in South Manchuria. Since the Japanese showed scant respect for the principle of the open door, they were held in check only by their agreement with Russia at Portsmouth to "restore entirely and completely

---

[64] *Ibid.*

[65] *Messages and Papers,* XVI, 7433.

[66] For an excellent discussion of the legal aspects of the San Francisco school order, upholding the view that the federal government had no power to grant by treaty with a foreign government any right to aliens to attend state educational institutions, see the speech of Senator Isadore Rayner of Maryland, in *Cong. Rec.,* XLI, December 12, 1906, pp. 297–304. See also the speech of Senator John M. Gearin of Oregon on the general problem of the Japanese in the United States, in *ibid.,* January 7, 1907, pp. 674–684.

[67] *Theodore Roosevelt: An Autobiography,* pp. 413, 414. See also Bailey, *op. cit.,* p. 144. It is probable that the efforts of the President were materially aided by the fact that anti-Japanese race riots had broken out in British Columbia; and Japan suddenly realized that her Western ally, Great Britain, might be seriously embarrassed by a war between the United States and Japan. See *Cong. Rec.,* XLII, April 21, 1908, p. 5013.

to the exclusive administration of China" all occupied territory in Manchuria outside the leased zone. But they soon nullified this restriction by convincing the Russian Government that its interests in Manchuria were identical with those of Japan and could be best promoted by joint action. Contrary to Roosevelt's expectations that Japan would not become an ally of Russia,[68] therefore, the two erstwhile enemies settled their outstanding differences in 1907 in a series of treaties designed to exclude other powers from Manchuria. "There could be no question any more of an 'open door' policy in Manchuria; the door was definitely slammed."[69] The same would be true, of course, in Korea and Mongolia.

The first agreements, signed on June 13, 1907, were intended to delimit and to regulate the respective railway interests of the two powers in Manchuria. The railway interests were interpreted by Russia and Japan to include political control over the railway zones, which embraced important coal mining properties; and Russian and Japanese troops were maintained within the zones to "protect" the railways and the mines. This affected the nationals not only of Russia, Japan, and China, but also of the other treaty powers, and was disputed by the powers affected, but with little success.[70] That these "political" rights were of paramount importance to Russia and Japan was evidenced by two further agreements, signed on July 30, 1907, only one of which was made public. These two treaties throw considerable light on the intentions of Japan and Russia, both because of their contents and because of the circumstances in which they were negotiated. The public treaty was clearly intended to make their political control permanent by pledging the contracting parties to "sustain and defend the maintenance of the *status quo*" in China. The secret treaty, on the other hand, apparently delimited the spheres of economic interest of the two powers, Japan's special interest in Korea being definitely recognized, as were Russia's interests in the Chinese Eastern Railway and, to a limited extent, in Mongolia. Moreover, a division line was drawn across Manchuria, north of which Japan agreed to

---

[68] Expressed in a letter to George von Lengerke Meyer, American Ambassador in Rome, February 6, 1905, and quoted in Dennett, *Roosevelt and the Russo-Japanese War*, p. 162.

[69] Baron Serge A. Korff, "Russia in the Far East," *The American Journal of International Law*, XVII (April, 1923), 272.

[70] Westel W. Willoughby, *Foreign Rights and Interests in China* (rev. ed.; Baltimore: Johns Hopkins Press, 1927), I, 164–168.

refrain from seeking railway or communications concessions; and Russia agreed to a similar restriction on her activities south of the line.[71]

To make the situation even more ominous, four of the powers chose this moment to enter into what appeared to be an alliance for the protection of their Far Eastern interests. France and Japan had signed a treaty on June 10, 1907, in which they engaged to "respect the independence and integrity of China, as well as the principle of equal treatment in that country for the commerce and subjects or citizens of all nations." They further agreed to maintain the *status quo* regarding their own possessions in the Far East in order to promote "the peace and security" of that region. Since France was already an ally of Russia and had entered into an *entente cordiale* with Great Britain in 1904, there was good reason to expect that these two powers would make every effort to bring Japan and Russia together. The British alliance with Japan, first consummated in 1902, had been renewed in 1905 during the Russo-Japanese War as a gesture of solidarity to prevent interference in that war by either France or Germany, especially by the latter. This process of international adjustment was rounded out on August 31, 1907, by an agreement between Russia and Great Britain, which composed differences over their respective spheres of influence in the Middle East.[72] Thus, the four great powers, Great Britain, France, Russia, and Japan, were bound together by their common interests in a loose alliance which boded little good for helpless China.

Long before the last of these agreements had been consummated, the United States Government became convinced that the Japanese were preparing for war. On June 18, 1907, the Joint Army-Navy Board frankly admitted that Japan possessed overwhelming superiority both on land and at sea in the Pacific Ocean and that the United States would be forced on the defensive until the battle fleet could be transferred to the Pacific Ocean from the Atlantic.

[71] Alfred L. P. Dennis, *The Anglo-Japanese Alliance*, University of California Publications, Bureau of International Relations, I, No. 1 (Berkeley: University of California Press, 1923), p. 28. The terms of the secret treaty as given here were reconstructed by Dennis from numerous references to its terms in other documents. See also *British Documents*, VIII, 485, for the text of a secret *Article Additionnel* to the treaty of 1907, which defines the boundary between Russian and Japanese spheres of influence in North and South Manchuria respectively.

[72] *British and Foreign State Papers*, C (1906–1907), 555–560.

Declaring that American forces in the Philippines were not strong enough to defend more than one place, the Board recommended that all preparations be concentrated on protecting the naval base in Subig Bay. Since Hawaii, Guam, and Samoa could not be defended, they were to be left as they were; but the Pacific Coast ports of the United States were to be made ready to resist an expected attack.[73]

In a conference with War and Navy Department representatives at Oyster Bay on June 27, President Roosevelt concurred in these recommendations and took prompt steps to carry them out. The Secretary of the Navy was instructed to store coal at Subig Bay, to mount advance base guns to defend the naval base, to recall the cruisers from the Orient to the safety of the Pacific Coast, and to prepare the Atlantic Fleet for an early transfer to the Pacific. The submarine mine defense of Subig Bay and the Pacific Coast was to be made ready by the War Department, fortifications at Subig Bay were to be pushed to completion, supplies for a field army were to be assembled at Subig Bay, and the regular Army was to be recruited to its full authorized strength.[74] The Army's Chief of Staff later asserted that these "orders of the President directing concentration of all elements of defense at Subig Bay were brought about by joint recommendations of the Army and Navy, which were inspired solely by the conditions then actually existing . . ."[75]

All these preparations were to be made quietly to keep from arousing suspicions abroad or at home that the United States was preparing for war in the Pacific.[76] When the Acting Secretary of War urged as a "policy of ordinary military prudence" the transfer of seacoast guns from the Atlantic Coast defenses to the Philippines and their mounting in completed emplacements, the President vetoed the suggestion because the operation would attract public attention.[77] But such feverish preparations for war could not wholly escape public notice. American newspapers during July were filled with stories of the "imminent war" with Japan. In the Philippine

[73] MS Letter, The Adjutant General to the Commanding General, Philippines Division, July 6, 1907.

[74] *Ibid.*

[75] See MS Memorandum, Chief of Staff to The Adjutant General, September 30, 1907.

[76] See MS Letter cited in note 73 above.

[77] MS Letter, Acting Secretary of War to the President's secretary, July 31, 1907; MS Memorandum, Secretary of War to the Chief of Staff, August 15, 1907.

Islands, the presence of troops and marines mounting the naval guns at Subig Bay so frightened the native workmen that they took to the hills, many not even stopping to collect their pay.[78]

The formation of the quadruple alliance among Great Britain, France, Russia, and Japan had, of course, done nothing to alleviate the tenseness between the United States and Japan, and only forced the United States into closer coöperation with Germany. The Kaiser was convinced that Japan was nearing her goal of "control of the Pacific Ocean, expansion of her territory to the southward, and predominance in China."[79] He therefore suggested either a political alliance or some other arrangement with the United States "in order to safeguard our similar economic interests in China against the predominance of the three entente powers."[80] The German Ambassador in Washington, Baron Hermann Speck von Sternburg, openly discussed with the President the possibility of German military and naval coöperation with the United States in the event of war with Japan.[81] At the Second Hague Conference, which was in session from June 15 to October 18, 1907, the United States and Germany also coöperated, and so closely as to attract serious attention, especially in the British delegation.[82]

The Hague Conference provides the background against which the changes in President Roosevelt's opinions on naval development may be traced as the American-Japanese crisis of 1906–1907 developed. In 1906, when the agenda of the conference was being

[78] MS Letter, District Engineer at Manila to the Chief of Engineers, July 13, 1907.

[79] *Die Grosse Politik,* XXV:1, 72. (Speck von Sternburg to the Imperial Chancellor, Prince von Bülow, September 9, 1907.) The Kaiser, in a marginal comment, said: "Richtig." As he later stated it himself, Japan's policy in the Far East was "L'Asie pour les Asiates (i[d] e[st] pour les Japonais)." See *ibid.*, p. 86. (Count A. von Rex, German Minister in Peking, to the Imperial Chancellor, December 7, 1907—marginal note.)

[80] *Ibid.*, p. 71. (Heinrich von Tschirschky, German Foreign Secretary, to Speck von Sternburg, September 15, 1907.) Why Russia was not mentioned as the fourth of the entente powers is not clear.

[81] *Ibid.*, pp. 78, 79. (Speck von Sternburg to the Foreign Office, November 8, 1907.) The Japanese Government was aware of the offers to the United States of German aid against Japan. See *British Documents,* VIII, 461. (Sir Claude M. MacDonald, British Ambassador in Tokyo, to Sir Edward Grey, British Foreign Secretary, November 27, 1908.)

[82] *British Documents,* VIII, 287, 288. (Eyre A. Crowe, member of the British delegation at the Hague, to William G. Tyrrell, private secretary to Sir Edward Grey, October 11, 1907.) Crowe reported that the "Americans have, except in the case of obligatory arbitration, also gone with Germany and against us in every possible way, most markedly in all naval questions, and often obviously in a sense quite opposed to their own interests."

discussed, and before the San Francisco school order aroused anew the anger of Americans and Japanese against each other, President Roosevelt had expressed the opinion that the United States could not reduce her land and naval armaments below the minimum level at which they then were; but he had offered to subscribe to a program merely of replacement of obsolete naval units in the future. To him, this meant "building about a battleship each year. Now and then we could omit a battleship."[83] He was even willing to limit the size of the battleships built.[84]

After the San Francisco school episode, however, his views changed. On October 27, 1906, he wrote to Senator Hale: "I most earnestly feel that we can not afford to let our navy fall behind"; and urged upon the Senator the necessity of laying down every year "two ships the equal of any laid down by any nation."[85] As the crisis continued and Congress refused, largely through the influence of Senator Hale, to heed his counsel, the President lost all patience with those who talked of peace when the nation was in danger. He wrote to Baron von Sternburg on July 16, 1907: "I am so utterly disgusted with the nonsense chattered by the extreme advocates of peace here that it was difficult for me to take a proper interest in the Hague proceedings."[86]

The failure of the Hague Conference to make any limitation of armaments offered the President a convenient pretext to carry his conversion to its ultimate and necessary extreme. In his annual message to Congress on December 3, 1907, he referred to the failure to agree on limitation and then said:

> . . . Such being the fact it would be most unwise for us to stop the upbuilding of our Navy. To build one battleship of the best and most advanced type a year would barely keep our fleet up to its present force. This is not enough. In my judgment, we should this year provide for four battleships. But it is idle to build battleships unless in addition to providing the men, and the means for thorough training, we provide the auxiliaries for them, unless we provide docks, the coaling stations, the colliers and supply ships that they need. We are ex-

[83] Nevins, *Henry White*, pp. 498, 499. (Roosevelt to Henry White, American Ambassador in Rome, August 14, 1906.)

[84] *British Documents*, VIII, 195. Report of a conversation on August 31, 1906, between the President and Count A. E. W. Gleichen, British Military Attaché in Washington. (Sir H. Mortimer Durand, British Ambassador in Washington, to Sir Edward Grey, September 7, 1906.) See also Sir Sidney Lee, *King Edward VII: A Biography* (London: Macmillan, 1925–1927), II, 437. (Count Gleichen to King Edward VII, September 1, 1906.)

[85] Bailey, *op. cit.*, pp. 82, 83. (Roosevelt to Senator Hale, October 27, 1906.)

[86] *Ibid.*, p. 236. (Roosevelt to von Sternburg, July 16, 1907.)

tremely deficient in coaling stations and docks on the Pacific, and this deficiency should not longer be permitted to exist.[87]

Thus the President not only urged Congress to authorize four new battleships and thereby make up some of the units by which the program of the General Board had fallen behind, but also stressed the need for Pacific bases for the fleet which was about to start on its cruise to the Pacific. As the President stated in his message, "This trip to the Pacific will show what some of our needs are and will enable us to provide for them."[88]

President Roosevelt had announced his decision to send the fleet to the Pacific on June 27, 1907, when the crisis with Japan was at its height. Later, in a letter to Secretary of State Elihu Root, the President said: "I am more concerned over the Japanese situation than almost any other. Thank Heaven we have the navy in good shape. It is high time, however, that it should go on a cruise around the world. In the first place I think it will have a pacific effect to show that it can be done . . ."[89] Although the President afterward believed that the cruise had had the desired effect upon Japan,[90] there were those who disagreed with him. For example, Sir Claude MacDonald, British Ambassador in Tokyo, reported to the Foreign Office:

The President's declaration that the reason the American Fleet was sent to the Pacific was to "impress Japan" with the seriousness of the situation is possibly only one more of those declarations which the President does not mean to be taken altogether seriously. Any way the arrival of the fleet in the Pacific

[87] *Messages and Papers*, XVII, 7494. Further proof of the danger which was thought to exist may be found in the following passage from the diary of George von Lengerke Meyer, Postmaster General in President Roosevelt's Cabinet:

"November 29, 1907—Cabinet Meeting. Good deal of discussion about the Japanese. Russian officers are offering their services, in case of war with Japan, in Philippine Islands. The President does not think that we will have war; if they should have such a purpose, they will have to attack before the fleet reaches San Francisco. We know that the Japs are buying ammunition in large quantities. I think they merely want to be ready in case the unexpected should occur." See M. A. DeWolfe Howe, *George von Lengerke Meyer: His Life and Public Services* (New York: 1919), p. 377.

[88] *Messages and Papers*, XVII, 7495.

[89] Bishop, *op. cit.*, II, 64. (Roosevelt to Root, July 13, 1907.) For a detailed account of the circumstances in which the cruise was made, see Bailey, *op. cit.*, chaps. x–xii.

[90] Bailey, *op. cit.*, pp. 301, 302. (Roosevelt to Whitelaw Reid, American Ambassador in London, December 4, 1908.) Roosevelt said: "The recent voyage of the fleet around the world was not the first occasion in which I have used it [big stick] to bring about prompt resumption of peaceful relations between this country and a foreign Power."

has certainly failed to impress Japan. The Japanese Government are fully impressed with the seriousness of the immigration question, and sooner than imperil friendly relations with America they would, I know, themselves prohibit emigration; but a menace such as the sending of a fleet, leaves them absolutely cold.[91]

Whatever the actual effect of the world cruise was, the fact remains that the immigration question between the United States and Japan was quickly settled, sealed only by Japan's promise thereafter to grant no more passports to the United States to Japanese of the laboring class, with certain reasonable exceptions.[92] In this so-called gentlemen's agreement of 1907, the President fulfilled his pledge to the people of California that the government would protect them against an influx of Japanese immigrants. The President described the agreement as "an arrangement with Japan under which the Japanese themselves prevented any emigration to our country of their laboring people, it being distinctly understood that if there was such emigration the United States would at once pass an exclusion law."[93]

The "gentlemen's agreement" was soon supplemented by the Root-Takahira exchange of notes on November 30, 1908, which were intended to end the distrust and ill feeling aroused by the activities of the Japanese and Russians in Manchuria and by the treaty concluded between those two powers on July 30, 1907. The United States and Japan pledged themselves "to the maintenance

[91] *British Documents,* VIII, 485. (MacDonald to Grey, March 17, 1908.) The Kaiser, on the other hand, thought that the sending of the American fleet into the Pacific had "overthrown all the calculations of the British and the Japanese." *Die Grosse Politik,* XXV:1, 87. (William II to Chancellor Bülow, December 30, 1907.)

[92] Report of the Commissioner General of Immigration, July 1, 1908, in *Reports of the Department of Commerce and Labor,* 1908, pp. 221, 222. See also the Report of the Secretary of Commerce and Labor of December 1, 1908, in *ibid.,* pp. 14, 15.

[93] *Theodore Roosevelt: An Autobiography,* p. 414. President Roosevelt sympathized with the people of California in their desire to exclude Japanese immigrants, but he did not approve of their methods of showing their dislike for the Japanese. He said that "the Japanese themselves would not tolerate the intrusion into their country of a mass of Americans who would displace Japanese in the business of the land." Evidence of the truth of this statement may be found in the action of the Japanese Government in banning the immigration of Chinese laborers into Japan except under special permits. This exclusion was authorized by Imperial Ordinance No. 352, of July 27, 1899. The term "laborers" was defined as "men engaged in labor in agricultural, fishing, mining, civil engineering, architectural, manufacturing, transporting, carting, stevedoring, and other miscellaneous work." See *Foreign Relations,* 1907, II, 768, 769.

of the existing status quo in the region" of the Pacific Ocean, "to respect the territorial possessions belonging to each other in said region," and to support "the independence and integrity of China and the principle of equal opportunity for commerce and industry of all nations in that Empire."[94] The two powers agreed to consult each other whenever any event threatened either the *status quo* in the Pacific or the principle of equal opportunity in China.

The Root-Takahira agreement gives a clear picture of the problems which were causing mutual distrust. The United States was interested primarily in maintaining the independence and territorial integrity of China and in preserving the principle of equal commercial opportunity in that country. The United States Government could therefore be elated at receiving a renewed pledge from Japan to respect these principles. Japan, on her part, was interested primarily in consolidating her position on the continent of Asia; hence, she must have felt triumphant in securing from the United States a recognition and a guarantee of "the existing status quo" in the region of the Pacific Ocean, which included Eastern Asia. This is particularly true in view of the secret Russo-Japanese treaty of 1907, the provisions of which seriously affected the existing *status quo* and of which the United States was unaware.

Although this agreement in reality settled nothing, the general consensus at the time was that it had prevented a war between the United States and Japan. Three days before the notes were signed, Sir Edward Grey, British Foreign Secretary, wrote: "This agreement would be a complete answer to all the apprehensions which have been aroused."[95] After the agreement was completed, T. A. Brassey, the eminent British naval authority, expressed the same opinion in more positive terms:

> The signature of the Treaty between the United States and Japan, by which each pledges itself to observe the territorial possessions of the other, and, in case of any threatened disturbance, to communicate with the other in order to arrive at a mutual understanding, considerably modifies the Naval situation in the Pacific. The possibility of a conflict between the United States and Japan appears to have been removed, at any rate for the present.[96]

---

[94] For the text of the notes, see *Foreign Relations*, 1908, pp. 510–512.

[95] *British Documents*, VIII, 462. (Grey to MacDonald, November 27, 1908.)

[96] *The Naval Annual*, 1909, pp. 27, 28. The German Minister in Peking, Count A. von Rex, interpreted the agreement in a different way; he attributed the notes to weakness on the part of the United States. He reported his views to the Foreign Office as follows: "Die Deklaration war das passende Mittel, sie erscheint mir vom amerikanischen Standpunkt als eine Art Waffenstillstand,

Meanwhile, Congress was acting in earnest upon the recommendations of the President in his annual message of December 3, 1907. Although the result was not wholly satisfactory, Congress did make more generous provision for the Navy, both afloat and ashore, than it had made for some years. Only two of the four battleships recommended by the President and the General Board were authorized, but twenty-three lesser units were to be added to the fleet. But the really important action was that Congress, after years of procrastination, authorized the construction of a great naval base at Pearl Harbor. The House Committee on Naval Affairs set forth the reasons for this step:

> In the judgment of your committee the new developments on the Pacific and among the nations that border its shores make it imperative that a strong operating base be established for our Navy at Pearl Harbor without further delay.
>
> A naval base at Pearl Harbor is not designed primarily for the protection of Hawaii. Its main purpose is to form a buffer of defense for our entire Pacific coast and to make possible our naval supremacy upon the Pacific. . . .
>
> The equipment of Pearl Harbor is therefore a matter of national prudence and not of extravagance. It affords the nation's least expensive way of defending our Pacific coast; *it will constitute one of the strongest factors in the prevention of war with any power in the Far East.*[97]

There could be little doubt about what was in the minds of the committee members, and memorials from organizations from coast to coast favoring the immediate development of Pearl Harbor indicated that the country at large was also aware of the danger imminent in the Pacific.

By the Naval Appropriation Act of May 13, 1908, the Secretary of the Navy was "authorized and directed to establish a naval station at Pearl Harbor, Hawaii"; and $1,000,000 was appropriated and made immediately available to start construction.[98] Nothing was done, however, toward developing a base in the Philippines.

---

welcher dazu dienen soll, die Flotte auszubauen und die Vorteile eines Panamakanals einem künftigen Kriege zu verschaffen. Ich sage Waffenstillstand, weil durch die Deklaration keine der zwischen Japan und Amerika strittigen Fragen geregelt worden ist. Die Reibungsflächen sind dieselben geblieben, sie haben nur durch die Erklärung die Aufrechterhaltung des Status quo im Stillen Ozean und der Integrität Chinas eine gewisse Beschränkung erfahren." See *Die Grosse Politik,* XXV:1, 98. (Count von Rex to the Imperial Chancellor, December 15, 1908.)

[97] *House Reports* (Ser. 5226), 60th Cong., 1st sess., No. 1385, April 4, 1908, pp. 2, 3. Italics mine.

[98] *U. S. Statutes at Large,* XXXV (1909), 141.

Congress had never accepted the recommendations of the Taft board and of the Navy Department that Olongapo on Subig Bay should be developed as the main Far Eastern base. Neither of the two stations in the Philippines was adequate as a fleet base; and, as the Secretary of the Navy, Victor H. Metcalf, reported in 1908, until the "uncertainty as to the location of the permanent naval station in the Philippines is definitely settled by Congress, the department does not view with favor any but absolutely necessary expenditures at its stations in the Philippines."[99] The crisis with Japan made it unnecessary for Congress to choose between Cavite and Olongapo.

The President revealed the attitude of the administration toward the Philippine Islands in a letter dated August 21, 1907, to Secretary of War Taft, whom he was sending to the Far East to observe conditions at first hand. He wrote:

> The Philippine Islands form our heel of Achilles. They are all that makes the present situation with Japan dangerous. . . . I think that to have some pretty clear avowal of our intention not to permanently keep them and to give them independence would remove a temptation from Japan's way and would render our task easier. . . .
>
> Personally I should be glad to see the Islands made independent, with perhaps some kind of international guarantee for the preservation of order . . . I would rather see this nation fight all her life than to see her give them up to Japan or any other nation under duress.[100]

The President clearly understood the weakness of the American position in the Far East, especially against so formidable an enemy as Japan. He believed, moreover, that he was speaking for the American people as a whole when he said he would never consent to give up the Philippines under compulsion. Since the islands admittedly could not be defended against a sea power dominant in Asiatic waters,[101] it was inevitable that the old question of relinquishing them should again be raised. The President apparently

---

[99] Report of the Secretary of the Navy, November 30, 1908. *Annual Reports of the Navy Department*, 1908, p. 34.

[100] Pringle, *Theodore Roosevelt*, pp. 408, 409. (Roosevelt to Taft, August 21, 1907.) Taft himself later said: "The occasion for my visit was the opening of the Philippine Assembly." See *Sen. Docs.* (Ser. 5240), 60th Cong., 1st sess., No. 200, January 27, 1908, p. 6.

[101] The Chief of Staff declared in December, 1907: "There is no avoiding the conclusion that we have not now, and never will have, sufficient troops in the Philippine Islands to defend Subig Bay from the land side against a land attack by the Japanese for any length of time to enable our fleet to reach the Philippine Islands from the Atlantic Ocean." See MS Memorandum, Chief of Staff to the Secretary of War, December 21, 1907.

was determined that the United States should not again be embarrassed by a similar situation.

As a result, the Army and Navy Joint Board made a study of the whole problem of American defenses in the Pacific. The difficulties with Japan and the deficiencies brought to light by the cruise of the fleet around the world naturally influenced the Board's conclusions. Secretary of the Navy Meyer, in commenting upon the work of the Joint Board in his report for 1909, said:

> Owing to the changed conditions, the past differences of opinion in regard to the establishment of a naval base in the Philippine Islands have been overcome. The joint board has recently considered this important matter, including the whole strategic field of the Pacific, and has made a report recommending that we maintain a small docking and repair station at Olongapo, in the Philippine Islands, but that our main naval base in the Pacific Ocean should be established at Pearl Harbor, Hawaii.
>
> This definitely disposes of any contention as to the locality for a repair station in the Philippines and enables us to concentrate effort on the building up of the naval base at Pearl Harbor and of the necessary defenses in connection therewith.[102]

The decision of the Board was, in effect, to abandon the Philippines to their fate and to concentrate major fleet facilities at a point which could readily be defended. The Joint Board stated that there were some sites on Manila Bay that "could be made into suitable naval bases at great expense"; but "the changed conditions in the Pacific made such expense unnecessary and undesirable." Olongapo was to be maintained, but the Board asserted that, by limiting its facilities to small repairs, "its defense would not become one of serious moment."[103]

By 1909 the transition was complete. The attitude of the United States toward the Pacific had changed completely. As the famous Spanish-American War hero, Richmond P. Hobson, said in the House debate on the naval appropriation bill for 1909, "... another ocean has come upon us."[104] The Far East had become the danger spot; and the broad Pacific, in the absence of a powerful American

[102] Report of the Secretary of the Navy, December 4, 1909, in *Annual Reports of the Navy Department*, 1909, p. 30.

[103] *Ibid.* The Army War College and the Joint Army-Navy Board had restudied Philippine defenses in 1907, and the Board had reversed its decision of 1904 by designating Cavite as the main Philippine base.

[104] *Cong. Rec.*, XLII, April 11, 1908, p. 4608. This was the appropriation bill in which Congress authorized two battleships for the first time since 1905 as a direct result of the Japanese crisis and President Roosevelt's first recommendation of four battleships in one year. See below, Appendix II, p. 177.

fleet in those waters, had become America's bulwark. The Philippine Islands, which had been considered defensible against a great European naval power, were relegated to a position of secondary importance, since the United States abandoned hope of defending them and established her major naval repair facilities at the more easily defended position of Pearl Harbor. The "gentlemen's agreement" and the Root-Takahira exchange of notes had settled nothing. The racial immigration problem remained an acute issue in Japanese-American relations; and, despite the Root-Takahira notes, Japan continued to encroach upon the administrative and territorial jurisdiction of China and to flout the principle of equal opportunity for the commerce of all. Japan had, in short, established herself in the American mind as the real "probable enemy" with whom the United States would eventually come into hostile conflict.[105]

---

[105] The Joint Army-Navy Board made the following statement in 1908: "It is believed that the change from the unanimous conclusion of 1903—that Subig Bay was suited for a naval base and station—to the reversal of that conclusion in 1907, was justified by the altered conditions of war, by the evident transition of a powerful nation close to that base from an attitude of strong friendliness to one of possible hostility, and because the whole question had received the best thought and thorough study of both services before the Joint Board reluctantly changed its views." See MS Letter, Joint Board to the Secretary of the Navy, March 5, 1908.

CHAPTER III

JAPAN, THE OPEN DOOR, AND THE ANGLO-JAPANESE ALLIANCE

... Die angelsächsische Rasse unter amerikanischer Führung als Beherrscherin der ganzen neuen Welt und des Stillen Ozeans, das ist das Hauptziel derjenigen Amerikaner, welche über die politischen Zukunft ihres Landes nachdenken. Zur Erreichung dieses Zieles muss indessen England der amerikanischen Leitung noch weiter folgen und aus einem Bundesgenossen Japans zu einem Gegner desselben werden.—COUNT JOHANN VON BERNSTORFF.

IN THE YEARS after 1908, the United States Government directed its efforts toward building up its naval defenses and toward checking Japan and Russia in their efforts to gain exclusive control of Manchuria and North China. The administration secured each year Congressional authorization for two battleships and numerous lesser craft in order to increase the striking power of the fleet. Work on the Pearl Harbor naval base was pushed unrelentingly in anticipation of the transfer of the fleet to the Pacific when the Panama Canal was completed. The annual appropriations for the construction of the base reached $2,262,000 in 1911.[1] Later in the same year, the Army and Navy Joint Board lent the weight of its expert opinion to the continued development of Pearl Harbor by once more stressing its strategic importance:

> This yard, owing to its advanced position and natural advantages as a naval base, is practically indispensable to our own fleet in any operation against an Asiatic power, and would be a great menace to us if it were permitted to fall into the hands of an enemy. It should be made as nearly as possible impregnable, in order that it may be safely held and that the fuel and other supplies of our fleet and its communications may be kept intact.[2]

With Congress willing to act upon such recommendations, the nation seemed to be well on the road to attaining a naval power commensurate with her world position.

Although the Taft administration favored and continued Roosevelt's policy of building up naval defenses, circumstances soon made it imperative to adopt other policies. First, the election of a Democratic majority in the House of Representatives in 1910

[1] In the Naval Appropriation Act of March 4, 1911. *U. S. Statutes at Large*, XXXVI (1911), 1276.

[2] *Cong. Rec.*, LI, May 1, 1914, p. 7587. Inserted by Representative Peter G. Gerry of Rhode Island in the debate on the naval appropriation bill for 1915. The report of the Joint Board was dated November 27, 1911.

ended the coöperation between the President and Congress. Consequently the Naval Appropriation Act passed by the new Congress in 1912 authorized only one battleship. Second, developments in the Far East gave impetus for adopting new methods of meeting the Japanese challenge.

To the Japanese, the renewed pledge in the Root-Takahira notes to observe the open door and to respect Chinese integrity was a small price to pay for the exclusive privilege of exploiting South Manchuria. Even if the United States had not intended to recognize such an exclusive privilege, the Japanese Government proceeded as if she had. The following facts give some idea of the methods and the extent of this politico-economic penetration of Manchuria:

> The exploitation of South Manchuria was not undertaken by the Japanese Government directly, but by a powerful joint-stock company in which the Government is the largest shareholder....
>
> The South Manchurian Railway Company engages largely in enterprises other than those implied by its designation. It runs a regular service of ships between Dairen (Dalny) and Shanghai, and owns the fleet of the Dairen Steamship Company coasting in the Gulf of Pechili. The Fushun Colliery, about twenty-five miles east of Mukden, is under its control. This is situated on an extensive coal bed with deposits from 75 feet to 180 feet thick, and a total storage estimated at 1,000 million tons. The output in 1913 was 3,000 tons per day.... It also owns the Yentai coal fields, north-east of Liaoyang. It owns and runs the great harbour works at Dairen and the wharves and shipping facilities of Port Arthur. It provides electric current for Hoshigaura, Changchun, Mukden, Dairen, and Port Arthur, and gas as well where required. It has large hotels at all these places. It owns about 50,000 acres of land, one third of which is let for building purposes. It maintains hospitals, with a central establishment at Dairen and twenty-five branch stations along its lines of railway. It provides fifteen primary schools and a medical college and a technical institute. It creates townships, erects public buildings, makes roads, constructs telegraph lines, and instals telephones. In short, this great concern runs South Manchuria for the Japanese Government.[3]

Such exploitation, possessing every element of permanency, did not betoken any Japanese intention to relinquish her rights in Manchuria when the time expired. The rights, obtained from Russia in the Treaty of Portsmouth in 1905, were the same as those which Russia had extorted from China in 1896 and 1898.

By the terms of the first agreement, dated September 8, 1896, Russia was granted the right to construct and to operate for eighty

[3] William Blane, "The Japanese in China," *The Nineteenth Century and After*, LXXVII (May, 1915), 1110, 1111.

years the South Manchurian Railway, and China the privilege of buying back the railroad at the end of thirty-six years by repaying the capital invested plus the outstanding indebtedness of the line. Similarly, in the second agreement, dated March 27, 1898, Russia was granted a twenty-five-year lease of the Liaotung Peninsula, including the ports of Talienwan and Port Arthur. But Japan proceeded to develop the territory as if she had permanent possession; and it is evident that the government did entertain such ideas. For example, the British Ambassador asked Prince Hirobumi Ito, a member of the Genro and a former premier, what Japan's attitude would be when the Liaotung lease expired. He replied, "I may not be alive then (1923) but I do not see how we can possibly return to China the Liao-tung Peninsula."[4] This evidence convinced the United States Government by 1909 that the Japanese pledge in the Root-Takahira agreement was without meaning and that American interests in China would have to be protected in some other way.

The United States had opportunity to assert her rights in May, 1909, after China had granted a concession to German interests to build the Hukuang Railways. These widespread projects included a line from Hankow to the Province of Szechwan, where the United States had an interest because of written promises exchanged in 1903 and 1904 between Edwin H. Conger, the American Minister in Peking, and the Chinese Government. The United States pressed this claim with such vigor that she eventually forced the inclusion of an American bankers' group in the four-power consortium of 1911. The State Department declared at the beginning that "the Government of the United States regards full and frank coöperation as best calculated to maintain the open door and the integrity of China . . ."[5] According to George E. Roberts, an official of the National City Bank of New York, the American bankers did not ask nor care to participate, because they doubted the salability of Chinese bonds in the American market. The government, however, had reasons for insisting on American participation, as Roberts explains:

The government at Washington . . . was interested in the Chinese situation. Our government has stood for the open door in China, and knowing that China

[4] *British Documents,* VIII, 467, 468. (MacDonald to Grey, May 13, 1909.)

[5] *Foreign Relations,* 1909, p. 152. (Knox to Whitelaw Reid, American Ambassador in London, June 9, 1909.)

was about to negotiate a large foreign loan in Europe, and realizing that this would give the countries participating special claims to consideration in Chinese trade, and probably lead to their obtaining a more intimate position in Chinese affairs than a non-participating country, it conceived the idea of having American bankers participate in the loan. The purpose was to obtain for this country the right to a seat at any council table at which Chinese affairs were under discussion. Our government acted in this matter upon the advice of the American diplomats most experienced in Asiatic affairs; it solicited the interest of the New York bankers, and asked of the Chinese government that American bankers be allowed to participate.[6]

Add to this the authority of the Assistant Secretary of State under President Taft, who asserted that, although the bankers would have profited from the investment, the loans "were so clearly a means to a greater end that the bankers had to be urged into the whole transaction and, during its difficult course, often urged to remain interested";[7] and it is apparent that American participation in the consortium was a government policy. It was a policy designed to check further encroachments by the powers upon the political independence of China, to safeguard the principle of equal commercial opportunity for all, and to increase American trade in China through the influence of financial interest. Through cooperative effort, the United States would escape all the responsibilities of unilateral action, and would be certain of support whenever American rights were brought into question. This energetic action by the United States may justly be called the first blow upon the wedge which was to be driven between Japan and Great Britain and which was ultimately to destroy the Anglo-Japanese Alliance. There were, however, complications in the negotiation of the Hukuang Railways loan, which served to make Japan's purposes in Manchuria so clear that even her ally could not fail to understand them.

While Great Britain, France, Germany, and the United States were negotiating an equitable distribution of the Hukuang Railways loan, the Chinese Government concluded on October 2, 1909, an agreement with an Anglo-American group of bankers for the construction of a railway from Chinchou by way of Tsitsihar to Aigun on the Russian Amur River border. Using this agreement

[6] "Property Rights and Trade Rivalries as Factors in International Complications," *Proceedings of the Academy of Political Science*, VII (July, 1917), 628.

[7] Huntington Wilson, "The Relation of Government to Foreign Investment," *The Annals of the American Academy of Political and Social Science*, LXVIII (November, 1916), 309.

as a bargaining tool, Secretary of State Philander C. Knox approached the interested governments with a plan to make effective the open door and the integrity of China in Manchuria by internationalizing the means of communication. Secretary Knox proposed to obtain an agreement among the powers to permit China to anticipate the dates upon which she was to be permitted by treaty to purchase control of the railways in Manchuria, and to make her a loan so that she could carry out the transaction. Under Chinese ownership, the railways would be operated for an indefinite period by an international commission to be set up by the interested powers.[8] The contribution of the United States to this international pooling of interests and responsibilities was to be the concession to build the Chinchou–Aigun Railway.

The State Department, confident that the proposal would be adopted after having received what was interpreted as a favorable reply from Great Britain, issued a statement to the press on January 6, 1910, stating the reasons "for this energetic action on the part of the United States Government." After pointing out the political implications of the original Hukuang loan agreement and the consequent importance to the United States of participation therein, the State Department asserted:

> There were, however, stronger reasons and broader grounds. In fact, the action of the Government in respect to the pending loan was but the first step in a new phase of the traditional policy of the United States in China and with special reference to Manchuria. As is well known, the essential principles of the Hay policy of the open door are the preservation of the territorial and jurisdictional integrity of the Chinese Empire and equal commercial opportunity in China for all nations. This Government believes that one of the most effective, if not the most effective, way to secure for China the undisturbed enjoyment of all political rights in Manchuria and to promote the normal development of the eastern provinces under the policy of the open door practically applied would be to take the railroads of Manchuria out of eastern politics and place them under an economic and impartial administration by vesting in China the ownership of its railroads . . .[9]

But the State Department's views were not consonant with those of the Japanese Government. If any doubt existed on this question or on the question of Japan's intentions in Manchuria, it was resolved by the Japanese reply to the Knox proposal. In this reply,

[8] *Foreign Relations*, 1909, p. 211. (Whitelaw Reid to Grey, November 9, 1909.) See also Willoughby, *Foreign Rights and Interests in China*, I, 175–187.
[9] *Foreign Relations*, 1910, p. 244.

delivered to the American Ambassador in Tokyo on January 21, 1910, Foreign Minister Komura stated that the proposal contravened the Treaty of Portsmouth which "was designed to establish in Manchuria a permanent order of things, and the Imperial Government believes that in a strict and loyal adhesion to its provisions are to be found the highest guarantees of enduring peace and repose in this part of the world and of the orderly advancement of Manchuria." Furthermore, the Japanese Government was unable to "see in the present condition of things in Manchuria anything so exceptional as to make it necessary or desirable to set up there an exceptional system not required in other parts of China." Finally, the government declared its intention to maintain its existing national control over South Manchuria for reasons which, although not necessarily inconsistent with the open door, actually confirmed the suspicion that that principle was a dead letter in Manchuria:

> In the regions affected by the Japanese railways in Manchuria there have grown numerous Japanese industrial and commercial undertakings which owed their inception, as they owe their continual existence, to the fact that the Imperial Government, possessing the railways in question, are able to extend to those enterprises and to the persons engaged in them due protection and defense against attack and pillage by lawless bands that still infest the country. In the development of these enterprises, which are contributing in such a marked degree to the prosperity and progress of Manchuria, a large number of Japanese subjects and large sums of Japanese money are enlisted, and the Imperial Government could not in good faith or with a due sense of their responsibility consent to surrender the means by which such protection and defense are made possible.[10]

In other words, the Japanese Government knew that under an impartial international administration of the Manchurian railways, the open door would become a reality; and the Japanese monopolistic control of the commerce of South Manchuria would thereby be destroyed.

When the Russian Government on the same day informed the State Department of its opposition to the Knox plan, for reasons very similar to those of Japan,[11] the neutralization scheme was

---

[10] *Ibid.*, p. 251. (Count Komura to Thomas J. O'Brien, American Ambassador in Tokyo, January 21, 1910.)

[11] *Ibid.*, pp. 249, 250. (William W. Rockhill, American Ambassador in St. Petersburg, to Knox, January 22, 1910, enclosing an *aide-mémoire* from the Russian Ministry of Foreign Affairs.) See also *Documents diplomatiques français, 1871–1914*, Series 3, II, 181, note 2. "Le 17 décembre 1909, M. Knox

dead; but there still remained the projected Chinchou–Aigun Railway. Here the opposition of Japan and Russia was equally effective. The Japanese Government agreed to permit the construction of the line on the condition that Japan should have the deciding voice in the location of the railway and a share in the management and in the furnishing of materials. These and other conditions were so stated as to make it impossible for China to accept.[12] The Russian Government used even less finesse in informing the State Department

that such a railroad would be exceedingly injurious both to the strategic and to the economic interests of Russia. China in 1899 engaged not to build railroads to the north of Peking with foreign capital other than Russian, and Russia could be willing not to insist on the execution by China of this obligation only under the conditions that railroads built with capital provided by international syndicates should not be an evident menace to the security of the Russian frontier and should not injure the interests of Russia's railroad enterprise in Manchuria.[13]

In addition, Japan and Russia brought the full weight of their diplomacy to bear upon the Chinese Government in an effort to prevent the consummation of the final agreement with the Anglo-American financial group. The Japanese minister in Peking informed the Chinese Foreign Office that before

the Chinese Government determines anything, *the consent of my Government must first be obtained.* If the position of my country is ignored and a decision is made *without referring the matter to my Government,* it will be hard to estimate the *seriousness of the trouble* that may be caused in the relations of the two countries.[14]

---

avait fait aux Puissances une proposition tendant à internationaliser la Mandchourie et à construire un chemin de fer de Kiao-Tchéou à Aïgoun. Cette proposition provoqua une protestation du Japon et surtout de la Russie. Le Gouvernement français contribua, par son attitude, à l'échec et à l'abandon de la proposition américaine."

[12] Thomas F. Millard, "America in China," *The Forum,* XLIV (July, 1910), 80. Millard, a resident of Shanghai, published in this article a number of documents from Chinese sources bearing upon the Knox plan and the Chinchou–Aigun Railway concession.

[13] *Foreign Relations,* 1910, p. 261. (Memorandum from the Russian Embassy to Knox, February 24, 1910.) As Willoughby points out, the Russian Government admits in this note that it deceived Japan in the Treaty of Portsmouth, when Russia declared in Article III, paragraph 2, that she had "not in Manchuria 'any territorial advantages or preferential or exclusive concessions in impairment of Chinese sovereignty or inconsistent with the principle of equal opportunity' . . ." See Willoughby, *op. cit.,* I, 181.

[14] Millard, *loc. cit.,* p. 74. January 31, 1910.

Russia adopted a similar course, notifying the Chinese Foreign Office "that the Russian Government expects that China will not settle any such matter *without first consulting Russia. Otherwise there will be trouble in the relationship between the two countries.*"[15]

It is apparent that neither Japan nor Russia was concerned with either the open door or the integrity of the Chinese Empire in Manchuria. Their main concern was to prevent any competition in Manchuria even by the permission of the nominal sovereign of that territory—the Chinese Government. Both the Japanese and the Russian Governments categorically denied that anything in the Manchurian situation either violated the principle of the open door or infringed the political rights of China. But they overlooked the fact that their very objections to the proposed Chinchou–Aigun Railway and to the plan of neutralization of all Manchurian railways constituted violations or infringements in themselves.

In order to clarify their relations in Manchuria and to make their opposition to the American proposals more pointed, Japan and Russia concluded a new treaty on July 4, 1910. Baron Ichiro Motono, Japanese Ambassador to Russia, referred to this project when he informed the Russian Ambassador at Tokyo on January 13, 1910, that he regarded *"the American proposal as a clear proof of the necessity of bringing about an understanding between Russia and Japan in the Manchurian question."*[16] Thus, the attempt of the United States to protect her rights in Manchuria was interpreted as a threat by those two powers; and the American proposals provided the primary impetus for the new treaty.[17]

[15] *Ibid.*, pp. 74, 75. February 2, 1910.

[16] *Entente Diplomacy and the World: Matrix of the History of Europe, 1909–1914*, documents collected and translated by Count Benno A. von Siebert [Zibert], and edited and arranged by George A. Schreiner (New York: 1921), p. 11. (Russian Ambassador in Tokyo to Alexander P. Izvolsky, Russian Foreign Minister, January 13, 1910.) Cited hereafter as *Entente Diplomacy*.

[17] Baron Komura maintained that the treaty would have been concluded regardless of the action of the United States. See *British Documents*, VIII, 485. (MacDonald to Grey, July 2, 1910.) Sir Edward Grey, however, in a minute inscribed on this dispatch, said: "Whatever the Japanese may say there can be little doubt that the policy adopted by the U[nited] S[tates] of A[merica] in China hastened if it did not bring about this arrangement." Sir Arthur Nicolson, British Ambassador in St. Petersburg, had discussed this question with the Russian Czar, Nicholas II, whose views had been reported to Grey as follows: "The United States of America, His Majesty observed, seemed disposed to pursue an active policy in the Far East which so far as it had been foreshadowed was not likely to be advantageous either to Russia or to Japan." *Ibid.*, p. 479. (Nicolson to Grey, April 15, 1910.)

The pact, intended to reinforce the Russo-Japanese treaty of 1907 and to consolidate the peace of the Far East, contained several noteworthy provisions. In Article I Russia and Japan agreed to coöperate in developing and improving their Manchurian railways, "and to refrain from all competition unfavorable to the attainment of this result." They further agreed, in the second article, to respect the *status quo* in Manchuria as it existed as a result of their treaties with each other and with China. This, of course, provided no protection for the rights of other nations, although China accepted it as a pledge to respect her sovereign rights. A final article provided that, in "case any event of such a nature as to menace the above-mentioned *status quo* should be brought about," the two governments would confer on the measures to be taken "for the maintenance of the said *status quo*." As in 1907, the public treaty was accompanied by a secret agreement in which Japan and Russia defined more clearly their respective spheres of interest in Manchuria and the restrictions upon the actions of each power within the sphere of the other power.[18] The Russian Minister of Foreign Affairs, Alexander P. Izvolsky, asserted that this treaty was being negotiated between the two powers *"in order to reinforce their mutual relations and to preserve the position proper to them in Manchuria from all interference on the part of other Powers."*[19] Certainly these aims were not consistent with the maintenance of the open door or with respect for the integrity of China, nor did the United States Government so interpret them.

Throughout the negotiations England occupied an anomalous position. She was in alliance with Japan; yet, her interests in the Pacific were closer to those of the United States. In fact, there were fundamental differences between Great Britain and her ally, just as there were between the United States and Japan. Canada had her own quarrel with Japan over immigration; for the people of British Columbia objected to the influx of Japanese immigrants, and serious anti-Japanese riots had occurred in Vancouver in 1907. Canada also opposed the Anglo-Japanese Alliance as a source of possible danger to her. Her surest guarantee of safety lay in cordial relations with the United States; but this safeguard might vanish should the United States be embroiled with Japan while the Anglo-

---

[18] The text of the secret treaty appears in *Entente Diplomacy,* pp. 17, 18.

[19] *Ibid.,* p. 16. (Izvolsky to Count Alexander Benckendorff, Russian Ambassador in London, June 24, 1910.)

Japanese Alliance remained in force.[20] Australia and New Zealand were rapidly being converted to this view, although they had at first welcomed the alliance with Japan. Australia had early adopted a policy of excluding the colored races, which was extended directly to the Japanese in the Commonwealth Immigration Act of 1901 by a general educational test for immigrants, who were required to read at least "50 words in a European language."[21] The Japanese Government had protested against these restrictions, both to the Australian Government and to the Imperial Government in London; but the British Government had refused to interfere. This friction, when added to the differences which later arose between Great Britain and Japan, had a tremendous influence in directing the British policy subsequently pursued in East Asia and in the Pacific.

When Secretary Knox proposed his plan for the neutralization of the railways of Manchuria, Great Britain was approached first. Sir Edward Grey expressed in reply Britain's agreement in principle not only to the neutralization plan, but also to the Chinchou–Aigun Railway project. His acceptance was qualified, however, by suggestions that the neutralization plan should await the outcome of the negotiations of the four powers for the Hukuang loan, and that the Japanese should be invited to participate in the Chinchou–Aigun project "as being the parties most interested."[22] It was apparent that Great Britain feared to take any action which might offend her ally. It later transpired that Russia had protested to the British Government against British participation in the proposed American arrangement, on the basis of an exchange of letters in 1899, by which England had agreed not to seek for herself or for her subjects any railway concession north of the Great Wall of China, Russia agreeing to be similarly abstentious in the Yangtze Valley.[23] Sir Edward Grey explained to the House of Commons on

[20] For the nature of Canada's laws restricting the immigration and privileges of aliens, see Norman MacKenzie, ed., *The Legal Status of Aliens in Pacific Countries* (London: Oxford University Press, 1937), chap. iii.

[21] For a scholarly account of the development of Australia's immigration policy, see Myra Willard, *History of the White Australia Policy*, in University of Melbourne Publications, No. 1 (Melbourne: 1923.) Chapters v and vi deal especially with the Japanese. See also MacKenzie, *op. cit.*, chap. ii.

[22] *Foreign Relations*, 1910, pp. 235, 236. (Grey to Whitelaw Reid, November 25, 1909.)

[23] Notes exchanged on April 28, 1899, between Sir Charles S. Scott, British Ambassador in St. Petersburg, and Count Michael Mouravieff, Russian Foreign Minister.

June 15, 1910,[24] that the Russian protest of December, 1909, had been rejected because the British Government was not actively supporting the British interests and because the project was not actually a concession, but a contract to carry out a Chinese Government railroad undertaking.[25] At the same time, Grey asserted that he had always favored Anglo-American coöperation; and he would welcome it if China could reach an understanding with Russia on the railroad problem in Manchuria.[26] Otherwise, his hands were tied.

Great Britain was aware of the intentions of Russia and Japan in Manchuria; for the texts of both the public and the secret treaties of July 4, 1910, had been communicated to the British Foreign Office in draft form even before they were signed.[27] Outwardly complaisant, the British Government announced its pleasure at this evidence of continuing friendship between Japan and Russia and accepted the assurances that the pacts would constitute "a new guarantee of peace and quiet in the Far East."[28] When Japan, encouraged by the Russian treaty and by the seeming acquiescence of Great Britain, took still further steps to consolidate her position in Asia, the reaction of the British Government and people was vastly different. On July 17, 1910, Japan gave Great Britain and a number of other nations a year's notice of the abrogation of her commercial treaties with them.[29] This action was part of a new policy which was aimed at the complete resumption of tariff autonomy by Japan. Earlier in 1910, a new tariff law had been adopted, which was to go into effect when the treaties expired on July 17, 1911; and this tariff had brought open threats of retalia-

[24] *The Parliamentary Debates: Official Report*, 17 H. C., 5 Ser., June 15, 1910, pp. 1388, 1389. Cited hereafter as *Parliamentary Debates*.

[25] For a Russian version of this protest, see *Entente Diplomacy*, p. 15. (Izvolsky to Benckendorff, January 13, 1910.)

[26] This statement represents a change in the early attitude of the British in approving the American proposals. The British Government had made known its approval before the attitude to be assumed by Japan and Russia had become known. See *Die Grosse Politik*, XXXII, 99, 100. "Sir E. Grey habe Whitelaw Reid direkt zugegeben, dass er sich in dieser Sache versehen hätte, da er seine Verpflichtungen Russland gegenüber vergessen habe, Staatssekretär [Knox] klagte sehr über England, mit dem jetzt nichts zu machen sei, und meinte, vielleicht liege Uebereinkunft Russlands, Japans und Englands vor, das Bahnprojekt zu Fall zu bringen." (Bernstorff to the German Foreign Office, received March 4, 1910.)

[27] June 28, 1910. See *British Documents*, VIII, 480–482.

[28] *Entente Diplomacy*, pp. 16, 17. (Izvolsky to Benckendorff, June 24, 1910.)

[29] The text of the notice is in *British and Foreign State Papers*, CIII (1909–1910), p. 571.

tion by Great Britain.[30] Britain's predicament was succinctly described in the House of Commons by Arthur James Balfour.

> . . . I believe it to be true that the Japanese Foreign Minister said there could be no negotiations with Great Britain on the subject, because Great Britain had nothing to give. The British Foreign Secretary, dealing with a nation like Japan in a matter of commercial bargaining, has the prospect of a very poor time before him if he has nothing to give. I certainly do not look forward with any satisfaction to the issue of the negotiations which, if this new tariff of Japan is left substantially unmodified, will inflict a very severe blow on some of the greatest of our staple industries.[31]

Moving swiftly, the Japanese Government next concluded, on August 22, 1910, a treaty of annexation with Korea, whose "independence and territorial integrity" Japan had explicitly guaranteed only five years earlier.[32] The Japanese Government thus further weakened Britain's confidence in her ally. In this instance, Japan had promised to await an opportune moment for annexation so as to avoid embarrassing Great Britain. Britain feared that premature annexation might be interpreted as an aggressive answer to the neutralization proposal of Secretary Knox.[33] When the annexation actually came, therefore, the British Government expressed surprise that Japan had acted without the promised notification and before the question of British commercial rights in Korea had been settled.[34] The London *Times,* which had approved the Russo-Japanese treaty only six weeks before, now expressed the conservative hope that Japanese statesmen would "remember that the world will watch their future policy in Korea with much expectancy and some anxiety."[35] Prominent British citizens, however, were not so conservative. For example, the Earl of Stanhope, in a letter to the editor of *The Times,* said that although the new situa-

[30] See *Parliamentary Debates,* 17 H. C., 5 Ser., April 25, 1910, pp. 5, 6.

[31] *Ibid.,* 19 H. C., 5 Ser., July 21, 1910, p. 1459. Baron Komura, the Japanese Foreign Minister, had said in a public address that, because of the British free-trade policy, Great Britain had nothing to offer Japan in the way of tariff concessions; hence, there was no basis for any negotiations with that country. He had at the time apparently not taken into account the possibility of retaliation in kind by Great Britain; but when he did recognize the possibility of such action, the tariff question assumed a significant place in subsequent Anglo-Japanese negotiations on other problems.

[32] The text of the treaty of annexation was communicated to the State Department on August 24, 1910. See *Foreign Relations,* 1910, pp. 682, 683.

[33] *British Documents,* VIII, 488, 489. (MacDonald to Grey, May 19, 1910.)

[34] *Ibid.,* p. 502. (MacDonald to Grey, October 10, 1910.)

[35] "The Annexation of Korea" (editorial), *The Times* (London), August 25, 1910, p. 7.

tion was covered by "the Anglo-Japanese Alliance, by which Japan promises to observe in Korea the principle of 'equal opportunities for the commerce and industry of all nations,'" it was "to be hoped that his Majesty's Government [would] . . . see that the pledge is carried out more in accordance with the letter and spirit of the clause than has recently been the case in Manchuria."[36]

Although all of these difficulties were eventually adjusted satisfactorily, they had had their effect upon the British Government. Japan's actions had made it much more difficult for the government to resist the opposition to the Anglo-Japanese Alliance in the Dominions of Canada, Australia, and New Zealand, and in the United States. The strong statement issued by the State Department in January, 1910, explaining the new policy of the United States in Manchuria, had apparently not been forgotten; and the danger of being drawn into a Japanese-American conflict was too real to be ignored. Whether by design or by fortuitous circumstance, President Taft provided a way out for Great Britain, a way which, incidentally, would also draw the British Empire into closer friendship with the United States.[37] The President had publicly stated that, in his opinion, "questions of . . . National honor" should not be excepted in treaties of general arbitration, which were then being much discussed.[38] In a private letter to Sir Edward Grey, Andrew Carnegie asked what would be the reaction of the British Government to such a broad arbitration proposal. Grey replied that, although he could not speak for the cabinet, he was sure such a proposal would be welcomed.[39] There the matter rested until after the Japanese annexation of Korea.

[36] *The Times* (London), August 27, 1910, p. 4.

[37] That this was an object earnestly desired in the United States is evidenced by a statement made by Secretary Knox in November, 1910, when he said to the counselor of the British Embassy in Washington: "Though keenly competitive as to commerce, we are animated by no jealousy. We desire nothing that England possesses, and Great Britain will find no power so ready to coöperate with her loyally and disinterestedly in every part of the world." See *British Documents,* VIII, 543. (Mitchell Innes to Grey, November 18, 1910.)

[38] At a meeting of the American Peace and Arbitration League in New York City on March 22, 1910, the President said: "I have noticed exceptions in our arbitration treaties, as to reference of questions of honor, of National honor, to courts of arbitration. Personally I do not see any more reason why matters of National honor should not be referred to a court of arbitration any more than matters of property or matters of National proprietorship." *The New York Times,* March 23, 1910, p. 2.

[39] These facts are from an editorial note in *British Documents,* VIII, 542. The Carnegie letter was dated July 11, 1910, and Grey's reply July 29, 1910.

On August 16, 1910, the Foreign Office received from James Bryce, British Ambassador in Washington, a report of a conversation which he had had with the President. Bryce said: "He [President Taft] seemed to think that a good example would be set to the rest of the world if the United States and Great Britain were to conclude a Treaty of Arbitration of the wider scope he had indicated; and I am inclined to believe that any intimation of a willingness on the part of His Majesty's Government to take such a step would be welcome to him."[40] Although these official views were important, the views expressed by officials of the British Foreign Office in minutes which they attached to Bryce's report were even more significant in revealing the attitudes of British ministers. The first of these minutes, undated, referred at once to the Anglo-Japanese Alliance:

> The agreement with Japan has five years to run and it would be very unfortunate to have to postpone negotiations all that time, supposing a real opportunity arose, although I recognize the paramount importance of maintaining our Treaty engagements unimpaired. It would be awkward to have to explain to the U[nited] S[tates] G[overnmen]t that we could not conclude this arbitration on account of our alliance with Japan but that may be the only way if the question is pressed.[41]

In a reply on September 14, 1910, however, Grey indicated that there was a way out of the difficulty—that of securing Japan's coöperation. He informed Baron Takaakira Kato, the Japanese Ambassador, that a general arbitration treaty with the United States was possible. He asked that the Japanese Government consider two alternatives to avoid a conflict between the new treaty and the Anglo-Japanese Alliance; first, if a conflict arose, the alliance should govern until its expiration, when the question would be reconsidered in discussing renewal, or, second, Japan should also enter into a general arbitration treaty with the United States.[42]

By January, 1911, the Japanese Government had decided that such a treaty was out of the question. It was suggested that, as an exception of the alliance in the Anglo-American treaty would tend to make the Anglo-Japanese pact unpopular "as an obstacle to arbitration," that agreement could be revised at any time to except

[40] *Ibid.*, p. 541. (Bryce to Grey, August 9, 1910.)
[41] *Ibid.*, p. 542. Initialed by Louis Mallet, Assistant Undersecretary of State for Foreign Affairs.
[42] *British Documents*, VIII, 503. (Grey to MacDonald, September 26, 1910.)

the United States from its provisions.[43] But as time passed and no American proposals materialized, the Japanese Government showed its apprehension. By mid-March, Baron Komura was suggesting that the alliance might be renewed, as well as revised, when the arbitration treaty was concluded.[44] Japan obviously feared that the alliance would become so unpopular in England that it would not be renewed. On the other hand, the British Government was unwilling to weaken the alliance unnecessarily at the very time when it would be most useful; for an outbreak of fighting between French troops and the natives in Morocco on March 16, 1911, was threatening to reopen serious questions with Germany. British officials, therefore, were quite ready to take advantage of Japan's anxiety and to discuss the renewal of the alliance.

The failure of Secretary Knox's plan for the international control of the Manchurian railways and the defeat of the Chinchou–Aigun Railway project by Japan and Russia had only increased the determination of the Taft administration to check Japanese aggression by any means short of war.[45] The very evident friction between Japan and the United States had had repercussions in Great Britain, where there was a large group who believed that, because of the Anglo-Russian Entente of 1907, the Anglo-Japanese Alliance had served its purpose. The fear of becoming involved in a war with the United States because of Japanese aggressions in China, coupled with the new Japanese tariff of 1910, increased the clamor against the Japanese. Fully conscious of the sentiment in England and America and confronted by a rising tide of Chinese resentment, which foreboded serious trouble in the Far East, Japan was finally compelled to make numerous concessions to appease her more powerful opponents.

At Japan's earnest request, the United States had consented to

[43] *Ibid.*, pp. 504, 505. (Grey to MacDonald, January 20, 1911.)

[44] *Ibid.*, p. 507. (MacDonald to Grey, March 16, 1911.)

[45] It was with reference to this situation that the German Emperor, William II, had written gleefully: "Die Reibungen zwischen Japs und Yankees mehren sich dadurch und das ist gut." *Die Grosse Politik*, XXXII, 98. Marginal comment. (Count A. Montgelas, First Secretary of the German Embassy in Tokyo, to Theodor von Bethmann-Hollweg, Imperial Chancellor, January 31, 1910.) Viscount Kikujiro Ishii, who was Japanese Vice-Minister of Foreign Affairs at the time, ignores the friction engendered by the Far Eastern situation and asserts that the "main subject of difference between Japan and America was the immigration question . . ." See his *Diplomatic Commentaries*, translated and edited by William R. Langdon (Baltimore: Johns Hopkins Press, 1936), p. 56.

negotiate a new commercial treaty at the same time as the other powers whose treaties Japan had abrogated. The consent had been conditioned in the first place upon Japan's promise to maintain in full effect the restrictions on the emigration of Japanese laborers to the United States; and this promise was appended to the treaty in a written declaration by Count Yasuya Uchida, Japanese Ambassador in Washington.[46] Other issues, such as revision of the customs tariff and the right of American citizens to hold real estate in Japan, were settled in a manner "highly satisfactory" to the United States.[47] Great Britain was equally successful in solving her commercial difficulties with Japan. In a treaty signed on April 3, 1911, Japan made substantial tariff concessions to prevent the levying of British retaliatory duties on Japanese products[48] and to insure successful negotiations for a renewal of the alliance. Sir Claude MacDonald reported from Tokyo on April 5, 1911, "that one of the main reasons" why Great Britain "received tariff concessions in [the] new treaty from the Japanese Gov[ernmen]t" was the fear that agitation aroused "by refusal to make such concessions would endanger the renewal of the alliance..."[49]

In the same telegram, Ambassador MacDonald declared that the Japanese Government was "exceedingly anxious to renew [the] Anglo-Japanese Alliance"; and, should Great Britain decline to renew the alliance until it expired in 1915, "the uncertainty of renewal would be [a] useful lever and also [a] check to any unnecessarily forward policy."[50] The British Government, however, had already committed itself to the immediate renewal of the alliance, because a refusal would have made the pact appear as an obstruction to arbitration and because "apprehension that it might not be renewed would have grown rapidly, and must have affected seriously both Japanese naval shipbuilding and our own in [the] next few years."[51] There was yet another important reason for Great Britain's willingness to renew the alliance, a reason which appeared when the British Government tried to convince Russia

[46] *Foreign Relations*, 1911, p. 319. The treaty was signed at Washington on February 21, 1911.

[47] Statement by President Taft in his annual message of December 7, 1911. See *Messages and Papers*, XVIII, 8046, 8047.

[48] *Parliamentary Papers*, 1911, CIII (Cmd. 5556), April 3, 1911.

[49] *British Documents*, VIII, 512. (MacDonald to Grey, April 5, 1911.)

[50] *Ibid.*

[51] *Ibid.*, p. 514. (Grey to MacDonald, April 7, 1911.)

that the alliance was no longer directed at her. The Russian Ambassador in London reported to his government that the

> ... *point in question was in reality a most delicate one, with special reference to the colonies, i.e., Australia. In view of the fact that the laws in the British colonies show but little consideration for the yellow race, a lapsing of the Treaty might have led to serious friction, which would have meant a continuous disquietude for England, even if it did not embody a direct danger of war.*[52]

Both powers, therefore, had reasons for renewing the alliance. The Japanese could not forget that, however small the actual use of the alliance had become to them, it had made possible their rise to power in the Far East and had immeasurably increased their prestige.[53] Furthermore, Japan and Russia, although virtually allies, still feared and distrusted each other. On her side, Great Britain still found the alliance useful in determining the disposition of her naval forces. Although the British Government recognized the grasping proclivities of the Japanese, it nevertheless felt safe in entrusting the protection of mutual interests in the Far East to Japan. This enabled England to concentrate her fleet in home waters as a powerful argument in British diplomatic relations with a Germany becoming increasingly vigorous and assertive. But the British no longer felt the old pressing need for the alliance; and, as their statesmen repeatedly remarked, they were in a position to use it to keep Japanese ambitions within reasonable limits. Since the extended treaty, which was signed on July 13, 1911, contained a new clause intended to release Great Britain from

[52] *Entente Diplomacy*, p. 32. See also *Graf Benckendorffs Diplomatischer Schriftwechsel*, edited by Count Benno von Siebert [Zibert] (Berlin and Leipzig: Walter de Gruyter, 1928), II, 126, 127. (Count Benckendorff to Anatole A. Nératoff, Russian Acting Minister of Foreign Affairs, July 17, 1911.) Benckendorff refers also to the advantage which Great Britain derived from the Anglo-Japanese Alliance of being able to withdraw her naval forces from the Far East and to concentrate them in home waters, where, according to Sir Arthur Nicolson, "they might eventually be needed."

[53] This view was generally entertained by statesmen of the time. See, for example, a record of a conversation on August 7, 1913, between the German Emperor and George von Lengerke Meyer, who had been Secretary of the Navy under President Taft. Referring to the Anglo-Japanese Alliance, the Kaiser said that it was "a most unwise action on England's part: it was brought about by fear of Russia, England not realizing that Russia had been bluffing. Why, Russia would not have been a dangerous commercial competitor in the East; and Japan is, and will seriously and finally impede English trade. But for that treaty Japan would not have dared to attack Russia." To this, Meyer replied: "Yes, Sire, I have always felt that England was in a great part responsible for Japan's present prominence as a world power." Howe, *George von Lengerke Meyer: His Life and Public Services*, pp. 499, 500.

going to war on the side of Japan against the United States, the British Dominions relaxed their opposition to it. In fact, they unanimously favored its continuance in 1911.[54]

While England and Japan were negotiating the renewal of their alliance, further proof of the unregeneracy of Russia and Japan was fast unfolding. The negotiations of the United States with Great Britain, France, and Germany for an equal share in the projected Hukuang Railways loan had finally succeeded with the signing of the Inter-Bank Agreement of May 23, 1910. This recognition of the equality of American rights in China was extended by the Quadruple Agreement of November 10, 1910, to include American participation in all consortium loans for railway purposes in China. Out of this negotiation arose another opportunity for Russia and Japan to demonstrate their good faith in their relations with China; and again they were found wanting.

After lengthy negotiations, the Chinese Government had finally decided to place a loan for Chinese currency reform with American bankers; and on September 22, 1910, the State Department was asked to approve the loan.[55] After its approval, the loan application was expanded on October 2 to include industrial developments in Manchuria,[56] a change of utmost importance. The Ameri-

[54] On July 20, 1911, Sir Edward Grey, in answer to a question, informed the House of Commons that the representatives of the Dominions had been consulted on the question of revision and renewal of the treaty and that they had unanimously favored it. *Parliamentary Debates*, 28 H. C., 5 Ser., July 20, 1911, p. 1257. The new clause in the treaty was as follows: "Article IV. Should either High Contracting Party conclude a treaty of general arbitration with a third Power, it is agreed that nothing in this Agreement shall entail upon such Contracting Party an obligation to go to war with the Power with whom such treaty of arbitration is in force." This text is from *British and Foreign State Papers*, CIV (1911), 174. The anticipated treaty between Great Britain and the United States was finally signed at Washington on August 3, 1911; but the Senate, in giving its advice and consent to ratification on March 7, 1912, made serious reservations which destroyed its unlimited character. See *British Documents*, VIII, 604, note. After the inauguration of Woodrow Wilson in 1913, Secretary of State William Jennings Bryan negotiated a series of treaties for the promotion of international peace, the so-called Peace Commission Treaties, or the Bryan Treaties. Great Britain was among the nations signing such a treaty with the United States on September 15, 1914; and the "British Government informed the Japanese Government that it regarded this treaty as equivalent to a treaty of general arbitration, and that the condition mentioned in Article IV of the treaty of 1911 had thereby become operative. This contention was accepted by the Japanese Government." *Ibid.*, p. 531, note.

[55] *Foreign Relations*, 1912, pp. 89, 90. (William J. Calhoun, American Minister in Peking, to Knox, September 22, 1910.) A brief résumé of the earlier negotiations may be found in *ibid.*, pp. 88, 89.

[56] *Ibid.*, p. 90. (Calhoun to Knox, October 2, 1910.)

can bankers agreed to make the loan, and a preliminary agreement was signed with the Chinese Government on October 27, 1910. When the other consortium powers were notified of the arrangement, France and Germany expressed the view that these loans should be quadripartite so that the consortium could continue to present a united front to the Chinese Government. The United States agreed; and in a conference at London on the eighth, ninth, and tenth of November, which resulted in the Quadruple Agreement already mentioned, the banking groups formulated a detailed plan for the participation of all four groups in the "industrial development loan" for Manchuria and, also, in the "currency reform loan," provided the consent of the Chinese Government could be obtained.[57] After China's objections had been overcome, the final contract for the dual-purpose loan was signed at Peking on April 15, 1911. This was followed five weeks later by a contract between the Chinese Government and the consortium for the construction of the Hukuang Railways, thus concluding three years of continuous negotiations.

With the publication of the results of the negotiations, the storm broke both upon the consortium powers and upon China. Japan and Russia protested to the powers what they maintained was an infringement by Article XVI of the Currency Loan Agreement of April 15, 1911, of their "special interests" in Manchuria. The article read:

> Article XVI.—If the Imperial Chinese Government should desire to obtain from other than Chinese sources, funds in addition to the proceeds derived from this loan, to continue or complete the operations contemplated under this agreement, the Imperial Chinese Government shall first invite the banks to undertake a loan to provide the funds required, but should the Imperial Chinese Government fail to agree with the banks as to the terms of such supplementary loan then other financial groups may be invited to undertake the same; and should the Imperial Chinese Government decide to invite foreign capitalists to participate with Chinese interests in Manchurian business contemplated under this loan, or to be undertaken in connection therewith, the banks shall first be invited to so participate.

The Japanese protest was based on what it charged was an unlimited grant of preferential rights in Manchuria to the consortium

[57] *Ibid.*, p. 92. It was after these negotiations that Willard Straight, formerly American consul general in Mukden, representing the American group of bankers at London, said: "We must now try to fortify ourselves in a position which we have attained by rather daring means." See Herbert Croly, *Willard Straight* (New York: Macmillan, 1924), p. 366.

instead of grants for specific projects to which no objection could be made. Forgotten apparently were the Japanese objections to the Chinchou–Aigun Railway and other projects, which had been dropped because of Japanese and Russian opposition. The Japanese Government declared

...Japan possesses in the region of southern Manchuria special rights and interests, and while she is fully prepared in the future as in the past to respect the rights of others, she is unable to view with indifference measures which tend not only to menace those special rights and interests but to place her subjects and institutions at a disadvantage as compared with the subjects and institutions of any other country.[58]

If any further indictment of Japanese policy in Manchuria were necessary, it is to be found here. Whereas in one sentence Japan asserted her willingness "to respect the rights of others," in the next she claimed for "her subjects *and institutions*" a privileged status in Manchuria which it was evident was being denied by Japan to all others, including the people and government of China.

The Russian protest showed an equal disregard for the actual situation existing in Manchuria:

...It seems that the syndicate pretends to a monopoly of financial and industrial enterprises in the region in which Russia possesses important special interests. The Imperial Government has always respected the right belonging to other nations in Manchuria, and for its part holds that there should be no disregard of its legitimate rights acquired in that country.[59]

The statement could have been accepted in better spirit if Russia's true designs on Manchuria and Mongolia had not been known. Accepting at face value the Russo-Japanese pledge in their treaty

[58] *Foreign Relations*, 1912, p. 100. (Uchida to Knox, July 11, 1911.)

[59] *Ibid.* (Prince N. Koudacheff, Russian Chargé d'Affaires in Washington, to Knox, July 11, 1911.) The fact that both the Japanese and Russian protests were delivered to the State Department on the same day indicates a previous consultation and agreement on joint action by the two powers. See also *Die Grosse Politik*, XXXII, 179, 180. See further, *Documents diplomatiques français, 1871–1914*, Series 3, I, 457–464. (J. de Selves, French Minister for Foreign Affairs, to George Louis, French Ambassador in St. Petersburg, January 9, 1912.) Prince Koudacheff reported to his government that the State Department had informed him that, if it should become apparent that the bankers were attempting to use Article XVI to create a monopoly for themselves, they would receive no encouragement from the United States Government. *Die Internationalen Beziehungen im Zeitalter des Imperialismus: Dokumente aus den Archiven der Zarischen und der Provisorischen Regierung, 1878–1917*, edited by the commission under M. N. Pokrovsky, chairman; German edition edited by Otto Hoetzsch (Berlin: Reimar Hobbing, 1931–1941), Series 3, I:1, 383. (Koudacheff to Nératoff, August 14, 1911.) Cited hereafter as *Die Internationalen Beziehungen*.

of July 4, 1910, to respect the *status quo* in Manchuria, the Chinese Government had formulated plans for reorganizing the provinces and strengthening government control over them. Russia's original disfavor toward this endeavor[60] was later expressed in an ultimatum demanding that China respect the treaty rights of Russia and of Russian subjects north of the Great Wall of China.[61] At the extraordinary meeting of the Russian Ministerial Council at which it was decided to send this ultimatum, however, the matter appeared in a different light, as the following report demonstrates:

> *The Minister of War confirmed the fact that, according to his information, Russia's position in Manchuria is an extremely difficult one. Japan is taking open measures for the annexation of Southern Manchuria.* China has begun to reorganize her military forces in Manchuria with the intention of dislocating our railway communications in Manchuria before we are in a position to guard them by a rapid strengthening of our Frontier Corps, stationed along the whole line. The progressing colonisation of Manchuria by the Chinese likewise follows strategic aims.... *The Minister of War is of the opinion that the present moment is all the more favourable for us to take possession of Manchuria in agreement with Japan, as the Japanese are very evidently preparing the annexation of Southern Manchuria.* Thus an end would be put to the presence of Chinese military in the vicinity of our railways, and also to Chinese colonisation. Should the annexation of North Manchuria be impossible at the present time, then it would be better for us voluntarily to withdraw from this territory before we are forced to do so.[62]

The Russian Minister of Foreign Affairs, however, was less pessimistic about Russia's position in Manchuria and was able to influence the council to favor a decision that Russia's *"stipulated privileges in Northern Manchuria must be maintained in full to permit eventually an annexation at some future date."*[63]

The Russian Government thus revealed its true intention, as well as that of Japan, which was to annex the territory comprising its sphere of influence in Manchuria. Incidental to such a change in

[60] "Wenn wir das oben Ausgeführte berücksichtigen, so brauchen wir gar nicht zu beweisen, dass die Umgestaltung der Mongolei in eine chinesiche Provinz, die mit dem Zentrum verbunden wäre und eine reichseinheitliche militärische Organisation hätte, vom russischen Standpunkt aus unerwünscht erscheint." *Graf Benckendorffs Diplomatischer Schriftwechsel,* I, 381, 382. (Ivan Korostovetz, Russian Minister in Peking, to Serge Sazonoff, Russian Minister of Foreign Affairs, November 16, 1910.) This dispatch is of further interest because Korostovetz mentions "Article 3 of the Secret Agreement of July 30, 1907." He asserts that in this instrument "Japan recognized our particular interests in Mongolia, and assumed the obligation herself to abstain from every interference which could injure these interests." *Ibid.*, p. 383.

[61] *Ibid.*, II, 30–33. (Sazonoff to Korostovetz, February 12, 1911.)

[62] *Entente Diplomacy*, pp. 24, 25.

[63] *Ibid.*, p. 27. December 2, 1910.

political status, the open door and the integrity of China would become of merely academic interest. Ostensibly the reason for urging annexation or the maintenance of Russia's "stipulated privileges" in Manchuria was fear of Chinese colonization and the increasing strength of Chinese military forces in the vicinity of Russia's railways in Eastern Asia. When these fears were broached to the Japanese Ambassador by the Russian Foreign Office, Baron Motono replied that the Chinese were not to be feared:

> ... *The only danger he can foresee would come from America whose fleet in the Pacific, on the completion of the Panama Canal, will be so powerful that the Japanese fleet might undertake a defensive action, but certainly not attack. The Ambassador believes that Russia and Japan will have to regulate definitely their position in China before the beginning of this period.*[64]

Obviously Russia and Japan were pursuing policies in Manchuria which they well realized could result in a future conflict with the United States; and, in the months following this communication, they directed their efforts toward the end suggested by Baron Motono—"to regulate definitely their position in China" before the United States could muster sufficient force to intervene.[65]

The long-smoldering resentment of the Chinese against their government for its weakness in the face of foreign aggressions, fanned into open revolt by the granting of the Hukuang Railways concession,[66] offered the Japanese and the Russians an opportunity to achieve their aims in China. To accomplish this, however, the favored position which the consortium had obtained in the control of Chinese finances had to be destroyed. Since neither Japan nor Russia had the financial resources to compete with the consortium and thereby restrict its influence, their only possible course of action was to disrupt the four-power group by working through their allies, England and France, who were members of the group. As events had already proved, there was little hope for Japan of weaning England away from her support of the consortium.

[64] *Ibid.*, p. 31. (Nératoff to Nicolas Malevsky-Malevich, Russian Ambassador in Tokyo, April 29, 1911.)

[65] Count Benckendorff, Russian Ambassador in London, reported to his government that in a conference with Sir Edward Grey and the French Ambassador, Paul Cambon, they had agreed: "The key to the situation lies in Washington. A complete guaranty of our interests can be reached only after friendly discussions with the Government of the United States." *Die Internationalen Beziehungen*, Series 3, I: 1, 106. (Benckendorff to Nératoff, June 6, 1911.)

[66] Croly, *op. cit.*, pp. 412–416. See also *Foreign Relations*, 1912, pp. 46, 47. (Calhoun to Knox, June 5, 1911.)

Alarmed over conditions in China, including the borrowing of $50,000,000 by China from the consortium under the agreement of April 15, 1911, Japan had approached her ally on the subject of coöperation should trouble arise in China.[67] The British reaction was not encouraging; in fact, Sir Edward Grey remarked flatly: "We do not want to be drawn into intervention in China."[68] Not only did Great Britain decline to coöperate with Japan in China, but, because of the concatenate circumstances in which the terms of the four-power loan agreement and of the renewal of the Anglo-Japanese Alliance had been published, many Japanese were convinced that Great Britain approved the policies of the United States in China and was actively supporting them.[69]

Russia, on her part, found her French ally more coöperative; but, like Japan, she was unsuccessful in bringing about a cleavage in the consortium. The French Government kept the Russian Foreign Office fully informed of the activities of the consortium,[70] and continually urged that a Russian group should enter the consortium. With a combination of the Russian, Japanese, and French groups and with the frequent coöperation of the English group, the policies of the consortium could be controlled to suit the aims of the three powers. So urged the French Government;[71] but the

[67] *British Documents,* VIII, 518, 519. (MacDonald to Grey, April 24, 1911.) In this dispatch, the British Ambassador in Tokyo reported a conversation which he had held with Marquis Komura, Japan's Minister for Foreign Affairs, and in which the latter had spoken "with great earnestness with regard to events in China which are undoubtedly causing the Japanese Government very great anxiety." It should be noted that this report was dated only nine days after the consortium had reached an agreement with the Chinese Government on the loans for currency reform and for industrial development in Manchuria. Japan, of course, had no share in these loans.

[68] In a minute inscribed on the above dispatch from MacDonald to Grey, *ibid.,* p. 520.

[69] *Ibid.,* p. 538. (Horace Rumbold, British Chargé d'Affaires in Tokyo, to Grey, July 29, 1911.) Rumbold reported the reaction of the Japanese press to the loan agreement and the renewed alliance, the substance being as follows: "England is freed by the Japanese Government from responsibility under the Treaty vis-à-vis America and the latter's activity in Manchuria seems to be approved."

[70] *Un livre noir: diplomatie d'avant-guerre d'après les documents des archives russes, novembre, 1910–juillet, 1914,* edited by René Marchand (Paris: Librarie du travail, 1922–1931), I, 79, 85 ff. *passim;* II, 480 ff. *passim.* Cited hereafter as *Un livre noir.*

[71] *Entente Diplomacy,* p. 36. (Sazonoff to Izvolsky, December 27, 1911.) See also *Der Diplomatische Schriftwechsel Iswolskis, 1911–1914, aus den Geheimakten der Russischen Staatsarchive,* edited by Friedrich Stieve (Berlin: Deutsche Verlagsgesellschaft für Politik und Geschichte, 1924), II, 66. (Izvolsky to Sazonoff [No. 232], March 14, 1912.)

Russians were not impressed. They had only two objectives: first, and most important, to break up the syndicate by inducing the French banking group to withdraw from it; and then, if the first could not be accomplished, to secure the admission of a Russian group to the consortium only on condition that the latter recognize Russia's privileged position in all enterprises north of the Great Wall of China.[72]

The first objective was not realized because the French refused to withdraw from the consortium. In the first place, they thought the consortium could be more easily controlled from within, as has already been indicated. Second, the French Government feared that the withdrawal of the French group might disrupt the long-standing close relationship between French banks and English financial interests, a relationship deemed essential to continued French participation in Chinese loans.[73] But Russian officials attributed other reasons for the French refusal to withdraw. Among them, and of the utmost significance, was Izvolsky's:

> ... The whole secret of the stubborn refusal of these banks to withdraw from the Syndicate of the four Powers and to join with us lies in their conviction that the Americans are stronger than we are in Peking and that they are disposing of large secret funds there in order to bribe the Chinese Ministers and high functionaries upon whom the conferment of concessions depends.[74]

The Russian Government thus failed to induce France to withdraw from the consortium; and the conviction prevailed that the aggressive policy of the United States in the Far East was responsible for the failure.

The policies of the United States, therefore, had aroused a degree of antagonism which caused considerable concern in Washington. Instead of their ideal of a friendly coöperation among the powers

[72] *Entente Diplomacy*, p. 36. See Chap. IV for the fate of the second objective.

[73] *Un livre noir*, I, 176, 177. (Izvolsky to Sazonoff, December 26, 1911.) The views expressed here are those of Georges Louis, French Ambassador in St. Petersburg, as reported by Izvolsky to his government.

[74] *Ibid.*, p. 152. (Izvolsky to Nératoff, October 26, 1911.) The views which Nératoff had expressed on this subject earlier are enlightening: "Wie Ihnen bekannt ist, ist bei uns der Gedanke aufgetaucht, die für unsere politischen Ziele schädlichen Folgen der Tätigkeit des Vierersyndikats dadurch zu paralyzieren, dass wir die Gebiete, wo wir spezielle Interessen haben, d. h. die Mandschurei, die Mongolei und Chinesisch-Turkestan, aus der Sphäre seiner Tätigkeit ausschalten, und zur Betätigung in ihnen wollten wir einer besonderes Syndikat mit der Russisch-Asiatischen Bank on der Spitze bilden. Die französische Regierung hat jedoch für diesen unseren Gedanken sehr wenig Sympathie gezeigt." See *Die Internationalen Beziehungen*, Series 3, I:2, 646. (Nératoff to Izvolsky, October 5, 1911.)

having interests in China, President Taft and Secretary Knox had seen their efforts to protect America's Far Eastern interests frustrated by Japan and Russia, who regarded the United States as an aggressive disturber of the peace in the Far East. That Japan and Russia intended to carry their opposition to American policies to extreme lengths was quite clear. Unfortunately for the United States, these developments came just at the time of the election of a Democratic majority in the House of Representatives, which made it obvious to Japan and Russia that the Taft administration did not have the united support of the American people. Further proof of the lack of unity in the United States was provided when the new Congress refused in 1912 to authorize the construction of more than one battleship, although the administration had recommended the usual two.[75] This position of diplomatic weakness on the part of the United States proved to be an open invitation to aggressive action in the Far East, and Russia and Japan were not slow in seizing the opportunity. So clearly was the situation in the United States connected with the subsequent course of events in the Far East that even before the end of 1912 President Taft remarked: "I do not think the world has yet reached a point where advantage would not be taken of our inability to resist attack, or to meet other nations on an equality in war . . ."[76] Time proved the accuracy of this statement, for the years 1912 and 1913 again brought the United States and Japan to the verge of war.

[75] See Appendix II, below, p. 178.

[76] In a speech at New York on the occasion of a review of the United States fleet, October 15, 1912. See *Annual Reports of the Navy Department*, 1912, p. 19.

CHAPTER IV

JAPAN, MANCHURIA, AND CALIFORNIA

We must be careful to . . . prepare ourselves with power to meet the struggle for existence. The people who cannot meet the struggle will be crushed. . . . Thus, those who are superior will govern those who are inferior. I believe within two or three centuries the world will have a few great governing countries and others will be governed by them—will pay homage to the mighty . . .

Woe to the nations which are governed. We should from now on prepare ourselves to become a governing nation.—COUNT SHIGENOBU OKUMA.

THE "GENTLEMEN'S agreement" and the Root-Takahira notes did not prove to be obstacles to Japan in consolidating her position in the Pacific area, as her activities after 1908 adequately demonstrated. Nevertheless, the Japanese found it increasingly difficult to carry out their plans in the face of determined opposition from the United States Government, an opposition certain to become much more effective with the completion of the Panama Canal and the transfer of the American fleet to the Pacific. The Taft administration made quite clear its intention of adhering to its original policy in the Far East despite the obstacles placed in the way by Japan and Russia. The President said: ". . . this Government is using its best efforts in continuance of its traditional policy of sympathy and friendship toward the Chinese Empire and its people . . ."[1]

By February, 1912, not only was it obvious to the Japanese and Russian Governments that their efforts to break up the consortium had failed, but also that they must enter the consortium and share in its decisions and enterprises in order to protect their own interests. A kaleidoscopic succession of events brought this conviction forcibly home to Russia and Japan. Western Europe was in turmoil. The sending of the warship *Panther* to Agadir by the Kaiser in July, 1911, and the subsequent international crisis, precipitated by Germany in the hope of gaining compensation to balance the widening French control of Morocco, had resulted in a humiliating diplomatic defeat for Germany. Italy had used the crisis in September, 1911, as a strategic moment to declare war on Turkey and to seize Tripoli and Cyrenaica, Turkish possessions. As a result of the diplomatic defeat, the German admiralty asked for a reorgani-

[1] In his message on foreign relations, December 7, 1911. See *Messages and Papers*, XVIII, 8046.

zation of the German fleet with an increase in capital-ship strength. The British Government, deeply concerned at the implied threat, sent Lord Haldane to Berlin in February, 1912, in an attempt to reach some agreement on relative naval strengths and to relieve the international tension. The mission failed, and the recommendations of the German admiralty were enacted into a new naval law on June 14, 1912. Russia, meanwhile, was becoming deeply involved in a Balkan situation which resulted, first, in a series of alliances among the Balkan nations and, ultimately, in the First Balkan War against Turkey in October, 1912. Thus, every great power with appreciable interests in the Far East, excepting only the United States,[2] was involved in a European tangle likely to result at any moment in general war. The powers had every reason to attempt to reconcile their differences in the Far East.

In addition, rapid developments in China made it imperative that friendly coöperation there should replace individual competition, which was so fraught with danger. The local outbreaks in the Province of Szechwan in September, 1911, after the signing of the Hukuang Railways loan agreement, blossomed into a real revolution. On February 12, 1912, the Manchu Emperor abdicated; and three days later the Nanking Republican Assembly elected Yüan Shih-k'ai as provisional president of the Chinese Republic. Two problems immediately confronted the powers: the question of the recognition of the new government and the loan policy to be pursued in China.

From the first the consortium powers had by mutual consent refrained "from independent action and from intervening in China's internal affairs," acting "in full accord with their mutual assurances that they would respect its [China's] integrity and sovereignty."[3] When it became obvious that the revolution would succeed, the Russians and the Japanese were quick to see an opportunity to improve their positions in North China before acknowledging the new government. Sazonoff, in a memorandum dated January 23, 1912, clearly expressed the Russian point of view:

> . . . Russia and Japan, as China's neighbors, possessing wider political interests in this country than all other Powers, are of especial importance to Yuan Shikai.

[2] Japan, it will be remembered, still had her alliance with Great Britain. For the interpretation placed upon the alliance by the two powers when war finally came, see below, pp. 117 ff.

[3] *Foreign Relations*, 1912, p. 64. (Knox to Bernstorff, February 3, 1912.)

Hence, Russia and Japan must use the present favourable moment to fortify their position in China and in this wise prevent the Chinese Government from continually opposing the political interests of Russia and Japan as has been the case during the past few years.[4]

According to Sazonoff, Russia was prepared to press vigorously three concrete demands upon China: an agreement on railroads to be built in Manchuria and Mongolia; an agreement on the strength of Chinese military forces in Manchuria; and an acknowledgment by China that the Chinese Eastern Railway possessed authority to "*assume the entire administration in the expropriated zone.*" Foreign Minister Sazonoff concluded: "*If we proceed in agreement with Japan, we shall be able to reckon all the sooner upon the fulfilment of our wishes as we succeed in assuring ourselves of the support of our French ally, just as England might also give her support to Japan.*"[5] At this early stage of the negotiations, Russia's willingness to coöperate was based on her desire to assure or improve her position in China. Russian plans apparently took no account of the principles for which the United States was contending.

Japan, however, first suggested to the powers that the recognition of the new government afforded an opportunity to secure a pledge from China to respect "the rights, privileges and immunities of foreigners at present enjoyed." To this proposal, no nation could object. But the Japanese Government went further, recommending "that the principle of joint action, adhered to so successfully during the present crisis, be extended to the recognition of any new government and to the above-mentioned conditions thereof, in order to secure guaranties more satisfactory than could be obtained otherwise."[6] The State Department, in its reply, agreed to continue the policy of concerted action, but added, the "Government of the United States will be glad to reply more definitely in regard to the other questions raised when more explicitly informed as to the nature and terms of the guaranties proposed."[7]

---

[4] *Entente Diplomacy*, p. 34.

[5] *Ibid.*, p. 35. It was in this memorandum that Sazonoff, referring to the Mongolian question, asserted that Russia would "*have to take into account* [her] ... *political interests which, in principle, are directly opposed to the maintenance of China's territorial integrity.*"

[6] *Foreign Relations*, 1912, p. 68. (Baron Sutemi Chinda, Japanese Ambassador in Washington, to Huntington Wilson, Acting Secretary of State, received February 23, 1912.)

[7] *Ibid.*, p. 69. (Memorandum, Department of State to the Japanese Embassy, February 27, 1912.) For an account of the policy pursued by the United States

Despite the reluctance of the Japanese Government to state specifically what it wanted, it was forced to do so by the action of the Russian Government. In accepting the principle of concerted action in recognizing the new Chinese Government, Sazonoff asserted Russia's right to take protective measures in North Manchuria, Mongolia, and Western China, where she claimed special rights and interests.[8] Japan countered the Russian reservation with one of her own, insisting upon the recognition of her special interests not only in South Manchuria, but also in adjoining Eastern Inner Mongolia.[9] The other powers acquiesced in the Russian and Japanese reservations, "on the understanding of course that the rights and interests referred to were those covered by treaty or convention."

Russia and Japan, however, were not so easily rebuffed; and an opportunity was at hand for them to renew their special claims. During the course of the revolution, Yüan Shih-k'ai was constantly hard pressed for money to finance his government; but the consortium refused to make any loans to China until a responsible government should be established there. Moreover, the four governments backing the consortium banking groups insisted that any loans to China be made through the consortium "in connection with some general plan by all the interested powers for the protection of the common interests in China."[10] When it became apparent that the Chinese Government would borrow money wherever it could,[11] the powers grew alarmed at the danger of reviving the old system

---

with respect to the recognition of the new Chinese Government, see Meribeth E. Cameron, "American Recognition Policy toward the Republic of China, 1912–1913," *The Pacific Historical Review,* II (June, 1933), 214–230.

[8] *Foreign Relations,* 1912, p. 74. (George Bakhméteff, Russian Ambassador in Washington, to Huntington Wilson, March 8, 1912.) For the instructions of Sazonoff to the Ambassador, see *Un livre noir,* II, 489; and *Der Diplomatische Schriftwechsel Iswolskis, 1911–1914,* II, 53, 54. (Sazonoff to Bakhméteff, March 6, 1912.)

[9] *Foreign Relations,* 1912, p. 79. (Memorandum of a conversation between Huntington Wilson and Chinda, May 16, 1912.) Significant is the fact that the United States first learned of the Japanese reservation through the German Ambassador in Washington, Count Johann von Bernstorff, on May 5, eleven days before the Japanese Ambassador communicated it to the State Department. See *ibid.,* p. 78. (Bernstorff to Wilson, May 5, 1912.)

[10] *Ibid.,* p. 103. (Knox to Bernstorff, December 7, 1911.)

[11] An attempt was made in December, 1911, to negotiate a loan of £2,000,000 sterling with an American company not connected with the consortium; but the State Department had frowned on this endeavor. On March 14, 1912, an agreement was actually concluded by the Chinese Government with a Belgian banking group for a loan of £1,000,000 sterling. It was this loan agreement which galvanized the consortium powers into action.

of uncontrolled international competition in China.[12] They finally agreed to approve a loan for China and to invite Japan and Russia to participate on an equal basis with the consortium powers.[13]

With the issuance of this invitation on March 11, 1912, Russia and Japan started a new drive to secure recognition of their special rights and interests in Manchuria and Mongolia. Russia made it clear that she regarded the advances already made to China as purely political in character. She believed that she should be permitted to participate in these loans on an equal basis, and that they "should be considered as entirely independent of future Chinese loans." As for future loans, Russia would discuss them only after the consortium powers had consulted her "in regard to the conditions of carrying out future financial operations in China."[14] Russia's acceptance, therefore, applied at this time only to the advances and not to any future loans to China.

France, however, was still urging upon the Russian Government the advantages of belonging to the consortium and controlling it from within. The French Government had supported Russia's opposition to Article XVI of the Currency Loan Agreement of April 15, 1911, and had repeatedly guaranteed her continued support of Russian interests in North China.[15] The new French Foreign Minister, Raymond Poincaré, assured his Russian allies that

> admission to the consortium, far from weakening the position of Russia and Japan, would enable them to participate upon a condition of perfect equality in all the advantages obtained, the alliance of Russia and France on the one

[12] The powers saw a similar danger in the demands of Russia and Japan for a recognition of their special rights and interests in China: "Les Puissances, tout en étant disposées à tenir comte des droits résultant pour chacune d'elles en Chine soit des traités, soit de frontières communes, soit d'accords spéciaux, ne peuvent reconnaître à la seule Russie une situation particulière au nord et à l'ouest de l'Asie; si cette procédure se généralisait, on reviendrait à la politique des sphères d'influence et du partage de la Chine, avec tous les dangers qu'elle comporte." See *Documents diplomatiques français, 1871–1914,* Series 3, II, 176. (Raymond Poincaré, French Premier and Minister for Foreign Affairs, to the French Chargé d'Affaires in St. Petersburg, March 11, 1912.)

[13] *Foreign Relations,* 1912, pp. 111, 112. (Huntington Wilson to Curtis Guild, American Ambassador in St. Petersburg, March 11, 1912.)

[14] *Ibid.,* pp. 112, 113. (Guild to Knox, March 15, 1912.)

[15] *Un livre noir,* I, 179, 180. (J. de Selves, French Minister for Foreign Affairs, to Izvolsky, January 4, 1912.) For an excellent résumé of relations between France and Russia on Far Eastern matters, see two departmental memoranda prepared by Philippe Berthelot, Underdirector for Asia in the Ministry for Foreign Affairs, in *Documents diplomatiques français, 1871–1914,* Series 3, II, 283–285 (March 31, 1912), and *ibid.,* pp. 339–341 (April 12, 1912). See also, *ibid.,* I, 457–464 (December 4, 1911).

hand, that of Japan and England on the other, and the friendship uniting the four powers, assuring to them a majority which would permit them to make effective their votes for or against the operations being considered.[16]

Poincaré added that England was also urging the Russian Government to join the consortium and that both powers were following a similar course in Tokyo.

Even the Russian ambassadors in London and Paris were pressing Sazonoff to enter the consortium. Benckendorff argued that, since Russia and Japan could not hope to provide an adequate market for Chinese loans, it would be advantageous to enter a sextuple consortium which they could control. They would be afforded guaranties "against the misuse of credits," and also against the extension of foreign political influence, especially by the United States.[17] Izvolsky in Paris was also convinced that Russia would benefit by joining the consortium:

> Passing to that question, allow me to express the opinion that, in the present circumstances, it is more advantageous for us to enter into the consortium than to sulk and to remain in the Anglo-Belgian group which has no serious financial importance. If, after having entered into the syndicate, it should appear that the elements which are hostile to us have the advantage there, we could always retire demonstratively, and in that case it would be easy to carry the French banks along with us.[18]

In an *aide-mémoire* of April 6, 1912, the Russian Government announced its willingness to participate, but qualified its acceptance by stipulating that in the future, loan agreements "should contain nothing that may be injurious in its nature to the rights and special interests of Russia in North Manchuria, in Mongolia and in West China."[19] The Japanese Government, in its acceptance made a similar reservation with respect to South Manchuria.[20] Thus, the two powers were once more in accord in protecting their respective interests in North China. When the Russian and Japanese banking representatives presented these reservations to the

---

[16] *Documents diplomatiques français, 1871–1914,* Series 3, II, 167. (Poincaré to the chargé d'affaires in St. Petersburg, March 8, 1912.)

[17] *Graf Benckendorffs Diplomatischer Schriftwechsel,* II, 326. (Benckendorff to Sazonoff, March 20, 1912.)

[18] *Der Diplomatische Shriftwechsel Iswolskis, 1911–1914,* II, 75, 76. (Izvolsky to Sazonoff, March 28, 1912.)

[19] *Foreign Relations,* 1912, p. 124. (Huntington Wilson to William J. Calhoun, April 8, 1912.)

[20] *Ibid.,* pp. 114, 115. (Charles Page Bryan, American Ambassador in Tokyo, to Knox, March 18, 1912.)

consortium, however, they were promptly rejected. The four consortium groups joined in stating that, as bankers, they "were unable to accept or consider either of these declarations upon the ground that they were not competent to deal with political questions."[21] In this, they were supported by their governments. The State Department announced that the "position of the Government of the United States in regard to these political questions is that they should be the subject of an understanding between the Governments concerned rather than between the bankers, although the bankers would doubtless be expected to subscribe to the agreement reached by the powers."[22]

The consortium notified Russia and Japan that it would hold its final meeting on June 15, 1912. If the acceptance of the two powers were not received by that time, the bankers would proceed without them.[23] This threat brought Japan's prompt adherence.[24] But Russia feared that the Chinese might use the loans for purposes inimical to Russian interests north of the Great Wall. Sazonoff demanded a greater safeguard by requiring unanimous approval of the groups for the transaction of consortium business in China.[25] Had this demand been granted, Russia and Japan would have been in a position to block all consortium activity in North China. However, the demand was rejected on June 18, 1912, by the German, English, and American representatives with nothing more than an expression of a hope that "any business done in China will be unanimously approved by the six groups and each group records its desire and will endeavor to bring about this result."[26] On the following day, the Russian and Japanese Governments agreed to the formula, "it being understood that we still preserve the possibility of withdrawing from the consortium in case its financial policies do not

---

[21] *Die Grosse Politik*, XXXII, 327, 328, note. At the instigation of Baron Takaaki Kato, Japanese Ambassador in London, the wording of this statement was subsequently changed. The words "not in a position to express their views upon" were substituted for "unable to accept or consider either of." (Report of Fr. Urbig, Director of the Disconto-Gesellschaft, and representative at Paris of the Deutsch-Asiatische Bank.)

[22] *Foreign Relations*, 1912, p. 80. (Knox to Whitelaw Reid, June 10, 1912.)

[23] *Un livre noir*, II, 511. (Izvolsky to Sazonoff, June 10, 1912.) See also *Documents diplomatiques français, 1871–1914*, Series 3, III, 105, 106. (Poincaré to Paul Cambon and Georges Louis, French Ambassadors in London and St. Petersburg, respectively, June 10, 1912.)

[24] *Un livre noir*, II, 512. (Izvolsky to Sazonoff, June 14, 1912.)

[25] *Ibid.*, pp. 513, 514. (Sazonoff to Benckendorff and Izvolsky, June 17, 1912.)

[26] *Ibid.*, p. 515. (Izvolsky to Sazonoff, June 18, 1912.)

correspond to our interests."[27] The consortium powers accepted this reservation, and it was extended to include all members of the syndicate. The general agreement establishing the six-power consortium was signed at Paris on June 20, 1912.[28]

Outwardly, the pact signaled the defeat of Russia's and Japan's ambitions in North China; actually, it did nothing of the sort. The two powers, it is true, had been compelled to admit the equality of the six powers in all consortium banking business in all parts of China. But Russia and Japan were in a position to disrupt the consortium whenever their interests were threatened. If the signing of the agreement represented a defeat for any nation, it was the United States. By the adhesion of Russia and Japan, the United States became a minority member in the consortium. The Russian Government frankly stated that

> one of the essential considerations which decided Russia to adhere to the consortium was the conviction that in all questions of vital importance for the Empire, the French representatives within the consortium would support their Russian colleagues and that the cabinet of Paris would use its influence in the same way with the British Government. . . . In case . . . of a joint action by Russia, France, and England, and with the support of Japan, whose interests are analogous to those of Russia, the group of four powers would have command within the consortium of a preponderant majority permitting them to regulate the destination of the funds conformably to their views.[29]

In reply, the French Government assured Russia that France would gladly continue to support Russian aims both in the consortium and with foreign governments.[30] The United States, therefore, could usually expect opposition from at least three of the six members of the consortium, especially when American action threatened the special rights and interests claimed by Russia and Japan.

The United States, in addition to her greatly weakened position,

---

[27] *Ibid.*, p. 516. (Sazonoff to Izvolsky, June 19, 1912.)

[28] The actual agreement had been signed by the representatives of all six groups on June 18, 1912; but the Russian and Japanese signatures had been affixed subject to the approval of their respective governments, which was given subject to the condition mentioned. For an official account of the negotiations leading up to the agreement, see *Documents diplomatiques français, 1871-1914*, Series 3, III, 168–171. (Poincaré to the French diplomatic representatives in St. Petersburg, London, Berlin, Peking, Tokyo, Washington, and Vienna, June 24, 1912.)

[29] *Documents diplomatiques français, 1871–1914*, Series 3, III, 203, 204. (*Aide-mémoire*, Izvolsky to the French Ministry of Foreign Affairs, July 3, 1912.)

[30] *Un livre noir*, II, 519. (Izvolsky to Sazonoff, July 8, 1912.)

had become extremely unpopular in both Russia and Japan during the negotiations. American motives were misconstrued and misrepresented; conditions existing in the Far East were attributed to American interference. Sazonoff indicated that Russia was highly suspicious of American plans, and complained that the "Americans showed not the slightest interest in the political side of the question, and always considered only their commercial advantage." He further declared that there was a strong belief in Russian circles that the United States would seize the opportunity afforded by the disorders in China to "promote as far as possible ... [her] railway projects in Manchuria."[31] This, of course, Russia was determined to prevent.

Sazonoff's assertions received confirmation from the Far East in a letter from Willard Straight to Henry P. Davison, a member of J. P. Morgan and Company. Straight wrote:

> Although the Japanese are now attacking Germany and are leaving us alone for the time being, the Russians are still damning us. They claim that our entry into the China field has been responsible for the present disorders. They assert that we still cherish the idea of neutralizing Manchuria, that the Currency Loan is but the old idea in a new form. Isvolsky at Paris, the officials in Petersburg, the people here, are endeavoring to play on French and Japanese susceptibilities, to create suspicion of our good faith and the honesty of our intentions.... They bombard the French Government and the banks with insinuations regarding American policy. It looks to me as if a serious attempt was being made to break up the quadruple combination which is not looked on with favor by either Russia or Japan.[32]

Even the French Government considered the United States the most hostile of all the powers to Russian and Japanese ambitions. French officials believed that fear of Russo-Japanese intervention in China during the revolution had restrained the United States and had forced her to agree to collective action in China by all the powers.[33]

The direct reports of the Minister in Peking, William J. Calhoun, to the State Department apprised Secretary Knox of the jealousy and suspicion rampant among the representatives of the powers

[31] *Die Grosse Politik,* XXXII, 302, 303. (Count Friedrich von Pourtalès, German Ambassador in St. Petersburg, to Bethmann-Hollweg, March 30, 1912.)

[32] Croly, *Willard Straight,* pp. 429, 430. This letter was written late in December, 1911, at which time, Russia and Japan were actively engaged in trying to disrupt the four-power consortium; so Straight's judgment proved sound.

[33] *Documents diplomatiques français, 1871–1914,* Series 3, II, 399. (Departmental memorandum by Philippe Berthelot, April 12, 1912.)

and of the tendency of Russia and France to coöperate with Japan and Great Britain, thereby isolating the United States and Germany. He summed up succinctly the general attitude of the powers toward the United States:

All of the powers are more or less suspicious of the Americans. They seem to think we have some exclusive or personal policy in mind; that our professions of altruism are a mere blind; and that we hope or intend, somehow or somewhere, to secure an advantage, either in prestige or substance, in which the rest will have no share. . . . It was all right so long as we released indemnities, educated Chinese youth at home, and sent missionaries to China. But when we rather forcibly injected ourselves into the Hukuang loan, tried to neutralize the Manchurian railways, proposed to build the Chinchow–Aigun railway, and finally negotiated a preliminary contract for the currency loan, we were then and are now believed to entertain an active and aggressive policy, which is competitive if not hostile to all other foreign interests in China. . . .[34]

Minister Calhoun concluded that the United States could expect for some time to come the strongest resistance to her policies in China.

To make the situation even more distasteful to the United States Government, the idea of coöperative action embodied in the original consortium had been radically altered. Coöperation for the laudable purposes of preventing international conflict in the Far East, of maintaining the open door, and of protecting the administrative and territorial integrity of China, had become coöperation for the questionable purposes of intimidating the Chinese Government and of interfering in the internal affairs of China. The consortium, as the only group able to supply the large sums necessary to reorganize and firmly establish the Chinese Government, had assumed a political character not originally intended by its founders.[35] This was accelerated by the admission to the consortium of Russia and Japan, who, backed by the French, immediately pressed the Chinese for "guaranties" and concessions. An example was the demand of Russia and France for the appointment of their nationals as advisers to administer Chinese finances in connection with the reorganization loan. The controversy became so heated that it threatened not only to defeat the loan but also to disrupt the consortium. This is evidenced by statements in Calhoun's reports to the State Department: "If this ends the consortium I

[34] *Foreign Relations,* 1912, pp. 64, 65. (Calhoun to Knox, February 12, 1912.)

[35] *Documents diplomatiques français, 1871–1914,* Series 3, II, 284. (Departmental memorandum by Philippe Berthelot, March 31, 1912.)

suggest that our country recognize the Chinese Government at once,"[36] and "This may end both the negotiations and the consortium."[37]

As the political importance of the consortium mounted and the powers became even more determined to control it for their own purposes, the United States was involuntarily becoming entangled in the *Machtpolitik* of Europe. Blamed by Germany for the stiff French resistance in the Moroccan crises, England was gradually forced into the open as an opponent of Germany and as an ally of France and Russia.[38] Nowhere was this more apparent than in the Far East, where England came to the support of France and Russia in the appointment of officials to supervise Chinese finances under the reorganization loan. Calhoun reported to the State Department that Britain had shifted her attitude on the appointments to accord with that of France and Russia. Moreover, France and Russia were suspected of plotting to disrupt the consortium so as to exclude Germany and the United States, thereby extending the "triple entente to China."[39] Calhoun, in reporting the later progress of the negotiations, said:

> . . . I believe Russian motive is unfriendly to China and has for its immediate purpose the enforcement of Mongolian demands. The French are cooperating with Russia and together they have forced England into line. The outlook is such that there can be no hope of early signature. To my mind it is no longer a question of friendly international cooperation to help China but a combination of big powers with common interests to accomplish their own selfish political aims.[40]

The United States, through the aggressive demands of two European powers, saw danger of being forced alongside Germany in opposition to the Triple Entente, a situation not at all to the liking of the United States Government. Also, it appeared that the United States was being drawn into the position, with the other powers, of forcing upon the Chinese Government a solution of the appointments problem by withholding the funds which China so badly needed.

In his reply to Calhoun, Secretary Knox attempted to clarify

---

[36] *Foreign Relations*, 1913, p. 147. (Calhoun to Knox, January 23, 1913.)

[37] *Ibid.*, p. 155. (Calhoun to Knox, February 10, 1913.)

[38] Heinrich Friedjung, *Das Zeitalter des Imperialismus, 1884–1914* (Berlin: 1922), III, 266.

[39] *Foreign Relations*, 1913, pp. 152, 153. (Calhoun to Knox, February 9, 1913.)

[40] *Ibid.*, pp. 163, 164. (Calhoun to Knox, February 21, 1913.)

the position of the United States on what seemed to be a reversal of the traditional American policies of isolation and the maintenance of the political independence of China. The State Department expressed regret that "political issues" had been introduced into the loan negotiations, and instructed the American Chargé d'Affaires in Peking to notify his diplomatic colleagues that the United States Government,

> while continuing to insist upon what it considers reasonable and general measures for the protection of the interests of all its nationals, including adequate guaranties for the lenders and efficient supervision of disbursements ... [was] not prepared to join in any coercive steps designed to compel China's acceptance either of the present loan or of any particular proposal as to advisers.[41]

In the face of a determined majority in the consortium eager to work its will upon the Chinese Government, however, the United States had no alternative but to withdraw from the consortium. The victory of the Democratic party in the election of November, 1912, with its reputation for opposing "Wall Street" and the "moneyed interests," made this action almost inevitable if not imperative.[42]

With the inauguration of Woodrow Wilson as President of the United States and the installation of William Jennings Bryan as Secretary of State on March 4, 1913, the American group of bankers, represented by Willard Straight, requested the State De-

---

[41] *Ibid.*, p. 166. (Knox to Edward T. Williams, February 27, 1913.) It is to be noted that, although Knox made this concession to appearances, he refused to believe that France and Russia had any "ulterior motives" or made any "deliberate efforts to impede the negotiations." The evidence, however, seems to contradict the conclusions of Secretary Knox. The activities of France and Russia were perfectly obvious even without an insight into their secret diplomacy. For example, Ambassador Herrick in Paris reported:

"It seems to me evident, on reviewing the history of the Chinese loan negotiations, that with the increase of the consortium from four to six powers began a persistent effort to disrupt the consortium, and that China is excluded from making loans in the world's financial markets as long as the six powers hold together.

"The desire, the interest and the policy of the United States have been to maintain the integrity of China and further her rehabilitation. In order to extricate ourselves from the false position in which these dilatory negotiations place us and to continue that policy, does it not seem proper to attempt to relieve China from this embargo of financial exclusion?

"To obtain this relief, the loan should be concluded forthwith or the six-power group should be dissolved and China be given a free hand to borrow where she will."

See *ibid.*, p. 168. (Myron T. Herrick to Bryan, March 8, 1913.)

[42] "The crucifixion of China upon a cross of gold would naturally be repugnant to an Administration whose foreign affairs are in the hands of the present Secretary of State ..." See *The Literary Digest*, XLVI (March 29, 1913), 691.

partment's views "as to the future conduct of these negotiations."[43] The administration replied with a press statement announcing that the government would no longer support the American group in the consortium, "because it did not approve the conditions of the loan or the implications of responsibility on its own part . . . The conditions of the loan seem to us to touch very nearly the administrative independence of China itself, and this administration does not feel that it ought, even by implication, to be a party to those conditions."[44] On the following day, March 19, 1913, the American group withdrew from the consortium.[45]

The withdrawal of the United States made clear her continued adherence to and support of the principle of respect for the administrative and territorial integrity of the Chinese Republic. Consequently, the withdrawal brought unstinted praise from the Chinese press and high officials.[46] At the same time, in her exit from the consortium, the United States confessed failure to achieve her original purpose as a member of the consortium—to maintain the Hay policies in the Far East through coöperative rather than dangerous unilateral action. Because of the perversion of the original purpose of the consortium, the United States had been forced to withdraw but not to abandon the principle of coöperative action in the Far East. For the very administration which led the American bankers out of the consortium was to lead them back again.

The full significance of the American withdrawal was not lost upon the Japanese Government. This was soon made manifest by Japan's bitter resentment of the new alien land law passed by the California State Legislature. The racial question between Californians and Japanese had again become acute because of the American-Japanese commercial treaty of February 21, 1911, which

[43] *Foreign Relations*, 1913, pp. 167, 168. (Straight to Bryan, March 5, 1913.) The American bankers had been aware for some time that the change of administrations probably held a threat for them. On February 20, 1913, Secretary Knox had informed Minister Calhoun in China that, owing "to uncertain political and financial conditions here in the near future, the American group is seriously contemplating withdrawal from the present loan negotiations unless the contract is signed without further delay." See *ibid.*, p. 163. (Knox to Calhoun, February 20, 1913.)

[44] *Ibid.*, p. 170. Statement to the press, issued by the President, March 18, 1913.

[45] *Ibid.*, pp. 171, 172. (Straight to Bryan, March 19, 1913.)

[46] *Ibid.*, pp. 174, 175. (Williams to Bryan, March 25, 1913.) For an opposite view, see Thomas W. Lamont, *Henry P. Davison: The Record of a Useful Life* (New York: Harper, 1933), pp. 163, 164.

apparently made it impossible for the United States to control the immigration of Japanese laborers. The earlier treaty of November 22, 1894, had granted the Japanese the usual most-favored-nation privileges of entry, travel, and residence in the United States, but stipulated that these privileges would not "in any way affect the laws, ordinances and regulations with regard to trade, the immigration of laborers, police and public security which are in force or which may hereafter be enacted in either of the two countries." The new treaty contained no such provision.

The reaction was instantaneous in California, the state most sensitive to the Japanese menace. On February 22, 1911, the day after the new treaty was signed, resolutions were adopted by the California State Senate which expressed regret at the omission of the protective feature from the new treaty, urged the President to withdraw the treaty from the Senate, appealed to the Senate to refuse ratification, and requested the Governor of California to notify the President and Congress of the resolutions.[47] President Taft allayed these fears temporarily by explaining that the declaration of the Japanese Ambassador, Baron Yasuya Uchida, which accompanied and was a part of the treaty, bound the Japanese Government just as effectively as had the older treaty to maintain "the limitation and control which they have for the past three years exercised in regulation of the emigration of laborers to the United States."[48]

The agitation continued, however; and the Magdalena Bay incident in 1912 revived the fears of the Pacific states.[49] When the Democratic administration took office on March 4, 1913, California's long-awaited opportunity had arrived. It was one thing for Republican-controlled California to yield its preferences to a Republican-controlled national administration in the interests of party harmony. But it was quite another thing to continue such coöperation with a Democratic President of the United States.[50] This was especially true when Japan took the lead in protesting

[47] The text of the resolutions as adopted is in *The Journal of the Senate* (California), 39th Session, February 22, 1911, pp. 1127, 1128.

[48] The texts of the telegrams exchanged by Governor Hiram Johnson and President Taft are in *ibid.*, February 23, 1911, pp. 1147–1149. The declaration by Baron Uchida is that referred to above, p. 80.

[49] See above, p. 3.

[50] Raymond L. Buell, "The Development of Anti-Japanese Agitation in the United States II," *Political Science Quarterly*, XXXVIII (March, 1923), 60, 61.

the decision of the new administration to recognize the Chinese Republic and to withdraw from the consortium.[51] The time seemed favorable, and the California leaders quickly seized the opportunity. The result was the California Alien Land Law of May 19, 1913, which denied to aliens ineligible to American citizenship the right to own land in California if the country of their origin barred Americans from owning land. Such aliens were to be permitted to lease land for periods of not more than three years.[52]

When it became apparent that the California State Legislature would pass the bill, President Wilson took the unprecedented step of sending Bryan to Sacramento to plead with the governor and the legislators not to embarrass the national government.[53] The President appealed directly to Governor Johnson "to act . . . in a manner that cannot from any point of view be fairly challenged or called in question."[54] Despite the President's appeal and Bryan's efforts, however, the California State Legislature passed the bill and the governor approved it. The use of the words "ineligible to citizenship" obviously directed the legislation at the Japanese, for European aliens were thereby specifically exempted. It was to this phraseology that the President had objected and to which Japan was to take such violent exception. To make the humiliation doubly bitter for Japan, the United States Government chose this particular time to recognize the new Chinese Republic, although the presidential election for which the other powers were waiting had not yet taken place.[55] This was looked upon by the Japanese as an

[51] *Documents diplomatiques français, 1871–1914,* Series 3, VI, 194. (Stephan Pichon, French Minister of Foreign Affairs, to the Ambassadors of France in London, Berlin, St. Petersburg, and Tokyo, April 1, 1913.) See also *ibid.*, p. 234. (Auguste Gérard, French Ambassador in Tokyo, to Pichon, April 4, 1913.) In a "Department Annotation" to this dispatch, it was stated: "It is the Japanese Government which has taken the initiative in the accord; it is they again who have taken the initiative to negotiate at Washington against the intention of President Wilson to recognize the Chinese Government of succession from the 8th of April, date of the meeting of the Assembly."

[52] The text of the act, which became effective on August 10, 1913, is in *The Statutes of California and Amendments to the Codes,* 40th Session, 1913, pp. 206–208.

[53] *The Journal of the Senate* (California), 40th Session, April 23, 1913, pp. 1785, 1786. See also the speech of Secretary Bryan before the Legislative Conference of the Governor, the Senate, and the Assembly of California on May 3, 1913, in *ibid.*, May 11, 1913, pp. 2900–2902.

[54] *Ibid.*, April 22, 1913, p. 1717.

[55] The note extending formal recognition was delivered to the Chinese Government on May 2, 1913. See *Foreign Relations,* 1913, p. 115. (Edward T. Williams to Bryan, May 2, 1913.)

unfriendly act, especially in view of the feeling aroused by the California land bill.[56] Obviously, therefore, Japan would center all her resentment against the action of the California Legislature.

The Japanese Government protested even before the act was approved, terming it "essentially unfair and discriminatory." Japanese Ambassador Chinda asserted that it was "impossible to ignore the fact that it was primarily directed against my countrymen."[57] So blunt was the protest that the United States feared war with Japan was imminent. At a meeting of the cabinet, there "was much doubt as to Japan's real purpose and meaning. Some thought that the protest was for home consumption; others that Japan wanted trouble before the Panama Canal was opened."[58] In spite of President Wilson's belief that there would be no war, the cabinet discussed the possibility on May 13, 1913, when Secretary of the Navy Josephus Daniels reported that the Navy was unprepared and that the Japanese could easily take the Philippines, Hawaii, and Alaska.[59] The President, however, continued to discount the possibility of war until, as Secretary of Agriculture David F. Houston says, "he noticed the extreme perturbation of the Japanese Ambassador" on May 15. On the following day, Secretary of War Lindley M. Garrison reported that the War Council thought "Manila could be defended for a year" with the support of some naval vessels then on the China station. But the President, fearing this might provoke hostilities, vetoed the suggestion that the ships should be moved.[60]

---

[56] "Der Aerger über Amerika's Vorgehen hat wohl nicht seinen Grund in der Sorge um die Wohlfahrt Chinas. Der Unmut über die Anerkennung Chinas durch die Vereinigten Staaten ist um so stärker, als diese sich China gegenüber gerade in dem Zeitpunkt freundlich zeigen, in dem Japan durch das kalifornische Gesetz gekränkt wird." *Die Grosse Politik*, XXXII, 277. (Count A. von Rex, German Ambassador in Tokyo, to Bethmann-Hollweg, May 9, 1913.)

[57] *Foreign Relations*, 1913, p. 629. (Sutemi Chinda to Bryan, May 9, 1913.)

[58] David F. Houston, *Eight Years with Wilson's Cabinet, 1913 to 1920* (New York: Doubleday, Page, 1926), I, 61. The view that "Japan wanted trouble before the Panama Canal was opened" was widely held. For example, the Kaiser asserted in an interview with the American Ambassador to Russia on February 3, 1907, that "Russia was attacked by the Japanese just as she had completed the Siberian Railroad and you, the United States, will be attacked as you are about to complete the Canal." See Howe, *George von Lengerke Meyer*, p. 339. For evidence that this view had some basis in fact, see above, p. 86.

[59] Houston, *op. cit.*, I, 65.

[60] *Ibid.*, pp. 66, 67. See also William C. Redfield, *With Congress and Cabinet* (New York: Doubleday, Page, 1924), pp. 71, 72; Ray S. Baker, *Woodrow Wilson: Life and Letters* (New York: Doubleday, Doran, 1927–1939), IV, 77–84; and Merle Curti, "Bryan and World Peace," *Smith College Studies in History*, XVI (April–July, 1931), 185, 186.

That actual preparations were made at Manila to defend the city against an expected Japanese attack soon became known. Representative Hobson of Alabama declared in the House of Representatives that "our gunners at Corregidor Island at the mouth of the Manila Bay slept on their guns for six weeks, and were on duty night and day; that the harbor was mined, and that every hour they expected the appearance of a hostile fleet. Furthermore, cipher instructions were sent to navy-yard commandants to be prepared to instantly put their station on a war basis."[61] On June 2, 1913, the Commanding General in Hawaii urgently requested the War Department to speed completion of Oahu's land defenses,[62] and the Chief of Engineers agreed, provided "circumstances are such as to warrant the additional expense . . ."[63] "In view of the urgent necessity for doing this work as soon as possible," affirmed the Chief of Staff, "I recommend that the expenditure be authorized." But the Secretary of War, on June 16, decided that "conditions now existing" made such measures unnecessary.[64] The California law had brought the United States and Japan close to a rupture; and probably only the moderation of Japan's peremptory demands enabled the two countries to bridge the gap peacefully.[65]

The belief was prevalent that Japan took a strong stand because of American weakness in the Pacific, and to many the incident seemed a national humiliation. Bryan's visit to California was described as "the spectacle of that great apostle of peace, the honorable Secretary of State, tiptoeing to California to advise its legislature against the passage of land laws depriving the Japanese residents of that State of the right to own land."[66] The government was castigated for not having been prepared to meet such international emergencies. President Taft, who had guided the nation

[61] In the House debate on the naval appropriation bill for 1916. See *Cong. Rec.*, LII, January 29, 1915, p. 2697. Representative Hobson further declared that he had made these statements before the House Committee on Naval Affairs in the presence of Secretary Daniels, and no denial had been made.

[62] MS Cablegram, District Engineer at Honolulu to the Chief of Engineers, June 2, 1913.

[63] MS Letter, Chief of Engineers to the Chief of Staff, June 4, 1913.

[64] *Ibid.*, Memorandum, Chief of Staff to the Secretary of War; and handwritten note by the Chief of Staff, June 16, 1913.

[65] David Lawrence, the news columnist, asserted that England had prevailed upon her ally to adopt a less belligerent attitude. See his *The True Story of Woodrow Wilson* (New York: Doran, 1924), p. 101.

[66] Remarks of Representative Michael E. Burke of Wisconsin on the naval appropriation bill for 1915. See *Cong. Rec.*, LI, May 7, 1914, p. 8264.

through the entire period of coöperative action in China, had realized that American diplomacy in the Far East needed real force behind it to make it effective. Shortly before the election of 1912, he had said:

> . . . I sincerely hope that whatever party comes into power the policy of two battleships a year will be continued until, through the Panama Canal and otherwise, the needs of the Pacific coast for its defense shall be satisfied and our people whose States abut on that great ocean may feel that they, too, are receiving the benefit of the sums expended from the National Treasury for adequate naval defense. . . . We provide a navy as we provide insurance, against a possible loss or a danger which we hate to anticipate, but which under present conditions we should be foolish not to treat as possible.[67]

After the experiences of American diplomacy in the Far East between 1908 and 1913, no official could possibly fail to understand the need for naval forces in the Pacific.

Japan's blunt protest, the uncertainty over her real intentions, and the indisputable fact that the United States was in no position to protect her outlying possessions in the Pacific, all led to feverish strengthening of the national defenses such as had accompanied the crisis of 1906 and 1907. Despite Secretary Daniels' pronounced preference for a naval construction holiday, he recommended to Congress the authorization of three battleships, eight destroyers, and three submarines, limiting himself, as he said, only by the prospective revenues available for naval construction.[68] Congress acted favorably upon the recommendations of the Navy Department, thereby demonstrating its awareness of the dangers confronting the nation. Representative Patrick H. Kelley of Michigan expressed clearly the views of those favoring the building up of the Navy:

> In considering our naval requirements we must also have in mind any National or State policies which have in the past given rise to controversies with foreign countries and which may cause trouble again. It so happens that certain policies which are deemed wise for the people of this country prove irritating to other nations. Our policy of excluding Asiatics falls within this class and is one of the most sensitive questions with which our Government is called

[67] In his address at the fleet review at New York, October 15, 1912. See *Annual Reports of the Navy Department*, 1912, pp. 18, 19.

[68] Report of the Secretary of the Navy, December 1, 1913, in *Annual Reports of the Navy Department*, 1913, pp. 10, 11. Secretary Daniels recommended two battleships in his annual report, but this was later increased to three when the old American battleships *Mississippi* and *Idaho* were sold to Greece and the proceeds of the sale became available for new construction.

upon to deal. Within a year the Secretary of State has appealed in person to the Legislature of the State of California urging upon that State the importance of doing nothing which would complicate our relations with Japan. Only recently, while the immigration bill was under consideration, the Members of this House were appealed to by the administration and by the leaders of both parties to the same effect. Members of the House fully realize the possibility of international complications growing out of anti-Asiatic legislation, either by Congress or any of the States. We can not ignore this question in considering our naval requirements.[69]

Representative Kelley's argument ran like a continuous thread throughout the debates on the naval appropriation bill. There was, of course, opposition. Representative Samuel A. Witherspoon of Mississippi sincerely believed that no nation on earth would go to war with the United States because American trade was too vital to the existence of other nations.[70] Others believed that the provisions of the bill were entirely inadequate and did not give the United States the naval strength to protect her interests. Alabama's Hobson, in support of this view, advocated a two-ocean navy with a fleet in the Atlantic superior to the German fleet and a fleet in the Pacific superior to that of Japan. In this way only could the United States be sure that these great naval powers, who also possessed large and powerful armies, would not threaten American security.[71] Supporting Representative Kelley's argument, however, Representative John R. Farr of Pennsylvania voiced the thought in the minds of many of those who voted for the bill:

The menace of Japan is due to the fact that she demonstrated fighting ability. She was prepared, and she defeated China. She was prepared, and she conquered Russia. It was after these victories that Japan loomed up as a world figure, and it is her ability to fight that makes that nation a possible menace to us on the Pacific coast. No one who knows human nature and who has followed the teachings of history believes that the California discrimination against that people is a closed incident. The unfriendliness of Japan's newspapers in this crucial period indicates that.[72]

With such arguments receiving bipartisan support from all sections of the country, the advocates of a stronger navy secured the authorization of three battleships as well as some auxiliary craft.

Work at the Pearl Harbor naval base on the power plant, barracks, magazines, shell houses, storehouses, a coal storing station,

[69] *Cong. Rec.*, LI, April 21, 1914, p. 7017.
[70] *Ibid.*, April 18, 1914, p. 6872.
[71] *Ibid.*, April 23, 1914, pp. 7147, 7148.
[72] *Ibid.*, April 25, 1914, p. 7264.

and fuel oil tanks proceeded apace.[73] In addition, the General Board called attention "to the present, and increasing, inadequacy of docking facilities for the fleet." Since the addition of new vessels to the fleet would only accentuate the deficiency, the Board expressed the "opinion that, in the event of war, the country would be in a most serious situation, especially in the Pacific, from its lack of docking facilities . . ." Accordingly the Board urgently recommended two docks large enough to accommodate the greatest of the new vessels of the fleet.[74]

The Joint Army and Navy Board, in its report of November 27, 1911, had pointed out the strategic value of Puget Sound and San Francisco Bay as naval operating and repair bases, and had urged the development of facilities at both points "in anticipation of the transfer of the battle fleet to that ocean."[75] There the matter rested until the crisis with Japan over the California land law and the resulting recommendation of two new docks by the General Board. Secretary Daniels then moved to supply the deficiency. In the estimates for the naval establishment for the fiscal year 1915, submitted to Congress on December 1, 1913, the Navy Department requested authority to enter into a contract with the Union Iron Works of San Francisco for the use by the Navy of a large dry dock to be built by that company at Hunter's Point on San Francisco Bay.[76]

The Secretary of the Navy, however, felt that the matter was too urgent to wait upon the normal course of the naval appropriation bill through Congress. In a letter dated January 9, 1914, to Senator Benjamin R. Tillman of South Carolina, Chairman of the Senate Committee on Naval Affairs, Secretary Daniels revealed the administration's anxiety over conditions in the Pacific. He wrote:

In view of the approaching completion of the Panama Canal and the ensuing arrival in the Pacific of our fleet, I consider the possession of a suitable dry dock on that coast a matter of such commanding importance that I must request your earnest consideration of the above provision.

You will note that the period of construction is to be two years from the

---

[73] Report of the Chief of the Bureau of Yards and Docks (Rear Admiral H. R. Stanford), October 24, 1913, in *Annual Reports of the Navy Department*, 1913, p. 102.

[74] Report of the General Board, in *ibid.*, p. 30.

[75] *Cong. Rec.*, LI, May 1, 1914, p. 7587. Inserted by Representative Peter G. Gerry of Rhode Island.

[76] *House Docs.* (Ser. 6600), 63d Cong., 2d sess., No. 398, December 1, 1913, p. 320.

date of signing the contract. This period is already longer than the interests of the Navy can well afford, and an effort will be made to reduce it as much as possible.

I therefore have to request that the proviso above quoted be taken from the naval bill and incorporated in a separate bill by itself.

With your familiarity with conditions on the Pacific, I need not urge the necessity of early action.[77]

The Senator complied with the Secretary's request, and the Senate actually passed the desired legislation on January 27, 1914.[78]

The Navy Department thus made clear its decision to transfer the fleet to the Pacific upon the completion of the Panama Canal. This is further evidenced by the government's provision for adequate facilities for servicing and supplying a great fleet. Secretary Daniels, in his annual report for 1913, pointed out the need for an assured fuel supply in the Pacific at a reasonable cost. The Navy, he said, should be producing and refining its own fuel oil on the two naval petroleum preserves in California by "the time the Panama Canal is opened and the fleet begins frequenting the Pacific . . ."[79] He deprecated the necessity of bringing coal all the way from Norfolk, Virginia, which had "always been a source of great expense and of considerable uneasiness to the department." The Navy Department, according to Secretary Daniels, was testing coals from the two major fields in Alaska, Bering River and Matanuska, and hoped that they would prove satisfactory. However, adequate transportation would have to be provided before they could be obtained in sufficient quantity. He urged Congress to provide suitable transportation as "economy and national security would seem to indicate this step to be both advisable and economical. From a strategical point of view it is imperative."[80]

As early as 1904, President Theodore Roosevelt had pointed out that, because of the sparse population, private enterprise could not be expected to provide the transportation needed to unlock the riches of Alaska. He recommended Congressional aid in the construction of wagon roads and a railway from the Gulf of Alaska

[77] *Sen. Reports* (Ser. 6552), 63d Cong., 2d sess., No. 163, January 21, 1914, pp. 1, 2.

[78] *Cong. Rec.*, LI, January 27, 1914, pp. 2367, 2368. The authorization was ultimately reincorporated in the naval appropriation bill and so enacted into law.

[79] Report of the Secretary of the Navy, December 1, 1913, in *Annual Reports of the Navy Department*, 1913, p. 15.

[80] *Ibid.*, p. 16.

to the Yukon River.[81] During the Japanese crisis of 1913–1914, President Wilson again urged these developments as "very pressing and very imperative." He also recommended that Congress, by suitable legislation, open up the resources of Alaska to exploitation under such safeguards as would conserve them in the public interest.[82] Bills to accomplish both purposes were duly enacted into law.

The chief reasons advanced in favor of the bill to authorize the President to locate, construct, and operate railroads in Alaska were strategic. James Wickersham, the Alaskan delegate in the House of Representatives, pointed out that the distance from Seattle to Yokohama by the Great Circle route, which passed through the Aleutian Islands, was 1,500 miles less than by way of Honolulu. Because of this and because of the coal supply in Alaska, he concluded that "there is an immediate necessity to create a naval base in Alaska, and the railroad provided for in this bill is the first unit in that great establishment for the defense of our Pacific frontier."[83] In calling the policy of the government "stupid and inexcusable" for bringing coal from the Atlantic Coast for use in the Pacific, Representative William E. Humphrey of Washington described succinctly the strategic value of Alaska:

> Alaska is the place where, above all others to-day, we need a new naval station. The great difficulty is in getting from the map the real situation of the countries on the Pacific and the real distance between them. A battleship fleet in Alaska is in a far better position to strike an enemy in the Orient than one at Hawaii. It is in a far better position to protect the coast of the United States. It is in a better position to intercept a fleet from the Orient.
>
> For naval purposes alone the construction of a railroad in Alaska is fully justified.[84]

On March 12, 1914, the President approved the bill authorizing the government to construct and operate railways in Alaska. This was followed some months later by a bill to permit the leasing of coal lands in Alaska. These lands had been withdrawn from entry by executive order on November 12, 1906, as a conservation measure.[85] The leasing bill, approved October 20, 1914, reserved for naval purposes over 12,500 acres of coal-bearing lands in the

[81] In his annual message to Congress, December 6, 1904. *Messages and Papers*, XVI, 7048–7050.

[82] On December 2, 1913. See *ibid.*, XVIII, 8291, 8292.

[83] *Cong. Rec.*, LI, January 14, 1914, p. 1676.

[84] *Ibid.*, January 28, 1914, p. 2436.

[85] Report of the Secretary of the Interior, December 23, 1908, in *Reports of the Department of the Interior*, 1907–1908, I:1, p. 15.

Bering River and Matanuska fields; and the unreserved coal lands were opened for leasing by private operators. Representative Scott Ferris of Oklahoma, Chairman of the House Committee on Public Lands, described the measure as "imperative to make the railway a success . . ."[86]

The problem of the status of the Philippine Islands was also accentuated by the Japanese crisis of 1913. The Democratic majority in the House, elected in 1910, had attempted to carry out the party pledge to free the islands from American control. Representative William A. Jones of Virginia, Chairman of the House Committee on Insular Affairs, had introduced a bill on March 20, 1912, to "establish a qualified independent government for the Philippines and to fix the date when such qualified independence shall become absolute and complete . . ."[87] In reporting the bill to the House on April 26, 1912, the committee declared its chief motive to be the repugnance to the principles upon which the United States Government had been founded "of holding and governing against their consent any people who aspire to independence and are capable of governing themselves."[88] Having satisfied their consciences, the committee then launched into a discussion of the real essence of the Philippine problem—could the United States defend the islands in a war with a first-class naval power? The committee itself admitted that even a country as rich as the United States could not afford to provide the ships, guns, and men necessary to defend the islands, and called them a "constant menace to the peace and well-being of the American people."[89] If the purpose in holding the islands was only to secure a base of military and naval operations in the Far East, the committee averred, that purpose could be as well served by retaining only such bases as were needed and granting independence to the islands generally.

Furthermore, the committee pointed out that it was "the opinion of our military experts that it would not be expedient, in the event of war with any strong naval power, for the United States to attempt to defend the Philippines."[90] The "strong naval power" referred to was obviously Japan, for the element of distance operated

[86] *Cong. Rec.*, LI, August 31, 1914, p. 14487.
[87] *Ibid.*, XLVIII, March 20, 1912, p. 3717.
[88] *House Reports* (Ser. 6131), 62d Cong., 2d sess., No. 606, April 26, 1912, p. 10.
[89] *Ibid.*, pp. 10, 11.
[90] *Ibid.*, p. 11.

just as effectively against the European powers as it did against the United States. Japan, because of her proximity to the Philippines, was the one power which could make the defense of the islands by the United States impracticable. Thus the committee concluded that if the United States would be forced eventually to abandon the islands to an enemy, it might just as well save the money expended on troops and fortifications by withdrawing immediately. The objection that the Philippines, if independent, would fall an easy prey of "some land-grabbing nation" could be met, in the opinion of the committee, by some international agreement for the neutralization of the islands.[91]

Congress took no action on this bill, and it died with the session. In his annual message of 1913, however, after the California Alien Land Law dispute had brought a crisis in American relations with Japan, President Wilson called the attention of Congress to America's obligation to the Philippines. He said: "We must hold steadily in view their ultimate independence, and we must move toward the time of that independence as steadily as the way can be cleared and the foundations thoughtfully and permanently laid."[92] Although this recommendation was not acted upon until after the opening of the World War, the debates on the Naval Appropriation Act approved June 30, 1914, indicate the complexity of the problem and of the views held by many. Representative Hobson, for example, referring to the Philippine Islands, stated simply that "whether we stay in them or not we must protect them."[93] It was apparently this complication to which the President had referred in his annual message. If the independence promised to the islands was to be placed on a really permanent foundation, the United States would have to be relieved of the sole responsibility for their defense. An international agreement to respect Philippine independence would, of course, have solved this problem at the moment.

Thus, the United States had commitments in the Far East which she would gladly have relinquished if a satisfactory method could have been devised. The Japanese Government, therefore, was in an anomalous position as America's *bête noire*. It was at once the cause of and the chief impediment to the desire of the United States to consolidate her position in the Pacific. Japan showed no inclination

[91] *Ibid.*, p. 12.
[92] *Messages and Papers*, XVIII, 8291.
[93] *Cong. Rec.*, LI, April 23, 1914, p. 7147.

to smooth the way for the United States to formulate permanent policies in Pacific waters. In fact, at the outbreak of the World War, Japan had broken off negotiations with the State Department for a conventional settlement of the California land dispute, and had returned to the exchange of diplomatic notes. The new Japanese Foreign Minister, Baron Takaaki Kato, reopened the correspondence with the State Department in a note clearly indicating the attitude of the Japanese Government. Baron Kato said:

> I have given the subject my most serious consideration and am consequently well satisfied that the enactment in question [California Alien Land Law] is not only in disregard of the letter and spirit of the existing treaty between Japan and the United States of America, but is essentially unfair and invidiously discriminatory against my countrymen and inconsistent as well with the sentiment of amity and good neighborhood which has always presided over the relations between the two countries.[94]

Thus, in a strained diplomatic situation in the Pacific, the World War began; and American-Japanese relations were to suffer further stress. Japan was not to forget the California land question, but the unique opportunity afforded her by the war was for a time to make such questions of minor importance. The attention of the Japanese Government was to focus entirely upon eliminating from the Far East a power which had humiliated Japan in 1895, and upon making Japan supreme in the Western Pacific while the other great powers were engaged elsewhere and, therefore, incapable of interfering. These activities of the Japanese, coupled with the naval publicity attendant on Germany's submarine warfare, were to bring the President, the Congress, the Navy, and the American people into agreement at last on the importance of the Navy in the national defense of the United States.

[94] *Foreign Relations*, 1914, pp. 426, 427. (Kato to Chinda, June 9, 1914.) A copy of this note was delivered to the State Department on June 10, 1914. The Yamamoto Ministry in which Baron Nobuaki Makino was Foreign Minister, had been driven from office on March 24, 1914; and a new ministry under Count Shigenobu Okuma had assumed office in Tokyo on April 16, 1914, with Baron Kato, formerly ambassador in London, as Foreign Minister.

CHAPTER V

JAPAN AND THE WORLD WAR

What Japan has now to do is to keep perfectly quiet, to lull the suspicions that have arisen against her, and to wait, meanwhile strengthening the foundations of her national power, watching and waiting for the opportunity which must one day surely come in the Orient. When that day arrives she will be able to follow her own course, not only able to put meddling Powers in their places, but even, as necessity arises meddling with the affairs of other Powers. Then truly she will be able to reap advantages for herself.—COUNT TADASU HAYASHI.

ALONE OF ALL the great powers the United States and Japan possess strategic positions which may be called insular. No nation strong enough to threaten American or Japanese security has her center of power within three to four thousand miles of their coasts. Early in her history the United States recognized the significance of this geographical fact; and the people, through the happy phraseology of James Monroe, became imbued with the idea that the safety of the nation depended upon the maintenance of that isolation. Consequently there grew up as a part of the permanent policy and tradition of the United States a national opposition to the establishment in this hemisphere of focal points of attack by any of the other great powers. So strong was this opposition and so well established the doctrine of Monroe that by the opening of the twentieth century the mere threat of foreign aggression on this continent was enough to ensure to the government the support of the whole people in resisting such encroachment. Thus, the United States was born in isolation, rose to power in isolation, and was in the fortunate role of being strong enough to protect her insular position throughout Europe's imperialistic expansion.

Japan, too, at one time possessed all of the attributes of insularity. But unlike the United States, Japan was unable to maintain her insular security; for first the great powers of Europe and then the United States moved in on her borders. Thus, when she was ready to emerge as a great power in her own right, she found herself surrounded by the territories and strongholds of the other great powers. And the establishment by peaceful methods of a Japanese "Monroe Doctrine" for East Asia had become impossible. This was made quite clear in 1894–1895, when Japan defeated

China but was robbed of the fruits of her victory by the intervention of Russia, Germany, and France. From that moment, Japanese statesmen accepted and followed the advice of Count Hayashi. The time would surely come, they thought, when Japan could show that she had not forgotten her diplomatic defeat. She kept quiet, and so well did she "lull the suspicions" of the powers that she was able to fight a victorious war against Russia without the intervention of any of the other powers.

But the triumph over Russia only complicated Japan's problem. Russia, although greatly weakened and driven back in the Far East, was not eliminated as a powerful force in that region. And Japan had manifested to the world her militaristic ambitions. As Theodore Roosevelt expressed it, there was no certainty "that the Japanese down at bottom do not lump Russians, English, Americans, Germans, all of us, simply as white devils inferior to themselves . . . to be treated politely only so long as would enable the Japanese to take advantage of our various national jealousies, and beat us in turn."[1] By her conduct during the war and by her surprising victory, Japan had aroused the very suspicions which Hayashi had warned should be avoided.

Japan's policy of "Asia for the Asiatics," or in the Kaiser's words, "pour les Japonais,"[2] finally became so obvious and roused such strong opposition, especially from the United States, that Japan's own ally, Great Britain, became alarmed at the prospect of being involved in a war at Japan's side against the United States. Accordingly, in 1911, the British Government secured a revision of its alliance with Japan in order to exempt from its terms any nation with which either party had negotiated a treaty of general arbitration. But the general arbitration treaty between Great Britain and the United States, which was to have relieved Great Britain of her obligations to Japan as against the United States, failed of approval by the United States Senate. Therefore, the Anglo-Japanese Alliance remained in full force, even against the United States, whose relations with Japan after 1911 steadily deteriorated.

This was the situation when war broke out in 1914; and the opportunity which Count Hayashi had predicted would "one day

[1] Gwynn, *The Letters and Friendships of Sir Cecil Spring Rice: A Record*, I, 444. (Roosevelt to Spring-Rice, December 27, 1904.)

[2] *Die Grosse Politik*, XXV:1, 86. (Count A. von Rex, German Minister in Peking, to Chancellor Bülow, December 7, 1907.) Marginal comment by the Emperor.

surely come in the Orient" had arrived. The great powers all recognized that war in Europe would for the time being make East Asia an open field for Japan. Many a foreign office official looked anxiously toward the Far East, wondering what Japan would do. The first reports from Tokyo were reassuring. On July 28, 1914, the government announced that Japan was on friendly terms with the countries involved and "would, as a matter of course, maintain the strictest neutrality."[3] But this was before France and Great Britain entered the struggle. The outlook began to change only three days later when Sir Edward Grey informed Katsunosuke Inouye, the Japanese Ambassador in London, that, although it appeared that Great Britain might be forced into the conflict, "it would be on the side of France and Russia, and ... [he] did not see that ... [Great Britain was] likely to have to apply to Japan under ... [their] alliance, or that the interests dealt with by the alliance would be involved."[4] This early notice to Japan was more than the mere courtesy of keeping an ally informed. It was rather the first step in what was to be a concerted attempt to keep Japan out of the war and to maintain peace in the Far East.

Subsequent negotiations between Japan and Great Britain hinged largely on their respective interpretations of their rights and obligations under the Anglo-Japanese Alliance of July 13, 1911. The purposes of the alliance, as defined in the preamble, were to preserve the peace of the Far East and India, to protect the interests of all powers in China by guaranteeing the integrity and independence of China and the principle of the open door, and to defend the territorial rights and "special interests" of each other in the regions mentioned. In Article II, both allies pledged full military assistance should either country be attacked by one or more powers "in defence of its territorial rights or special interests mentioned in the preamble of this Agreement ..."; that is, in Eastern Asia or in India.[5] Needless to say, when the crucial moment

[3] "The Austro-Hungarian Red Book," in *Collected Diplomatic Documents Relating to the Outbreak of the European War* (London: 1915), p. 515. (Baron Ladislas von Müller de Szentgyörgy, Austro-Hungarian Ambassador in Tokyo, to Count Leopold Berchtold, Austro-Hungarian Foreign Minister, July 28, 1914.) This is the original *Oesterreichisch-Ungarisches Rotbuch* in English translation, published by the British Foreign Office.

[4] *British Documents*, XI, 256. (Grey to Sir Conyngham Greene, British Ambassador in Tokyo, August 1, 1914.)

[5] The text of the alliance is in *British and Foreign State Papers*, CIV (1911), 173, 174. It should be noted that the secret naval provisions of the earlier alli-

came, each power interpreted these provisions in the light of her own interests; and in 1914, they were not in agreement.

The British desire to keep Japan out of the war was motivated largely by her fear of repercussions in the United States and in the Dominions. The British Foreign Secretary, Sir Edward Grey, later explained the situation:

> In the early days [of the war] the Japanese Alliance was a matter of some embarrassment and even of anxiety. Japan was ready to take her part in the war as our Ally; the Far East and the whole of the Pacific Ocean lay open to her and were her natural sphere of operations. But the prospect of unlimited Japanese action was repugnant to Australia and New Zealand. They already regarded Germany, her position and transactions in the Pacific with misgiving; they would have viewed the substitution of Japan for Germany with positive alarm. Equally important, the effect of Japanese action on public opinion in the United States might be disastrous; it might even make American sentiment definitely antagonistic to us. It was unthinkable that we should not have the most scrupulous care for the interest and feelings of British Dominions that were taking their part in the war, ready to face danger and to make sacrifices with so much patriotism. We dared not risk offending the United States. We had, therefore, to explain to Japan that her help would be welcome, but that her action must be limited and her prospective acquisition of German territory must not extend beyond certain bounds.[6]

These views were translated into an agreement between the two allies that the alliance would become operative only in the contingency of an attack on the British possessions at Hong Kong or Weihaiwei, or "a similar concrete act of aggression . . ."[7] This agreement confirmed and emphasized the statement of Baron Kato,

---

ance of 1902 that each of the allies must maintain in the Far East at all times a fleet greater than that maintained there by any third power had been omitted from the second and third alliances; and Great Britain had withdrawn all her battleships from Asiatic waters. See *British Documents,* II, 119, 120; IV, 131, 169.

[6] Sir Edward Grey, Viscount of Fallodon, *Twenty-Five Years, 1892–1916* (London: Hodder and Stoughton, 1925), II, 99, 100.

[7] The agreement came on August 3 and 4, 1914, in an exchange of notes in which the British Government announced that it would rely on the support of the Japanese in the event any of the contingencies mentioned arose, and the Japanese Government announced its readiness to render such assistance "if called upon." See *British Documents,* XI, 298. (Grey to Greene, August 3, 1914.) Also, *ibid.,* pp. 327, 328. (Greene to Grey, August 4, 1914.) The Russian Ambassador in Tokyo reported to the Russian Foreign Office on August 7, 1914, that "in the opinion of the British Ambassador [Greene] the Japanese were preparing 'without awaiting a communication from their ally, an attack upon Kiauchow' and only sought 'for a suitable pretext in order to strike at the German possessions in the Far East.'" See *Die Internationalen Beziehungen,* Series 2, I:1, 8, note 2. (Malevsky-Malevich to Sazonoff, August 7, 1914.)

Japan's Foreign Minister, to Count von Rex, the German Ambassador in Tokyo, "that Japan desired to remain neutral as long as possible," and would open hostilities only in the event of a German attack on British possessions in the Far East.[8] When Baron von Rex assured Kato that Germany contemplated no aggressive action in the Far East,[9] the possibility of Japan's becoming involved in the war seemed remote.

On August 6, however, Great Britain inadvertently opened the way for Japan's entry into the war; and the Japanese immediately seized the opportunity. Sir Edward Grey sent to the British Ambassador in Tokyo the following telegram:

> As our warships will require some time to locate and destroy the German warships in Chinese waters it is essential that the Japanese should hunt out and destroy the German armed merchant cruisers who are attacking our commerce now.
>
> If the Japanese Gov[ernmen]t would employ some of their warships in this way it would be of the very greatest assistance to us. It means of course an act of war against Germany, but we do not see how this is to be avoided.[10]

The British Government, it should be noted, was careful to specify exactly the aid desired of Japan—the destruction of German commerce raiders until the British fleet was able to protect British shipping in Far Eastern waters. Baron Kato, however, had other plans. To the British request, he replied that he "thought that an attack upon Tsingtau would be the quickest way of settling the business."[11] To the Imperial Premier, Count Okuma, Baron Kato recommended "that (1) Japan should enter the war, (2) that the

---

[8] *Outbreak of the World War: German Documents Collected by Karl Kautsky,* edited by Count Max Montgelas and Walter Schücking and translated by the Division of International Law, Carnegie Foundation for International Peace (New York: Oxford University Press, 1924), p. 558. (Count A. von Rex to Gottlieb von Jagow, German Foreign Secretary, August 3, 1914.)

[9] *British Documents,* XI, 305. (Greene to Grey, August 3, 1914.)

[10] *Ibid.,* X:2, 823. (Grey to Greene, August 6, 1914.)

[11] *Ibid.* (Greene to Grey, August 7, 1914.) According to the German Chargé d'Affaires in Peking, Russia and Japan had concluded an agreement in 1912, at the time of the Balkan crisis, in which Russia had consented to Japanese annexation of South Manchuria and acquisition of Kiaochow, and Russia retained freedom of action in North Manchuria. The Chargé d'Affaires further averred that Great Britain had later consented to Japan's acquisition of Kiaochow in return for Japanese aid in the Pacific in a possible war against Germany. *Foreign Relations,* 1914 Supplement, p. 164. (John V. A. MacMurray, American Chargé d'Affaires in Peking, to Bryan, August 7, 1914.) The Russian Ambassador in Tokyo, Nicolas Malevsky-Malevich, however, denied that there was any "agreement of any kind between Japan and Russia concerning China." *Ibid.,* p. 165. (George W. Guthrie, American Ambassador in Tokyo, to Bryan, August 29, 1914.)

scope of the military and naval operations should not be confined to the destruction of German war vessels in Chinese waters, and that (3) negotiations should be entered into with the British Government concerning the grounds upon which Japan should join the war."[12]

The Japanese cabinet considered the British request for aid in a series of conferences on August 7 and 8, 1914. Baron Kato expressed his frank opinion that "the general conditions were not such as to impose upon Japan the duty to join the war under treaty obligations"; but he "welcomed it as an opportunity to destroy the German influence from Eastern Asia and to enhance the international position of Japan."[13] These statements are important since Japan later insisted that under the terms of her alliance with England she was obliged to go to war against Germany, and that she had no selfish aims in doing so. The cabinet reached the decision on August 8, 1914, that Japan should enter the war against Germany. In informing the British Government, Baron Kato asked Britain to agree to Japan's entry into the war under the "general principles" of the Anglo-Japanese Alliance, and not to impose any limitations on the scope of Japanese aid.

On the following day, August 9, Great Britain replied, urging Japan not to declare war, and for the time being merely to protect her commerce from raiders. Grey also expressed to Ambassador Inouye the fear that a declaration of war by Japan would result in widespread disturbances in the Far East with inevitable losses in British trade. Kato retorted that Japanese entry into the war would constitute no threat to British trade and that Japan "entertained no territorial ambition."[14] When the British Government, on August 11, asked the Japanese to reconsider their decision, Kato replied that public opinion in Japan, demanding revenge on Germany for her part in the intervention of the powers in 1895, was too strongly in favor of war for the cabinet to risk such action. Britain, therefore, had no choice but to acquiesce in a declaration of war by Japan, but, in an effort to prevent Japan's seizure of Germany's island possessions in the Pacific, again attempted to

[12] Takeuchi, *War and Diplomacy in the Japanese Empire,* p. 169. This work contains an excellent account of the entrance of Japan into the war from the Japanese standpoint, based largely on Seitoku Ito, ed., *Kato Komei,* or *Life and Letters of Count Komei Kato* (Tokyo: 1929).

[13] Takeuchi, *op. cit.,* pp. 169, 170.

[14] *Ibid.,* pp. 171, 172.

restrict the field of Japan's warlike activities to the coastal waters of Asia. Baron Kato protested that Japan could not prosecute the war effectively nor protect her commerce in the Pacific if her sphere of action were thus limited.[15] There the matter rested until after the Japanese ultimatum to Germany on August 15, 1914.

Meanwhile, at the suggestion of the Chinese Government, the State Department undertook to secure the consent of the belligerents to a neutralization of "Chinese territory and marginal waters" and "adjacent leased territories."[16] Sir Edward Grey objected to a general neutralization as impracticable, suggesting instead an agreement to maintain the *status quo* in China to prevent the disturbances incident to hostilities.[17] Germany went even farther by agreeing on August 13, to a complete neutralization of the whole Pacific area;[18] but it was too late. Japan assured the British Government that, although she found it impossible to refrain from hostilities in the Far East, she was "anxious to respect both the neutrality and the integrity of China."[19] But the Japanese Government said only that it was "anxious" to do this things, not that it *would* do them.

China feared the worst, as the American Chargé d'Affaires in Peking reported to the State Department on August 13. The Japanese, it seemed, were looking for pretexts for dealing with the Chinese Government independently of the other powers. They were charged with "creating daily provocative incidents" in Manchuria. Even more indicative of the Japanese attitude was their reaction to China's request that the United States bring about the neutralization of the Pacific area. Although China, at the same time, had also requested the Japanese Government to coöperate with the United States toward the desired end, Japan informed China that she regarded "it as an unfriendly act that the Chinese Government

[15] *Ibid.*, pp. 172, 173. See also *The Times* (London), August 11, 1914, p. 6.

[16] *Foreign Relations,* 1914 Supplement, p. 162. (MacMurray to Bryan, August 3, 1914.) The Chinese Minister in Washington had spoken to the Secretary of State as early as August 1, 1914, "in regard to the feasibility of securing an agreement among the belligerents that the Far East should be neutralized." *Foreign Relations,* "The Lansing Papers, 1914–1920," I, 1. (Memorandum by Robert Lansing, Counselor for the Department of State, August 7, 1914.)

[17] *Foreign Relations,* 1914 Supplement, pp. 165, 166. (Walter H. Page, American Ambassador in London, to Bryan, August 11, 1914.)

[18] *Ibid.*, pp. 169, 170. (James W. Gerard, American Ambassador in Berlin, to Bryan, August 13, 1914.) The German offer was transmitted to Tokyo on August 15, 1914, the day on which the Japanese ultimatum was delivered to the German Government.

[19] *Ibid.*, pp. 167, 168. (Page to Bryan, August 11, 1914.)

so far disregarded the friendly disposition of Japan as to seek in the first instance good offices of the United States in the attempt to exclude the area of hostilities from the Far East."[20] In the circumstances this attitude boded little good for China.

Having convinced herself, if not her ally, that she should enter the war, Japan delivered an ultimatum to Germany on August 15, 1914, couched in the language of "friendly" advice which the three powers had used in 1895. Germany was advised to withdraw her armed vessels from Asiatic waters or to disarm them and to turn over to Japan not later than September 15, 1914, "without condition or compensation the entire leased territory of Kiaochow, with a view to eventual restoration of the same to China."[21] In informing the United States Government of the ultimatum, Baron Kato, according to Ambassador Guthrie, "requested me to impress on you [Bryan] as strongly as possible that in taking the present action Japan was not animated by any selfish purpose but was acting strictly in pursuance of the alliance with Great Britain and would not seek any territorial aggrandizement or selfish advantage in China and would carefully respect all neutral interests."[22] Thus, while Kato admitted privately that under the alliance Japan's obligations were not affected by the crisis in the Far East, he was willing to use the alliance as a pretext to allay American fears of Japan's actions.

The assurances of Foreign Minister Kato, however, did not create the effect he so ardently desired. *The New York Times,* for example, in a long editorial on August 18, 1914, declared that not only was Japan not acting under the terms of the alliance but was actually assuming the role of a disturber of the peace the maintenance of which was one of the main objects of the alliance. The editor pointed out that, although Japan had demanded the surrender of Kiaochow alone, nations at war "strike at each other where they may." Since Germany possessed a great number of Pacific islands which would become the legitimate prey of Japan in a war with Germany, the editor foresaw danger to the United States. "The possession of these islands would give her [Japan] coaling and naval stations on the direct line between the Panama

[20] *Foreign Relations,* 1914 Supplement, p. 169. (MacMurray to Bryan, August 13, 1914.)

[21] *Ibid.,* p. 170. (Guthrie to Bryan, August 15, 1914.) Germany was given until August 23, 1914, to reply to Japan's "advice."

[22] *Ibid.,* pp. 170, 171.

Canal and the Philippines. It is not to be supposed that we could view such changes of territorial ownership without anxiety." Japan's assurances that her action would in no way threaten American interests were accepted by the editor, "of course," especially in view of the British announcement that Japan would confine her operations to Asiatic waters. But, said the skeptical editor, "there is a general belief that it is the policy of Japan to assert and maintain for herself supremacy and control in the Asiatic waters of the Pacific with a view, probably, to the ultimate exclusion of the influence of Western nations."[23]

In addition to such evidence of the public distrust of the Japanese Government and its assurances, the State Department made known its own misgivings. In reply to the Japanese ultimatum to Germany, Secretary Bryan expressed the satisfaction of the United States Government that Japan intended to return Kiaochow to China and that she had no selfish interest to gratify. But, he reminded the Japanese Government, in the event of disturbances in China requiring action by Japan, the latter would, in accordance with the Root-Takahira agreement of 1908, wish to consult the United States.[24] Rumors were spread in the Far East, however, that "the United States regards Japanese promise to restore Kiaochow to China as satisfactory."[25] The State Department promptly denied making any such statement. Secretary Bryan declared that no opinion at all had been expressed on "the merits of the question."[26]

Congress was not so diplomatic in letting the Japanese know they were being watched with some concern. On August 17, 1914, Representative Fred A. Britten of Illinois introduced a resolution in the House in which the Secretary of State was directed "to inform the Japanese Government that the United States views with concern the transfer by force of arms of any Chinese territory to Japan or other foreign power . . ."[27] Four days later Senator Jacob H. Gal-

[23] "Japan's Intentions" (editorial), *The New York Times*, August 18, 1914, p. 8.

[24] *Foreign Relations*, 1914 Supplement, p. 172. (Bryan to Guthrie, August 19, 1914.) See also Harley Notter, *The Origins of the Foreign Policy of Woodrow Wilson* (Baltimore: Johns Hopkins Press, 1937), pp. 332, 333.

[25] *Foreign Relations*, 1914 Supplement, pp. 172, 173. (MacMurray to Bryan, August 19, 1914.)

[26] *Ibid.*, p. 173. (Bryan to MacMurray, August 19, 1914.)

[27] *Journal of the House of Representatives of the United States*, 63d Cong., 2d sess., August 17, 1914, p. 867. The Russian Ambassador in Washington, George Bakhméteff, reported to Sazonoff: "Die japanische Ultimatum an Deutschland hat auf die hiesige Regierung einen starken Eindruck gemacht."

linger of New Hampshire presented a set of resolutions intended to clarify the attitude of the United States toward the recent Far Eastern developments. The first resolution reaffirmed the traditional policy of the United States on the open door and the integrity of China, thus revealing the disquietude in Senatorial minds. The second resolution was more explicit and far more indicative of the fears prevalent in the United States. It read as follows:

> *Resolved,* That the United States could not view with indifference any suggestion looking to the alteration of the existing territorial status quo of the islands of the Pacific and Oceania or to any change in the character of their present occupation and settlement.[28]

None of these resolutions was considered by either branch of Congress, but they showed that Congress, like the State Department, was alive to the dangers consequent upon Japan's activities.

Meanwhile, the British Government still hoped to circumscribe the warlike activities of its ally. Accepting the Japanese reply of August 13, 1914, as an assent to restriction under protest, the British Foreign Office issued a statement to the press on August 17 announcing that Japan would coöperate with Great Britain under the alliance in view of the imminent threat to the general interests of the allies in the Far East. It concluded:

> It is understood that the action of Japan will not extend to the Pacific Ocean beyond the China Seas, except in so far as it may be necessary to protect Japanese shipping lines in the Pacific, nor beyond Asiatic waters westward of the China Seas, nor to any foreign territory except territory in German occupation on the continent of eastern Asia.[29]

The London *Times* commented hopefully that there "is every reason to believe that the military and naval action of Japan will be

---

He also said that "although the President had expressed the opinion that he had no reason to doubt the honesty of Japan's declaration that, in connection with her declaration to Germany, she did not intend to infringe the integrity of China, a resolution was introduced in Congress which required that the Secretary of State should protest the occupation by Japan of the German leased territory in China." *Die Internationalen Beziehungen,* Series 2, I:1, 91. (Bakhméteff to Sazonoff, August 17, 1914.) Malevsky-Malevich later reported from Tokyo that, "in the words of Baron Kato, the Japanese Government 'attached no importance to the introduction of the resolution in Congress; according to a declaration of the Secretary of State to the Japanese Ambassador in Washington, it will have no effect.' " *Ibid.,* p. 91, note 1. (Malevsky-Malevich to Sazonoff, August 21, 1914.)

[28] *Cong. Rec.,* LI, August 21, 1914, p. 14074.

[29] *Foreign Relations,* 1914 Supplement, p. 171. (Sir Colville Barclay, British Chargé d'Affaires in Washington, to Bryan, August 18, 1914.)

limited to the removal of the Germans from Kiaochau. Japan in her own interests will assuredly refrain from all action likely to arouse the legitimate susceptibilities of the United States or of the British Dominions in Australasia."[30] These hopes soon proved to be too sanguine.

On August 19, the Japanese Government presented to the British Foreign Office as its reply the text of part of a speech delivered by Premier Count Okuma the day before, once more denying that Japan had any selfish motives or that she coveted any territories. Okuma declared that Japan intended to fight her war against Germany wherever it might become necessary in order to protect "her own legitimate interests"; but he coupled with this an assurance that Japan would "take no action such as to give to the Powers any cause for anxiety or uneasiness regarding the safety of their territories or possessions."[31] To make the Japanese reply even more emphatic, Baron Kato informed the British Ambassador in Tokyo that Japan considered the statement merely as the British interpretation which, of course, would not bind Japan in any way.[32] By this time there could be little doubt that Japan was acting independently and even against the wishes of her ally.

In an atmosphere of suspicion and doubt, Japan declared war on August 23, 1914, Germany having failed to reply to the Japanese ultimatum. In making the declaration, however, Premier Okuma thought it necessary to give some further explanation to the American people. His statement, dated August 24, read in part:

> It is my desire to convince your people of the sincerity of my Government and of my people in all their utterances and assurances connected with the present regrettable situation in Europe and the Far East.
>
> Every sense of loyalty and honor oblige Japan to cooperate with Great Britain to clear from these waters the enemies who in the past, the present and the future menace her interests, her trade, her shipping and her people's lives.
>
> This Far Eastern situation is not of our seeking....
>
> *As Premier of Japan, I have stated and I now again state to the people of America and of the world that Japan has no ulterior motive, no desire to secure more territory, no thought of depriving China or any other peoples of anything which they now possess.*

[30] *The Times* (London), August 18, 1914, p. 6.

[31] *Ibid.*, August 21, 1914, p. 7. See also Takeuchi, *op. cit.*, p. 173.

[32] Takeuchi, *op. cit.*, p. 174, note 25. See also, *Foreign Relations*, 1914 Supplement, p. 210. (Guthrie to Bryan, December 31, 1914.) In this dispatch, Ambassador Guthrie forwarded a copy of summaries of interpellations of the Japanese Foreign Minister in the Diet on December 10, 1914, which contains a paragraph on the subject *The Sphere of Warlike Operations.*

My Government and my people have given their word and their pledge, which will be as honorably kept as Japan always keeps promises.[33]

Japanese actions did not confirm the assurances of the premier. The cry was immediately raised in Japan that, since Germany had rejected the ultimatum, Japan was no longer bound by her promise to return Kiaochow to China.[34] This attitude became official in September when, in answer to a question in the Diet, Baron Kato replied that, "with reference to Kiaochow after the war, there is no agreement between the two Governments [Japan and Great Britain] outside the provisions of the alliance."[35] Japanese troops promptly took over the Shantung railway as far west as Tsinan-fu, alleging that as German property it was subject to seizure. Early in October the Japanese Navy captured and occupied the strategic island of Jaluit, the seat of the government of the Marshall Archipelago, although it was asserted that the occupation "was temporary and for military purposes only."[36] Japan subsequently occupied other strategic islands in the south Pacific.

The British Government had failed to restrict the area of Japan's operations, but publicly expressed confidence in the honesty of Japan's purposes. Some of these expressions, however, were in reality admonitions. After the occupation of Jaluit, for example, "official quarters" in London reported that Japan was adhering to her promises, "because Japan certainly will not utilize this war to aggrandize herself in the Pacific. This is the belief of the British Government, which through the alliance naturally has great influence with Japan."[37] The British Government, seeing the imminent

[33] "The Premier of Japan to the American People: A Message from Count Okuma," *The Independent*, LXXIX (August 31, 1914), 291.

[34] *Foreign Relations*, 1914 Supplement, p. 179. (Guthrie to Bryan, September 1, 1914.)

[35] *Ibid.*, p. 185. (Guthrie to Bryan, September 22, 1914.)

[36] *Ibid.*, pp. 183, 184. (Guthrie to Bryan, October 6, 1914.) Baron Kato informed Malevsky-Malevich that, although the occupation was temporary, "in any case, we do not intend to give them back to Germany." Malevsky-Malevich reported to Sazonoff that the Japanese press had rejoiced at the occupation of the Pacific islands as "a sign of the freeing of Japanese policy from the 'tutelage of Great Britain.' However, this newspaper fuss did not last long. As soon as a rumor appeared that the Japanese had occupied another island, all reports in the press were silenced, obviously from fear of objections on the part of the United States." Baron Kato had assured Malevsky-Malevich, however, that up to that time the United States had made "no observations of any kind with regard to the occupation of the Marshall Islands by the Japanese." *Die Internationalen Beziehungen*, Series 2, I:1, 315, 316. (Malevsky-Malevich to Sazonoff, October 17, 1914.)

[37] *The New York Times*, October 9, 1914, p. 3.

friction in the Pacific, had already taken more practical steps to protect itself from involvement in war because of Japan. Two days after Japan's declaration of war, Sir Cecil Spring-Rice, British Ambassador in Washington, urged the Foreign Office to sign one of the "peace commission" treaties with the United States as a general safeguard against untoward incidents arising out of the war.[38] These so-called Bryan treaties, which Secretary Bryan had been urging upon the British Government for more than a year,[39] provided that all disputes between the parties should be referred to a permanent international commission for investigation; and the parties agreed not to begin hostilities until the report of the commission could be submitted. The British readily saw the advantage of the agreement and soon accepted the treaty, which was signed at Washington on September 15, 1914.[40] Japan was promptly notified that the treaty was considered the equivalent of the general arbitration treaty mentioned in Article IV of the Anglo-Japanese Alliance of 1911. The Japanese government accepted the interpretation, and consequently Great Britain was no longer obligated to support Japan in a war against the United States.[41]

In the face of Japan's activities in the Pacific, the United States determined to strengthen her international position. Congress, first of all, attempted to carry out the President's recommendation with respect to the Philippine Islands.[42] Representative Jones of Virginia, who introduced the earlier measure of 1912, presented a bill on August 20, 1914, providing for greater power for the native government and pledging the United States to recognize Philippine independence "as soon as a stable government shall have been established therein."[43] This meant that independence would come only through demonstration by the Filipinos of the ability to govern themselves. But the majority of the House Committee on

[38] Gwynn, *The Letters and Friendships of Sir Cecil Spring Rice: A Record,* II, 220. (Spring-Rice to Grey, August 25, 1914.)

[39] *British Documents,* VIII, 605, 606. (James Bryce, British Ambassador in Washington, to Grey, April 24, 1913.)

[40] The text of the treaty, with the President's proclamation of November 11, 1914, is printed in *Foreign Relations,* 1914, pp. 304–307.

[41] *British Documents,* VIII, 531, note. Also, see above, Chap. III, note 54. For a different view of the reason for the willingness of Great Britain to sign the Bryan treaty at this time, see Merle Curti, "Bryan and World Peace," *Smith College Studies in History,* XVI (April–July, 1931), 157–161.

[42] In his annual message for 1913. *Messages and Papers,* XVIII, 8291.

[43] *House Reports* (Ser. 6560), 63d Cong., 2d sess., No. 1115, August 26, 1914, p. 1.

Insular Affairs urged that the natives were already capable, and with an opportunity to demonstrate their competence, "the date of complete independence will not be long deferred."[44]

The committee minority, however, pointed out that the war in the Far East made it inexpedient for Congress to discuss in public debate the future relations of the United States to the Philippines. They declared:

> It is true that Japan has stated that her offensive operations would be confined to Kiaochow; but why should they from Japan's point of view? If, angered by a stubborn resistance, severe losses, and pressed by an already aroused war spirit among her people, Japan should seize all Germany's Pacific possessions, no one would be surprised.
>
> To enter upon a debate in which all our relations and interests in the Pacific would be discussed and our rights in the Philippines, Hawaii, Samoa, and Guam challenged, would be to encourage disregard to our interests and lead nations with opposing interests to believe the United States would not go far in defense of possessions so lightly regarded by those in control of the Government. To make the nations of the world believe we are anxious to get rid of the Philippines, do not desire to keep them, have little or no interest in their retention, is to invite aggression which would mean war.[45]

Despite the force of these arguments, the sentiment in favor of starting the Philippines on the road to ultimate independence was stronger; and the bill was debated and passed by the House on October 14, 1914.[46]

National defense was also receiving critical attention during this period. In fact, so widespread was the demand for preparedness that a large part of President Wilson's annual message to Congress concerned that subject. He warned the people not to go to extremes which would indicate "that we had lost our self-possession, that we had been thrown off our balance by a war with which we have nothing to do, whose causes can not touch us, whose very existence affords us opportunities of friendship and disinterested service which should make us ashamed of any thought of hostility or fearful preparation for trouble."[47] The President pointed out that the Navy was the "natural means of defense" for the United States; but with the rapid development of new types of naval craft in the

[44] *Ibid.*, p. 2.
[45] *Ibid.*, No. 1115:2, August 31, 1914, p. 6.
[46] *Cong. Rec.*, LI, October 14, 1914, p. 16629. The bill was reported in the Senate in the following short session, but was never reached on the Senate calendar.
[47] December 8, 1914. See *Messages and Papers,* XVIII, 8402.

war, no one could predict with certainty what kinds of ships should be built. Wilson concluded by outlining the policy which the government would pursue:

> ... We shall not alter our attitude toward it [the subject of national defense] because some amongst us are nervous and excited. We shall easily and sensibly agree upon a policy of defense. The question has not changed its aspects because the times are not normal. Our policy will not be for an occasion. It will be conceived as a permanent and settled thing, which we will pursue at all seasons, without haste and after a fashion perfectly consistent with the peace of the world, the abiding friendship of states, and the unhampered freedom of all with whom we deal. Let there be no misconception. The country has been misinformed. We have not been negligent of national defense. We are not unmindful of the great responsibility resting upon us. We shall learn and profit by the lesson of every experience and every new circumstance; and what is needed will be adequately done.[48]

President Wilson undoubtedly had in mind the reports of the General Board and the Secretary of the Navy for 1914. The General Board, refusing to be unduly influenced by naval developments in the Atlantic, still kept to its original purpose of acquiring a fleet of ships that could engage an enemy on even terms at great distances from American shores. This, the Board maintained, was the true mission of the fleet; for "command of the sea can only be gained and held by vessels that can take and keep the sea in all times and in all weathers and overcome the strongest enemy vessels that may be brought against them."[49] In other words, the Board still believed that the battleship remained the backbone of the fleet, although other types of vessels had their legitimate functions. The development of the battleship fleet, therefore, should continue unabated. The Board recommended that four new dreadnaughts be authorized. In view of the demonstrated effectiveness of the submarine and the airplane for certain types of work in the European war, the Board also recommended the further expansion of these arms of the American fleet, but not to the exclusion of the new dreadnaughts, as many were demanding. Finally, the Board stressed the importance of trade rivalry as a cause of war. No nation had ever been able to maintain its overseas commerce in time of war without adequate sea power; and this, the Board pointed out, "has a particular bearing on the United States at the present time,

[48] *Ibid.*, pp. 8402, 8403.

[49] Report of the General Board, November 17, 1914, in *Annual Reports of the Navy Department*, 1914, p. 63.

when such strenuous efforts are being made to build up a national merchant marine and extend our foreign commerce."[50]

The Secretary of the Navy, however, was inclined to share the then prevalent belief that the submarine had made the battleship obsolete; but he was unwilling to disregard the advice of the General Board. Accordingly, he merely reduced the number of vessels of each type recommended by the Board.[51] But he qualified the reduction by urging Congress to make "a larger increase in the submarine craft, appropriating generously therefor without reducing the appropriations for other craft."[52] Such differences of opinion led President Wilson in his annual message to ask skeptically: "When will the experts tell us just what kind [of ships] we should construct—and when will they be right for ten years together, if the relative efficiency of craft of different kinds and uses continues to change as we have seen it change under our very eyes in these last few months?"[53] There can be little doubt that the President sincerely believed that the war was revolutionizing the value of various types of naval craft. Nevertheless, within the year, not only was he to revise his opinion, but he was also to come to an understanding of, and to agreement with, the policy long advocated by the General Board.

By the time Congress could act upon the program of naval construction recommended by the Navy Department, the Japanese Government had begun the series of acts which were to give final direction to a new United States naval policy. First, the question of the California Alien Land Law was still very much alive. In the last diplomatic note of 1914 on the subject, the Japanese Government concluded its argument with the warning that "the Imperial Government deem it to be a matter of grave importance that no efforts on their part as well as on that of the United States Government should be spared to meet the question with entire rectitude, and to prevent any possible future complications which might arise and result in perplexing the situation and aggravating the susceptibilities of the two nations."[54] Consistent with this warning,

---

[50] *Ibid.*

[51] For a comparison of the recommendations, see below, Appendix II, p. 179.

[52] Report of the Secretary of the Navy, December 1, 1914, in *Annual Reports of the Navy Department*, 1914, p. 9.

[53] December 8, 1914. See *Messages and Papers*, XVIII, 8403.

[54] *Foreign Relations*, 1914, p. 434. (Chinda to Bryan, November 25, 1914.)

the Japanese Ambassador offered finally to accept a treaty with the United States in which such discriminatory laws should be prohibited in the future. This idea appealed to Secretary Bryan, who recommended it to President Wilson, saying: "I think such a treaty would go a long way toward answering the 'jingos' who are always insisting upon our getting ready for war with Japan."[55]

The President readily agreed with Bryan that the United States should eventually make some such concession to Japan in order to settle the dispute. But he qualified his approval by adding that "there are many things to consider first: among the rest her [Japan's] present attitude and intentions in China and her willingness or unwillingness to live up to the obligations she has assumed towards us with regard to the open door in the East."[56] The President's disquietude was amply justified. Japan's obvious eagerness to assume the status of a belligerent was enough in itself. Her flagrant violation of Chinese neutrality, her seizure of the Shantung–Tsinan Railway, and the discrimination of the Japanese against American shippers in the matter of rates on the South Manchurian Railway[57] were other subjects of concern for the United States Government.

The move which the Japanese Government was about to make had been in preparation at least since January, 1913. At that time, Baron Kato, on the verge of leaving his post as ambassador in London to become foreign minister in the Katsura cabinet, held two conferences with Sir Edward Grey. He informed Grey "that Japan entertained vital political and psychological concern in the Kwantung Peninsula and the concessions of the South Manchuria and Antung–Mukden Railways," and "that the Japanese people were determined to maintain a permanent occupation of the Kwantung Province."[58] Japan awaited only a "psychological moment"

---

[55] *Foreign Relations*, "The Lansing Papers, 1914–1920." II, 400. (Bryan to Wilson, January 23, 1915.) The earlier attempt to negotiate a treaty had been dropped by the Japanese Government because the United States had refused to include a provision partially to invalidate the California statute.

[56] *Ibid.*, p. 400. (Wilson to Bryan, January 27, 1915.)

[57] On the question of rate discrimination, see Paul H. Clyde, "An Episode in American-Japanese Relations: the Manchurian Freight-Rate Controversy, 1914–1916," *The Far Eastern Review*, XXVI, Pt. 1 (August, 1930), 410–412; Pt. 2 (September, 1930), 480–483. The correspondence between the two governments is printed in *Foreign Relations*, 1915, pp. 594–625; *ibid.*, 1916, pp. 446–450.

[58] The conferences were held on January 3 and 10, 1913. See Takeuchi, *op. cit.*, pp. 184, 185. Also, see above, p. 67, for the views of Prince Ito on this question.

to open negotiations with the Chinese Government; and this moment came with the fall of Tsingtao on November 7, 1914. Instructions were given to Eki Hioki, Japanese Minister in Peking, on December 3; and the "negotiations" began with the presentation by Hioki of the Twenty-one Demands to President Yüan Shih-k'ai on January 18, 1915.[59]

These demands, arranged in five groups, were designed to give Japan a stronger foothold in South Manchuria and Eastern Inner Mongolia, to secure China's consent to the transfer to Japan of Germany's rights in Shantung, and to gain for Japan certain rights and privileges in these areas and even in China itself. Many of the demands were inconsistent with Japan's treaty pledges to respect the territorial and administrative integrity of China and to observe the principle of equal opportunity in China. The most objectionable, and the ones that touched most closely the sovereign independence of the Chinese Republic, were those in Group V, which would have given Japan a strong hold on Chinese finance, military and police administration, and control of schools and hospitals. China was to buy a large percentage of her war munitions from Japan and was to grant to Japan what amounted to a new sphere of influence in the Province of Fukien.[60] In the words of Bertram L. Simpson, a man with an intimate knowledge of the Far East, "the gleaming knife of the Japanese surgeon is to aid the Japanese teacher in the great work of propaganda; the Japanese monk and the Japanese policeman are to be dispersed like skirmishers throughout the land; Japanese arsenals are to supply all the necessary arms . . . Japanese advisers are to give the necessary advice in finance, in politics, in every department—foreshadowing a complete and all-embracing political control."[61]

In presenting the demands, the Japanese Government took extraordinary precautions against any counteraction by the United States, the only great power in a position to offer effective resistance. Although urged by the British, Russian, and French Govern-

[59] Takeuchi, *op. cit.*, pp. 187, 188.

[60] The text of the demands, subsequent correspondence, and proposals exchanged between the two governments, as published by each government, are printed in *Foreign Relations*, 1915, pp. 159–204. See also *The Sino-Japanese Negotiations of 1915: Japanese and Chinese Documents and Chinese Official Statement*, Division of International Law, Pamphlet No. 45 (Washington: Carnegie Endowment, 1921).

[61] B. L. Putnam-Weale (pseud. for Bertram L. Simpson), *The Fight for the Republic in China* (New York: 1917), p. 99.

ments to send troops to the European theater of war,[62] Baron Kato informed the British Government that, "since Japan has important interests to protect in the Far East, she must retain her armed forces there intact . . ." Sir Edward Grey told Cambon "very confidentially, that among the motives which deterred Japan from sending her troops away, one of the most important concerned the United States. They fear in Japan, if the Japanese army were away, that California could take advantage of the opportunity for anti-Japanese legislative measures, which are always to be feared and which will be prevented chiefly by the dread which Japan inspires."[63] Without doubt the Japanese actually were concerned about the United States; but it was not because of any action California might take, but because of what Japan herself intended to do and the way in which she intended to do it.

Every effort was made by the Japanese to keep the negotiations secret. The Chinese Government was warned that the nature of the demands must be kept secret "on pain of serious consequences to China." In informing the State Department of this restriction, Paul S. Reinsch, the American Minister in Peking, characterized the demands as "such as could not be granted without abandoning entirely the open-door policy as well as independence in political and industrial matters."[64] Thus, within five days of the presentation of the demands, knowledge of them was leaking out. In fact, on January 23, 1915, the Japanese police suppressed an extra edition of the Tokyo *Asahi Shimbun,* which carried a dispatch from

[62] *Die Internationalen Beziehungen,* Series 2, I:2, 542 and note 3. (Izvolsky to Sazonoff, December 10, 1914.) Also, *ibid.,* pp. 479, 480. (Sazonoff to Vladimir A. Suchomlinoff, Russian Minister of War, November 25, 1914.)

[63] *Ibid.,* pp. 549, 550. (Benckendorff to Sazonoff, December 14, 1914.) Malevsky-Malevich reported later from Tokyo that "should the European powers really call upon Japan for help, she would not fail to utilize her service extensively, not in financial, but in political and territorial interests. Japan will not be satisfied with the occupancy of Tsingtau and of the small islands in the Pacific Ocean." See *ibid.,* p. 623. (Malevsky-Malevich to Sazonoff, January 4, 1915.)

[64] *Foreign Relations,* 1915, p. 79. (Reinsch to Bryan, January 23, 1915.) See also *Die Internationalen Beziehungen,* Series 2, II:1, 94. (Vassily N. Krupensky, Russian Minister in Peking, to Sazonoff, January 29, 1915.) In this dispatch, Krupensky said that Lu Cheng-hsiang, China's Foreign Minister, had told him that "die japanischen Forderungen, die aus 21 Punkten bestünden, seien sehr schwer, und die Japaner beständen besonders darauf, dass die chinesische Regierung sie den anderen Mächten nicht mitteilte, indem sie mit dem schwersten Folgen drohten." Lu Cheng-hsiang had just replaced Sun Pao-chi as Foreign Minister, the latter having resigned because of the Japanese demands. See *ibid.,* note 3. (Krupensky to Sazonoff, January 28, 1915.)

Peking with an outline of the demands.[65] Furthermore, the Japanese Government, in its efforts to maintain secrecy, failed to observe its treaty obligations to consult the United States under the Root-Takahira agreement and Great Britain under the Anglo-Japanese Alliance.[66]

When, in spite of the attempts at secrecy, the sweeping nature of the demands, especially of those in Group V, gradually became known, the Japanese Government communicated to the interested governments on February 8, 1915, a memorandum containing a summary of the demands in the first four groups.[67] Nothing was said about Group V, even to her own British ally; and when Secretary Bryan inquired of the Japanese Ambassador whether larger demands had been made, as was being reported in the newspapers, Chinda "expressed himself as certain that the memorandum included everything."[68] Japan's Far Eastern ally, Russia, also suspicious about the rumors, inquired of Baron Kato whether the list communicated to Russia, England, and France contained all the demands. Baron Kato replied that "by this list the demands of the Japanese Government had been completely set forth; but at the same time Japan had expressed the desire to resolve a series of other questions in relation to China, which had been discussed between China and Japan for a long time."[69] The Chinese Government, however, made further secrecy impossible by communicating to the

[65] *Die Internationalen Beziehungen,* Series 2, II:1, 66, 67. (Malevsky-Malevich to Sazonoff, January 24, 1915.)

[66] *Foreign Relations,* 1915, p. 82. (Bryan to Page, February 2, 1915.) *Ibid.,* p. 88. (Page to Bryan, February 13, 1915.)

[67] *Ibid.,* pp. 83, 84. Ichiro Motono, Japanese Ambassador in St. Petersburg, had urged upon Baron Kato the desirability of notifying "at least Russia and France of the substance of the negotiations." Sazonoff had informed him, so Motono reported, that "he doubts not at all that this step runs counter to none of Russia's interests, but from reports from England and America—especially from America—they entertain profound suspicion, and Japan should pay earnest attention to that if her public opinion will permit." See *Die Internationalen Beziehungen,* Series 2, II:1, 102, note 3. (Motono to Kato, February 2, 1915.) Count Benckendorff reported from London three days later that Sir Edward Grey knew nothing of any Japanese "wishes for privileges or monopolies which would extend over the whole of China"; but the British Foreign Secretary was worried about the possibility of future difficulty with Japan "not so much because of China as of the English possessions in the Pacific Ocean, in Australia and Canada, on racial grounds . . ." See *ibid.,* p. 126. (Benckendorff to Sazonoff, February 5, 1915.)

[68] *Foreign Relations,* 1915, p. 92. (Department memorandum of a conversation between Secretary Bryan and Ambassador Chinda, February 16, 1915.)

[69] *Die Internationalen Beziehungen,* Series 2, II:1, 193. (Malevsky-Malevich to Sazonoff, February 16, 1915.) Kato also indicated the general nature of these "desires."

State Department in mid-February, 1915, a complete list of the demands in all five groups.[70] When the State Department inquired about the accuracy of the Chinese memorandum, the Japanese Government admitted that Group V had been a part of the original communication to China; but, as Ambassador Guthrie reported, Baron Kato "was particularly anxious that you [Secretary Bryan] should understand that the reason for confining the statement sent you strictly to Japan's 'demands' was that the other items were 'requests' and were so designated when presented to China."[71] The Japanese Government then followed this up by communicating to the State Department on February 22, 1915, the text of the "requests."[72]

Despite the complaints of Japanese leaders that Japan's motives had been misunderstood,[73] the Japanese Government clearly had adopted a policy which it knew would be opposed by the other powers as derogatory to their interests. The bold attempt to coerce the Chinese Government into maintaining secrecy, the unwilling communication of the complete set of demands when there was no longer an alternative, and finally the obvious attempt to explain away the most flagrant of the demands by calling them "requests"—all attest to the truth of this statement. Japan had thus violated her agreement of 1908 to consult the United States in such circumstances,[74] not to mention the more serious offense of seeking monopolies and privileges in violation of the principle of equal opportunity and the maintenance of the administrative independence of China. Japan had, moreover, acted unilaterally by failing even to consult Great Britain, just as she had acted unilaterally in entering the

---

[70] *Foreign Relations,* 1915, pp. 93–95. (Memorandum, undated.) A similar list was communicated to the Russian Government on February 24, 1915. See *Die Internationalen Beziehungen,* Series 2, II:1, 229–231. (Krupensky to Sazonoff, February 24, 1915.)

[71] *Foreign Relations,* 1915, p. 96. (Guthrie to Bryan, February 21, 1915.)

[72] *Ibid.,* p. 97. A similar communication was made to the Russian Foreign Office on February 24, 1915. See *Die Internationalen Beziehungen,* Series 2, II:1, 231, note 1.

[73] Baron Ishii, at the time Japanese Ambassador in Paris, later wrote: "Perhaps no other subject has given rise to so much world-wide misunderstanding as these negotiations." See his *Diplomatic Commentaries,* p. 85.

[74] Paragraph 5 of the Root-Takahira agreement of November 30, 1908, read as follows:

"5. Should any event occur threatening the status quo as above described or the principle of equal opportunity as above defined, it remains for the two Governments to communicate with each other in order to arrive at an understanding as to what measures they may consider it useful to take."

war against the wishes of her ally.[75] Russia, of course, received no more consideration than did the United States and Great Britain. Well might the President of the United States say that it was necessary to consider Japan's "present attitude and intentions in China and her willingness or unwillingness to live up to the obligations she has assumed towards us with regard to the open door in the East."[76]

In the meantime, Japan's conduct was having its effect in the United States. When news of the demands became public, Representative Hobson of Alabama introduced a resolution on February 10, 1915, in which the Secretary of State was requested to provide the House with any information in the possession of the State Department about any demands which, "if enforced, would imperil the 'open-door' policy or the integrity and sovereignty of China."[77] When the House Committee on Foreign Affairs failed to take any action on his resolution, Hobson, on February 18, introduced a second resolution which proclaimed

> ... That the people of the United States would look with disfavor upon any effort to change the status quo in China while so many of the high contracting parties pledged to maintain that status quo are distracted by war, and that the people of the United States would view with grave concern as an unfriendly act any aggressive move on the part of a foreign Government against the integrity and sovereignty of China.[78]

Representative Hobson urged in support of his resolution that Japanese aggression must be curbed before the grave crisis in the Far East involved the United States in hostilities. He said: "At this juncture our foreign relations are perhaps in a more critical condition than they have been for many decades, possibly for more than a century. The importance of those relations is not confined to Europe, the chief theater of war. The most important and critical situation of all is the one in the Far East, as it has developed in the course of this war."[79] Many of his colleagues agreed with his

---

[75] Benckendorff, reporting a conference in London with French Ambassador Cambon and Sir Arthur Nicolson, British permanent Undersecretary of State for Foreign Affairs, said: "Cambon antwortend hat Nicolson gesagt, die japanische Regierung habe die britische Regierung in dieser Frage in keiner Weise um Rat gefragt." See *Die Internationalen Beziehungen*, Series 2, II:1, 234. (Benckendorff to Sazonoff, February 25, 1915.)

[76] See above, p. 131.

[77] *Cong. Rec.*, LII, February 18, 1915, p. 4053.

[78] *Ibid.*, p. 4054.

[79] *Ibid.*, p. 4046.

estimate of the gravity of the situation, but they disagreed with his solution. Representative James R. Mann of Illinois, the Republican leader in the House, asserted that he was fully aware of the matters referred to, but that President Wilson was entrusted with the conduct of foreign relations and that Congress should not interfere. Mann declared: "I believe that he [the President] wants to preserve peace and uphold our rights and the dignity of our country. I hope that we will be able both to uphold our rights and dignity and preserve peace; but the only thing that we can do under the circumstances is to have faith in the administration."[80]

The House agreed with Representative Mann, and nothing came of the resolution. But Congress did not let the matter rest there. In fact, Representative Hobson had already raised the question in connection with the naval appropriation bill then being discussed in the House. In recommending an enlarged program of submarine and destroyer construction, the House Committee on Naval Affairs stressed the fact that these vessels had demonstrated their effectiveness for certain tasks, but that the battleship fleet must be maintained to control the seas.[81] Hobson supported the committee's views by showing the need for ships which could fight at great distances from American shores. The effect of the Anglo-Japanese Alliance upon American naval policy was, in his view, greatly increased by new conditions arising out of the war. The war had brought the United States and Great Britain into conflict over the freedom of the seas and neutral rights; therefore, since the United States had no general arbitration treaty with Japan, a war with Great Britain would mean a war with both allies. Because of this and because Japan had made demands upon China, Hobson drew the conclusion that eventually the United States would need a two-ocean navy. Since the European nations were engaged in a life and death struggle, the United States alone was confronted with the task of defending the open-door policy in China. He said: "America has vital interests in the Far East. No one can deny it. America can not sit still and see the Chinese Republic made a vassal nation of a military monarchy."[82] Only a greater fleet of capital ships could achieve the ends of American policy.

[80] *Ibid.*, p. 4054.

[81] *House Reports* (Ser. 6766), 63d Cong., 3d sess., No. 1287, January 16, 1915, p. 2.

[82] *Cong. Rec.*, LII, February 5, 1915, p. 3109.

But Congress as a whole was not yet convinced, although both branches approved the naval appropriation bill authorizing the construction of the usual two battleships. Unwilling "to sit still and see the Chinese Republic made a vassal nation of a military monarchy" but without sufficient force to back up its remonstrances, the administration readily foresaw the failure of its efforts. Nevertheless, the State Department persevered. On February 22, 1915, the day after the Japanese Government informed Ambassador Guthrie that the matters touched upon in Group V were merely "requests," not "demands," Secretary Bryan suggested to President Wilson that this notification provided the United States an excellent opportunity to set forth its views. Since Group V comprised only "requests," thought the Secretary of State, "our discussion of them upon their merits will not be objectionable."[83] This suggestion drew from President Wilson the observation that he fully approved "of taking advantage of the opening to present to Japan very frankly our views on her 'suggestions' or 'requests'." Continuing, he said: "I think those views can be made very weighty and conclusive. *We shall not have uttered a more important state paper.*"[84]

The State Department accordingly drew up a long note which was delivered to the Japanese Ambassador in Washington on March 13, 1915.[85] Reminding Japan of the various treaties, to many

[83] *Foreign Relations*, "The Lansing Papers, 1914–1920," II, 407. (Bryan to Wilson, February 22, 1915.)

[84] *Ibid.* (Wilson to Bryan, February 25, 1915.) Italics mine. It should be noted that the United States was not the only power which found the "requests" objectionable. Guthrie reported from Tokyo a conversation he had held with British Ambassador Greene: "The Ambassador also said that Great Britain had given Japan notice of her established rights in China and as she expected that these would be respected she had not taken any further action although she would have preferred that the negotiations had not been taken up at the present time or at the very least that the Allies had been consulted in advance." See *ibid.*, p. 416. (Guthrie to Bryan, April 6, 1915.) Russia, too, with whom Japan had agreements concerning China, had found several of the points in Group V "unsuitable from the standpoint of Russian interests." See *Die Internationalen Beziehungen*, Series 2, II:1, 232. (Sazonoff to Izvolsky and Benckendorff, February 25, 1915.)

[85] The text is printed in *Foreign Relations*, 1915, pp. 105–111. (Bryan to Chinda, March 13, 1915.) The President had revealed his concern three days earlier in a short note to the Secretary of State in which he said: "I am anxious to know whether our note to Japan about the 'requests' she made of China has gone forward or not. The twelfth (Thursday of this week) is the day named in the despatches on which China must yield or ———? It would be well to have our note in Japan's hands by that date." See *ibid.*, "The Lansing Papers, 1914–1920," II, 409. (Wilson to Bryan, March 10, 1915.)

of which she was also a party and under which the United States had acquired rights in China, the United States Government pointed out how the "requests" violated these treaties and then declared:

...It is difficult for the United States, therefore, to reconcile these requests with the maintenance of the unimpaired sovereignty of China, which Japan, together with the United States and the Great Powers of Europe, has reaffirmed from time to time during the past decade and a half in formal declarations, treaties and exchanges of diplomatic notes. The United States, therefore, could not regard with indifference the assumption of political, military or economic dominion over China by a foreign Power, and hopes that your excellency's Government will find it consonant with their interests to refrain from pressing upon China an acceptance of proposals which would, if accepted, exclude Americans from equal participation in the economic and industrial development of China and would limit the political independence of that country.[86]

The Japanese Government, however, refused to consider the note as a protest and assured the Japanese public that the United States was merely seeking information.[87] Baron Kato, in addition to attempting to explain away the serious nature of the Japanese demands on China, revealed to Ambassador Guthrie Japan's fear that the United States still intended to establish a naval station on the coast of Fukien Province.[88] These fears could easily be removed, Wilson believed, since his administration had no intention of establishing such a base; but the other Japanese explanations elicited from the President this remark: "Frankly, I do not think that the explanations of the other 'requests' which are offered... are convincing, and I hope that a candid discussion of them by the two governments may result in putting them in a more satisfactory light."[89] That this hope was vain was soon evident.

[86] *Foreign Relations*, 1915, p. 111. (Bryan to Chinda, March 13, 1915.)

[87] *Ibid.*, p. 115 (Guthrie to Bryan, March 21, 1915.) Guthrie reported that Baron Kato had even "expressed regret at the published report that information as to our objections had been given out at Washington by authority saying that public belief on this point would seriously embarrass the administration here [Tokyo]..." Moreover, Kato informed the Russian ambassador that "it [the American note] had the character of a friendly solicitation with the request to explain several points of the Japanese demands." See *Die Internationalen Beziehungen*, Series 2, II:1, 385. (Malevsky-Malevich to Sazonoff, March 23, 1915.)

[88] For the origin of these fears, see *Foreign Relations*, 1915, pp. 113 ff., note 42.

[89] *Ibid.*, "The Lansing Papers, 1914–1920," II, 411. (Wilson to Bryan, March 24, 1915.) For the proposed solution of the Fukien problem, see *ibid.*, 1915, pp. 116, 117. (Bryan to Guthrie, March 26, 1915.)

Although the Japanese Government had informed the powers that the demands in Group V were only "requests," it proceeded in Peking as if there were no such distinction. But the American protest of March 13 had already given the Chinese Government sufficient encouragement to resist the Japanese demands.[90] When it was reported in news dispatches that the United States had acquiesced in some of the Japanese demands, the United States Government seized the opportunity to encourage the Chinese even more strongly. President Wilson, deeply concerned because the Japanese were pressing the demands in Group V, asked Secretary Bryan to express to the Japanese Government the "grave concern" of the United States at the steps being taken in China. The President, in his note to Bryan, said: "In short, I feel that we should be as active as the circumstances permit in showing ourselves to be champions of the sovereign rights of China, now as always, though with no thought of seeking any special advantage or privilege for ourselves."[91] The result was an announcement by the State Department on the following day, April 15, 1915, which read: "The American Government has not surrendered any of its treaty rights in China or abated one iota of its friendly interest in all that concerns the industrial and political welfare of China."[92] From this, the Chinese took further encouragement.[93] But the Japanese Government had interpreted the assertion in the American protest of March 13, 1915, that the United States was seeking no concession for herself and had no intention of obstructing the legitimate aims of Japan, as an indication that the United States would not interfere in the negotiations nor encourage the Chinese to resist.[94]

These conflicting interpretations of the views of the United States finally led President Wilson to declare that "the real weakness of our influence in this matter lay in the *privacy* of our rep-

[90] From Peking, Krupensky reported to the Russian Foreign Office: "The Chinese have recently become markedly confident, and they hope apparently that they will succeed in evading the acceptance of the most oppressive of the Japanese demands." He attributed this change in attitude to the moral effect which the American note had had in China. See *Die Internationalen Beziehungen,* Series 2, II:2, 590, note 1. (Krupensky to Sazonoff, March 31, 1915.)

[91] *Foreign Relations,* "The Lansing Papers, 1914–1920," II, 416. (Wilson to Bryan, April 14, 1915.)

[92] *Ibid.,* p. 417. (Bryan to Reinsch, April 15, 1915.) Reinsch was authorized to release this statement "informally and unofficially."

[93] "The Chinese looked upon the American declaration as a very favorable omen for them." See *Die Internationalen Beziehungen,* Series 2, II:2, 590. (Malevsky-Malevich to Sazonoff, April 22, 1915.)

[94] *Ibid.,* p. 591.

resentations to Japan with regard to it." Continuing, the President told the Secretary of State that it might be well, therefore, to notify the Japanese Ambassador that, since the United States possessed interests in the Far East which gave her a right to speak, it might become necessary for the United States Government to make its views public. Although the matter was to be handled in such a way as to indicate to the world at large that "no friction from this source is involved so far as our two governments at present are concerned," the President revealed that his own opinion was in direct contrast to this statement, when he concluded:

> This, I am convinced, is the only means we have of reassuring China, our own people, and other governments at present less free than we to protest.
>
> I think, too, that we ought to instruct Reinsch to assure the Chinese government that it has our sympathy in resisting any demands which too seriously impinge upon its sovereignty, its administrative independence, or its territorial integrity.[95]

Unfortunately for China, the sympathy of the United States was not equal in influence to the troops and battleships of Japan.

The Japanese Government finally withdrew for future discussion all the "requests" in Group V except the one dealing with Fukien Province, and then presented an ultimatum to China on May 7, 1915, in which an unqualified submission was demanded by six o'clock on the evening of May 9. Failing this, the Japanese Government declared that it would "take such independent action as they may deem necessary to meet the situation."[96] The State Department, informed of the ultimatum on the preceding day, took immediate steps to avert what it feared was to be another war in the Far East. The Chinese Government was urged by Secretary Bryan, at the personal request of the President, to make every endeavor to find a peaceable solution of the problem;[97] and the Secretary of State made a direct personal appeal to Premier Okuma to continue to negotiate in the interest of peace.[98] An appeal was also

---

[95] *Foreign Relations,* "The Lansing Papers, 1914–1920," II, 417, 418. (Wilson to Bryan, April 27, 1915.)

[96] For the text of the ultimatum, see *Foreign Relations,* 1915, pp. 168–170. The Japanese Government had decided to postpone its "requests" in Group V for future discussion, "as further insistence upon them might lead to a war between Japan and China and also might invite greater suspicion from the powers." See Takeuchi, *op. cit.,* p. 189, note 30.

[97] *Foreign Relations,* "The Lansing Papers, 1914–1920," II, 422. (Bryan to Reinsch, May 6, 1915.)

[98] *Ibid.,* pp. 422, 423. (Bryan to Post Wheeler, American Chargé d'Affaires in Tokyo, May 6, 1915.)

directed to the governments of Great Britain, Russia, and France to join with the United States in urging upon Japan and China a peaceable solution of their differences.[99] Britain had already informed Japan of her concern at the danger of war's imperiling the objects for which the Anglo-Japanese Alliance had been negotiated, and had asked to be consulted before any final action was taken.[100] Thus, the British Government made evident its awareness of the dangers of the Far Eastern situation, and showed as well its lack of confidence in the purity of Japan's motives. But Russia, long in agreement with Japan on the spoliation of China, refused to join the United States in an appeal to Japan to maintain peace in Asia.[101]

Because of the anticipated failure of the Allies to coöperate, Robert Lansing, Counselor of the State Department, suggested on May 7, 1915, that a note be sent to Japan and China which would protect American interests and keep the questions involved open for future discussion.[102] President Wilson approved this suggestion in a note to Secretary Bryan after the Chinese Government accepted the Japanese ultimatum. The President said:

> In view of the situation as a whole (I mean the situation of the world, politically) I think that it would be wise to file such a caveat as Mr. Lansing suggests. It will not do to leave any of our rights indefinite or to seem to acquiesce in any part of the Japanese plan which violates the solemn understandings of the nations with regard to China.[103]

The result of Lansing's suggested reservation and its approval by President Wilson was a note from Secretary of State Bryan on May 11, 1915, addressed to the governments of Japan and China, which read as follows:

> In view of the circumstances of the negotiations which have taken place and which are now pending between the Government of Japan and the Government of China, and of the agreements which have been reached as a result thereof,

[99] *Ibid.*, p. 423. (Bryan to the American ambassadors in London, St. Petersburg, and Paris, May 6, 1915.)

[100] *Ibid.*, pp. 424, 425. (Page to Bryan, May 7, 1915.)

[101] *Die Internationalen Beziehungen*, Series 2, II:2, 710. (Sazonoff to Malevsky-Malevich, May 10, 1915.) Sazonoff wrote: "Ich lehnte die Zustimmung zu diesem Vorschlage ab, unter Hinweis auf die zwischen uns und Japan bestehenden Bündnisbeziehungen."

[102] *Foreign Relations*, "The Lansing Papers, 1914–1920," II, 424. (Lansing to Bryan, May 7, 1915.)

[103] *Ibid.*, p. 426. (Wilson to Bryan, May 10, 1915.) The President, in another note on the same day, had expressed to the Secretary of State his appreciation of the action of Sir Edward Grey in supporting the appeal of the United States Government to Japan to maintain peace in the Far East. *Loc. cit.*

the Government of the United States has the honor to notify the Imperial Japanese Government that it cannot recognize any agreement or undertaking which has been entered into between the Governments of Japan and China, impairing the treaty rights of the United States and its citizens in China, the political or territorial integrity of the Republic of China, or the international policy relative to China commonly known as the open door policy.[104]

From subsequent actions of the United States Government, it became evident that little faith was placed in the efficacy of such declarations, their value lying rather in the legal effect of having placed the case of the United States on record. Indeed, the reaction of the Japanese Government to the American declaration makes clear the futility of such measures. Baron Kato called it "impudent" and said that "Japan needs no recognition of her treaty with China, especially by America."[105] If any other evidence were needed to prove that power was the only diplomacy Japan heeded, it may be found in the fact that the Okuma cabinet yielded on the demands in Group V not to the protests of foreign powers, but to the internal pressure of the powerful influence of the Genro, the "Elder Statesmen" of Japan.[106] In short, the Japanese Government intended to achieve its aims regardless of the dangers of war, the violation of solemn treaties, or the force of world opinion.

In these circumstances, the Wilson administration had no further hesitation. Diplomacy had been tried, and it had failed. There remained only one alternative: namely, to build up the naval power of the nation so that the United States Government could speak the only language which the Japanese seemed to understand—the language of force. But Congress and the people remained to be convinced, as the General Board of the Navy Department had so powerfully insisted not two years earlier, when it declared:

In the opinion of the General Board any rational and natural development of the Navy looking to the continuance of peace and the maintenance of our national policies demands the adoption of, and the consistent adherence to, a governmental naval policy founded on our national needs and aims. To give life to such a policy requires the support of the people and of Congress; and

[104] *Foreign Relations,* 1915, p. 146. (Bryan to Guthrie, May 11, 1915.)

[105] *Die Internationalen Beziehungen,* Series 2, II:2, 765. (Malevsky-Malevich to Sazonoff, May 18, 1915.)

[106] *Ibid.,* p. 684, note 4. (Malevsky-Malevich to Sazonoff, May 10, 1915.) According to the Russian Ambassador in Tokyo, "Japans Verzicht auf die letzte Gruppe der Forderungen ist veranlasst durch das Drängen des Genro, der mit dem Kabinett des allzu selbstständigen Okuma und namentlich mit Kato unzufrieden ist."

this support can only be obtained by giving the widest publicity to the policy itself and to the reasons and arguments in its support, and taking the people and the Congress into the full confidence of the Government, inviting intelligent criticism as well as support.[107]

To the task of formulating such a policy and of gaining for it the support of the public and of Congress, the President now turned his earnest attention.

[107] Report of the General Board, December 1, 1913. See *Annual Reports of the Navy Department*, 1913, p. 30.

CHAPTER VI

JAPAN AND AMERICAN NAVAL POLICY

Restricted to the Pacific basin, where its major elements must be worked out, the problem of the relations of Japan and the United States comprises two principal factors—direct contacts of the two governments and peoples, and conditions involved with the fate of China. Both factors are surcharged with forces making for international friction and war, yet I am amazed to find American public opinion little concerned about them. Americans are so engrossed with the terrific spectacle presented in Europe that they seem to be blind or indifferent to a more sinister and more imminent menace to our peace and security that is creeping upon us from the opposite side.—THOMAS F. MILLARD, 1916.

THE AMERICAN people by long tradition have opposed the establishment and maintenance of large military forces. They have always looked on the Navy as their bulwark of defense, but without a true conception of the fleet's mission as an offensive arm of the national defense. Whenever anyone in public life advocated building up the Navy as a protection against foreign dangers, the cry was immediately raised that he was an alarmist or that he was in league with steel and munitions makers. As a result, the average American had been led to believe that no dangers threatened from abroad and that any attempt to strengthen the national defenses would impose an unjust burden upon the taxpayer. Andrew Carnegie, the stanch pacifist, expressed this view in 1915: "To build a great Navy or increase the Army would, in my opinion, be folly only equaled by one who declined to walk outside without a lightning rod down his back because once there was a man struck by lightning."[1] That at a time when all Europe was in flames and the Far East loomed as a serious menace.

President Wilson as late as December, 1914, had cautioned the country in his annual message to Congress against precipitate action indicating "that we had been thrown off our balance by a war with which we have nothing to do, whose causes can not touch us, whose very existence affords us opportunities of friendship and disinterested service which should make us ashamed of any thought of hostility or fearful preparation for trouble."[2] But the demands

[1] In a letter to Chairman Tillman of the Senate Committee on Naval Affairs, January 27, 1915, in *Cong. Rec.*, LII, March 3, 1915, p. 5251.
[2] December 8, 1914, in *Messages and Papers*, XVIII, 8402.

of the Japanese Government upon China had a profound effect upon the President's views. With the delivery of the Japanese ultimatum to China on May 7, 1915, he abandoned his former position.

The relations of the United States with Germany reached a crisis with the sinking of the *Lusitania* on May 7, 1915, the very day of the Japanese ultimatum to China, and provided a convenient shield for the United States Government's action. While the Japanese press and public railed at the United States and Great Britain for interfering in the negotiations with China,[3] President Wilson was laying the groundwork for an epoch-making reversal in American policy. In a notable address at a review of the United States fleet in New York on May 17, 1915, he said:

> The interesting and inspiring thing about America, gentlemen, is that she asks nothing for herself except what she has a right to ask for humanity itself. We want no nation's property. We mean to question no nation's honor. We do not wish to stand selfishly in the way of the development of any nation. We want nothing that we cannot get by our own legitimate enterprise and by the inspiration of our own example; and, standing for these things, it is not pretension on our part to say that we are privileged to stand for what every nation would wish to stand for, and speak for those things which all humanity must desire.[4]

Almost every word of this statement points an accusing finger at Japan; yet, the passage is even more significant for what was left unsaid. The President clearly was warning that the United States, although she wanted the property of no other nation, would not submit to the usurpation of any of her own rights. Thus, when the Japanese propagandist asserted Japan's policy to be "the protection, so far as it is within her right and privilege, of her neighbor against European aggression,"[5] it was apparent that the President interpreted the term "European" to include the United States. The Chinese, however, using every device to protect themselves against Japanese aggression, had started a widespread boycott of Japanese goods, which boded ill for the future peace of the Far East.[6]

---

[3] *Die Internationalen Beziehungen,* Series 2, III:1, 59, 60. (Malevsky-Malevich to Sazonoff, June 3, 1915.) The condemnation was directed especially at Great Britain; for, as an ally, she had been expected to support Japan's desires.

[4] Ray S. Baker and William E. Dodd, eds., *The Public Papers of Woodrow Wilson* (New York: Harper, 1925–1927), III, 330.

[5] Toyokichi Iyenaga, "The New Chino-Japanese Treaties and Their Import," *The American Review of Reviews,* LII (September, 1915), 341.

[6] Charles F. Remer and William B. Palmer, *A Study of Chinese Boycotts with Special Reference to Their Economic Effectiveness* (Baltimore: Johns Hopkins Press, 1933), chap. vi. The Russian Ambassador in Tokyo reported:

On July 21, 1915, President Wilson took the first concrete step toward securing an adequate navy. He suggested to Secretary of the Navy Daniels the need for "a wise and adequate naval program, to be proposed to the Congress at its next session . . ."[7] Whereas in his annual message for 1914, the President had ridiculed the naval experts for their inability to predict with any accuracy the probable developments in naval craft, he now insisted that "first we must have professional advice." This to him meant the men in the Navy Department "who have been most directly in contact with actual modern conditions, who have most thoroughly comprehended the altered conditions of naval warfare, and who best comprehend what the navy must be in the future in order to stand upon an equality with the most efficient and most practically serviceable." These experts were to advise on policy and were to suggest a program "formulated in the most definite terms." Although Congress might not authorize the full program, the President stressed that the "important thing now is to know fully what we need," and to formulate a program "planned for a consistent and progressive development of this great defensive arm of the nation . . ."[8]

The General Board accordingly submitted a report on July 30, 1915, containing the following celebrated statement: "The Navy of the United States should ultimately be equal to the most powerful maintained by any other nation of the world," the equality to be "attained not later than 1925."[9] To carry out this policy, the

"By official estimates, Japanese exports to China have declined by 30 million yen in the first half of the present year as compared with the same months in the past year, a decline of 53 per cent . . . The Japanese press demands further energetic measures against China and sharply criticises the cabinet of Count Okuma and especially Japanese diplomacy for inactivity." See *Die Internationalen Beziehungen,* Series 2, III:1, 285, 286. (Malevsky-Malevich to Sazonoff, July 12, 1915.)

[7] The Sixty-third Congress had expired on March 4, 1915, and apparently the President intended to test the sentiment of the people as expressed through the members of the newly elected Congress scheduled to meet early in December. Undue significance should not be given to the fact that this letter to Secretary Daniels was written on the same day the third *Lusitania* note was dispatched to Germany, because that crisis had passed its critical point. See Baker, *Woodrow Wilson: Life and Letters,* V, 367, note 4. See also Charles Seymour, *American Diplomacy during the World War* (Baltimore: Johns Hopkins Press, 1934), pp. 97, 98.

[8] "Professional Notes," *United States Naval Institute Proceedings,* XLI (September–October, 1915), 1654. (Wilson to Daniels, July 21, 1915.)

[9] Report of the General Board, July 30, 1915, in *Sen. Docs.* (Ser. 6951), 64th Cong., 1st sess., No. 231, January 5, 1916, p. 1.

Board recommended the addition of ninety-six new vessels to the fleet by authorizations in the coming fiscal year, a program limited only by the shipbuilding facilities of the country. Among the vessels recommended were four dreadnaughts, four battle cruisers, six scout cruisers, twenty-eight destroyers, thirty coast submarines, and seven fleet submarines. It was natural that a board of naval officers of the richest country on earth should want the greatest navy on earth, and it is possible that the General Board really wanted a "navy second to none." The administration, however, had no intention of competing with Great Britain for the mastery of the seas, nor is there any proof that President Wilson had so intended when he said that the United States Navy should "stand upon an equality with the most efficient and most practically serviceable." As to hostile action against the United States, the "most practically serviceable" fleet in the world was that of Japan, lying safely in her home ports unopposed by any enemy and with defenseless American territory within easy reach.

At any rate, the administration was not ready to adopt such an extreme policy. Neither was it willing to wait until 1925 to achieve its naval aims, especially in view of further Japanese unregeneracy. When the Chinese people, seeking a continuing form of government in order to secure internal peace, determined to abandon the Republic in favor of a constitutional monarchy with Yüan Shih-k'ai as Emperor, Japan interfered. On October 27, 1915, when the United States was asked to join in representations in Peking, President Wilson suggested to Robert Lansing, the new Secretary of State, that Japan should be informed that the United States agreed with China "that a change in their form of government, however radical, is wholly a domestic question and that it would in our opinion be a serious breach of China's sovereignty to undertake any form of interference or even protest . . ."[10] But this did not deter the Japanese. Since England was in no position to block Japan, and Russia was disinterested so long as she was not threatened in the north, Japan sought to utilize the opportunity to gain complete freedom of action in China. Minister Reinsch reported to the State Department:

. . . The preoccupation of Great Britain in Europe, the fact that Japan could easily become dangerous to her in Asia, the indifference of Russia, the en-

[10] *Foreign Relations*, "The Lansing Papers, 1914–1920," II, 429. (Wilson to Lansing, October 31, 1915.)

deavors of Germany further to weaken British influence in China and to keep China from joining the Allies, leave growing material power of Japan the one positive factor in the situation, foreshadowing irretrievable loss of European influence in China should the war continue. American interests would suffer together with European and the question arises whether it is, under the circumstances possible to give sufficient backing to the European Entente Powers enabling them to preserve the status of International Rights in China and of Chinese sovereignty itself intact until the end of the war.[11]

President Wilson's reaction was brief, to the point, and ineffective. He suggested to Secretary Lansing that since "the interests and the treaty rights of the United States would be very directly and unfavourably affected by the foreshadowed change of political suzerainty in China," the Japanese Government should be informed of the views of the United States "in all friendly frankness."[12]

The Japanese Government already knew the views of the United States on China; so the President's suggestion was merely a repetition of what had gone before and made no more impression upon the Japanese than his previous warnings. The Navy Department had already expressed the administration's concern over the weakness of American diplomacy as well as its dissatisfaction with the program submitted by the General Board, by ordering that group on October 7, 1915, to submit "a building program for the Navy that will continue over a period of five years, with an expenditure of about $100,000,000 each year for five years, on new construction only."[13] The Board responded on October 12 by recommending the program shown in table 1. In a later report, the reasons for the recommendations were discussed. The course of the war in

[11] *Ibid.*, pp. 429, 430. (Reinsch to Lansing, December 4, 1915.) As early as October 13, 1915, the Russian Minister in Peking, after reporting the latest developments in China to his government, said: "Alles oben Gesagte nötigt zu der Annahme, dass die Japaner die Aenderung der Regierungsform in China benutzen wollen, um von letzterem auf diese oder jene Weise neue Zugeständnisse zu ihren Gunsten zu erlangen." See *Die Internationalen Beziehungen*, Series 2, III:2, 798. (Krupensky to Sazonoff, October 13, 1915.) For some indication of the type of proposals being made by Japan, see Komissiia po izdaniiu dokumentov epokhi imperializma, *Mezhdunarodnye otnosheniia v epokhu imperializma: dokumenty iz arkhivov tsarskogo i vremennogo pravitel'stv. 1878–1917 gg.* (Moskva-Leningrad: Gosudarstennoe Sotsial'no-Ekonomicheskoe Izdatel'stvo, etc., 1931–1940), Series 3, IX, 468, 469. (Memorandum of the Japanese Foreign Office, December 6, 1915.)

[12] *Foreign Relations*, "The Lansing Papers, 1914–1920," II, 430. (Wilson to Lansing, December 5, 1915.)

[13] Report of the General Board, November 9, 1915, in *Annual Reports of the Navy Department*, 1915, p. 73.

Europe had convinced the members that their views on the proper size of the Navy would have to be modified. They declared: "A navy strong enough only to defend our coast from actual invasion will not suffice. Defense from invasion is not the only function of the Navy. It must protect our sea-borne commerce and drive that

TABLE 1

FIVE-YEAR NAVAL CONSTRUCTION PROGRAM*

Vessels	First year 1917	Second year 1918	Third year 1919	Fourth year 1920	Fifth year 1921
Dreadnaughts	4	2	2	2	..
Battle cruisers	3	..	1	2	..
Scout cruisers	4	2	1	3	..
Destroyers	10	10	10	14	6
Fleet submarines	2	2	2	2	1
Coast submarines	20	10	10	10	8
Fuel ships, oil	1	..	..	2	..
Repair ships	..	..	..	1	..
Transports	..	..	..	1	..
Hospital ships	1	..	..	..	..
Destroyer tenders	1	..	..	1	..
Fleet submarine tenders	..	..	..	1	..
Ammunition ships	1	..	..	1	..
River gunboats	2	..	..	..	..

Aircraft service—$3,000,000 first year; $1,000,000 a year thereafter.
Reserve ammunition—$11,000,000 first year.

* Report of the General Board, October 12, 1915, in *Annual Reports of the Navy Department*, 1915, p. 80.

of the enemy from the sea." There was only one conclusion: "The current war has shown that a navy of the size recommended by this board in previous years can no longer be considered as adequate to the defensive needs of the United States. Our present Navy is not sufficient to give due weight to the diplomatic remonstrances of the United States in peace nor to enforce its policies in war."[14]

The Secretary of the Navy, in his annual report for 1915, approved the recommendations of the General Board as to numbers of capital ships to be authorized, but made some changes in their distribution over the five-year period because of the congestion in the nation's shipyards. Secretary Daniels thought a more uniform distribution of the capital ships would facilitate early completion

[14] *Ibid.*, p. 74.

of more of the smaller craft. His demand for more destroyers and submarines, as shown in table 2, was clearly influenced by the war in the Atlantic. Finally, the growing consciousness of the future world-wide role of the United States was made evident by Daniels' request for more scout cruisers: "While, under the conditions of the past, attacks upon the overseas merchant marine of the United States, in case of war, would have done little damage owing to its limited size, it is to be hoped that by the time these vessels are built

TABLE 2

FIVE-YEAR NAVAL CONSTRUCTION PROGRAM*

Vessels	1917	1918	1919	1920	1921
Dreadnaughts	2	2	2	2	2
Battle cruisers	2	..	1	2	1
Scout cruisers	3	1	2	2	2
Destroyers	15	10	5	10	10
Fleet submarines	5	4	2	2	2
Coast submarines	25	15	15	15	15

* Report of the Secretary of the Navy, December 1, 1915, in *Annual Reports of the Navy Department*, 1915, p. 5. In other respects, the recommendations approximated those of the General Board except in regard to reserve ammunition. The Secretary recommended the expenditure of $8,000,000 for this purpose in the first year, $5,000,000 each year for the second, third, and fourth years, and $2,000,000 in the fifth year, or a total of $25,000,000.

our overseas merchant marine will be more extensive."[15] A militant Congress was soon to place both problems on the road to ultimate solution.

Meanwhile, President Wilson had begun a long series of public addresses designed to impress on the American people the need for a naval policy closely integrated with the other elements of the national strategy. In New York, on November 4, 1915, the President had emphasized that no matter how large the Navy it would never be used "for aggression of any kind, nor for the satisfaction of any political or international ambition, but merely to make sure of our security."[16] The building up of the Navy ought to be accelerated, thought President Wilson; and he advocated "a definite policy of development, not made from year to year but looking well into the future and planning for a definite consummation." In addition, there was the problem of "the mobilization of the

[15] *Ibid.*, p. 7.

[16] In a speech before the Manhattan Club. See Baker and Dodd, *op. cit.*, III, 386.

resources of the nation at the proper time if it should ever be necessary to mobilize them for national defense."[17] Although the President was obviously feeling his way, he was already giving direction to the mounting chorus of demands for adequate preparation for war.

Wilson returned to the attack in his annual message to Congress on December 7, 1915. Pointing out that "democracies are not belligerent" and that they resent aggression from any direction, he declared:

> ... We insist upon security in prosecuting our self-chosen lines of national development. We do more than that. We demand it also for others. We do not confine our enthusiasm for individual liberty and free national development to the incidents and movements of affairs which affect only ourselves. We feel it wherever there is a people that tries to walk in these difficult paths of independence and right.[18]

The President could have referred only to China and her continuing resistance to Japanese aggression. To meet such situations, Wilson asserted that the policy previously adhered to would have to be speeded up. The plan to be submitted to Congress, therefore, did not alter the fundamental policy of maintaining a navy equal to that of any great military power. The only innovation was to be the adoption of a definite long-term plan of development in order to reach the required strength. "It seems to me very clear," said the President, "that it will be to the advantage of the country for the Congress to adopt a comprehensive plan for putting the navy upon a final footing of strength and efficiency and to press that plan to completion within the next five years."[19]

With Congress in session, the fruit of the administration's efforts began to appear. Demands for preparedness and warnings of imminent disaster poured in from all sides. The long and ominous silence on Far Eastern affairs gave way to open condemnation of Japan's acts and fear of her intentions. The Japanese, it seemed, were doing everything they could to provoke such outcries. Premier Okuma chose this inauspicious moment to remind the American people that Japan considered the California land question far from a closed issue. In fact, according to Count Okuma, only the patient forbearance of the Japanese Government prevented this

[17] *Ibid.*, pp. 388, 389.
[18] *Messages and Papers*, XVIII, 8485.
[19] *Ibid.*, p. 8487.

issue from being made a *casus belli.*[20] In China, the open door had acquired a doorman in uniform—a Japanese uniform. Japan's doctrine of paramount political interest in China was being carried to such lengths that Americans interested in development enterprises in China were systematically blocked by Japan.[21] Finally, the news of the rapid development of the Japanese Navy, even during the war, had its effect in the United States. The statement that Japan "may well be proud of her growing fleet, composed, as it will be in a short time, of vessels which can give battle to any of the best vessels afloat of foreign powers," was not calculated to allay fears in America.[22]

The result was inevitable. Even the stanch pacifist, Samuel Gompers, president of the American Federation of Labor, publicly stated that he had been wrong. The United States must be prepared to defend her heritage. "Freedom and democracy dare not be synonymous with weakness."[23] When the president of the Kansas Women's Christian Temperance Union urged Representative Jouett Shouse of Kansas to vote against the preparedness program, his reply expressed the thoughts of many sincere advocates of peace:

> I said a while ago that I believe this continent is not in serious danger of attack from a European nation when the present war closes; but I do not feel the same degree of complacency with reference to Japan. Since she became victorious out of the Russian war, Japan has been preparing herself carefully with the idea of ultimate world domination. She has grown rich during the European war; rich beyond her wildest dreams. She has supplied to the allies every article that she could manufacture, and nothing has been bought from us by them until Japan had been given the first opportunity to furnish it. . . .
>
> Japan is not a Christian nation. She is a nation of materialists, a nation

[20] "Okuma Appeals to United States to Drop Racial Barriers," *The New York Sun*, December 4, 1915, as inserted by Senator James D. Phelan of California in *Cong. Rec.*, LIII, January 10, 1916, pp, 754, 755. The article was datelined at Tokyo, October 28.

[21] George B. Rea, "Closing the Open Door," *The North American Review*, CCIII (May, 1916), 690, 691. An example of this may be found in the Japanese demand in the case of the proposed improvement of the Grand Canal in Shantung that "application must first be made to Japan." See *Foreign Relations*, 1916, p. 123. (Reinsch to Lansing, September 25, 1916.)

[22] "Our Eastern Ally," *The Straits Times*, Singapore, September 1, 1915, as inserted by Senator Jacob H. Gallinger of New Hampshire in *Cong. Rec.*, LIII, January 12, 1916, p. 937. This item, significantly, was referred to the Senate Committee on Naval Affairs.

[23] Speech at Washington, January 18, 1916, before the annual meeting of the National Civic Federation. See *Sen Docs.* (Ser. 6951), 64th Cong., 1st sess., No. 311, February 7, 1916, p. 4.

of believers in force, a nation that clings to the tenet that might makes right. Suppose when this war is over all of Europe is prostrate. Will not the opportunity come that Japan has perhaps been waiting for, and will it not be necessary for us to contest with her the ambition of ultimate world domination which she is said to have cherished for 10 years or more?[24]

Confronting such an openly acknowledged threat, the United States would certainly act; but the American people were not yet convinced of the necessity of preparation. British Ambassador Spring-Rice informed Sir Edward Grey that "there is no widespread feeling of insecurity [in the United States], or of fear that such undefended riches are a great danger to the possessor. This fear, however, prevails very widely in thinking circles."[25] The President himself assumed the task of enlightening the people. "Democracy," he said, "is the most difficult form of government, because it is the form under which you have to persuade the largest number of persons to do anything in particular."[26] In a series of magnificent addresses in cities from New York to Topeka, President Wilson used all of his rare persuasive powers. At Pittsburgh on January 29, 1916, he asked: "What is it that we want to defend?" And in reply, "We want to defend the life of this Nation against any sort of interference."[27] He pointed out that the failure to maintain a merchant marine had made the United States dependent for the movement of American commerce upon the nations then at war. Inevitable friction had arisen out of this fact the importance of which he fully acknowledged; but, not to overlook the aggressive acts of Japan, he said: "Wherever the ordinary rules of commerce at sea and of international relationship are thrust aside or ignored, there is danger of the more critical kind of controversy."[28]

At Milwaukee on January 31, 1916, the President boldly told his audience why the United States needed a larger fleet:

. . . There is no sudden panic, there is no sudden change of plan; all that has happened is that we now see that we ought more rapidly and more thoroughly than ever before to do the things which have always been characteristic of America. For she has always been proud of her Navy and has always been

[24] *Cong. Rec.*, LIII, January 6, 1916, Appendix, p. 99. (Jouett Shouse to Mrs. Lillian Mitchner, January 5, 1916.)

[25] Gwynn, *The Letters and Friendships of Sir Cecil Spring Rice: A Record*, II, 329. (Spring-Rice to Grey, April 14, 1916.)

[26] Address at Washington, September 28, 1915. See Baker, *op. cit.*, VI, 1.

[27] Baker and Dodd, *op. cit.*, IV, 18.

[28] *Ibid.*, p. 24.

addicted to the principle that her citizenship must do the fighting on land. We are working out American principle a little faster, because American pulses are beating a little faster, because the world is in a whirl, because there are incalculable elements of trouble abroad which we cannot control or alter. I would be derelict to the duty which you have laid upon me if I did not tell you that it was absolutely necessary to carry out our principles in this matter now and at once.[29]

Here the President included the Pacific as well as the Atlantic as is proved by his later reference to the naval defense of "the enormous stretch of coast from the Canal to Alaska—from the Canal to the northern corner of Maine."[30] Throughout his tour, President Wilson frequently declared that "America cannot afford to be weak," and urged his audiences to see that "the President, not as a partisan but as the representative of the national honour, shall be backed up by the whole force that is in the Nation."[31]

On the very day of the President's return to Washington, the Senate passed the bill which set the Philippines on the road to ultimate independence. In his annual message to Congress in December, 1915, the President had said of the Philippine Islands:

There is another matter which seems to me to be very intimately associated with the question of national safety and preparation for defense. . . . Our treatment of them and their attitude towards us are manifestly of the first consequence in the development of our duties in the world and in getting a free hand to perform those duties. *We must be free from every unnecessary burden or embarrassment;* and there is no better way to be clear of embarrassment than to fulfill our promises and promote the interests of those dependent on us to the utmost. . . . there are few measures you could adopt which would more serviceably clear the way for the great policies by which we wish to make good, now and always, our right to lead in enterprises of peace and good will and economic and political freedom.[32]

In reporting a measure to the Senate on December 17, 1915, to carry out the President's recommendation, the Senate Committee on the Philippines declared that it was "the opinion of the committee that there is an urgent need for action on the pending bill at this session."[33]

The bill was debated in the Senate from January 5 to February

[29] *Ibid.*, pp. 53, 54.
[30] Speech at St. Louis, February 3, 1916, in *ibid.*, p. 113.
[31] Speech at Pittsburgh, January 29, 1916, in *ibid.*, p. 27.
[32] *Messages and Papers*, XVIII, 8490, 8491. Italics mine.
[33] *Sen. Reports* (Ser. 6897), 64th Cong., 1st sess., No. 18, December 17, 1915, p. 3.

4, 1916, and in the House on May 1. All the old arguments both for and against retention of the islands were used once more, but with greater emphasis because of the war. The separation of the islands from the control of the United States seemed so vital to some that Democratic Senator James P. Clarke of Arkansas introduced an amendment, which the Senate adopted, to grant complete independence to the Philippines within four years from the date of the act.[34] The need for immediate action was pointed out by a number of Senators, cutting through the old arguments on commercial advantage, national pride, and responsibility to the Filipinos. Senator Frank B. Brandegee of Connecticut, referring to the Japanese demands on China in 1915, which, according to reports, had been reasserted in January, 1916, declared that "the other powers of the world are distracted at this time . . . [and] China has appealed to us to protect them against those demands made upon them by Japan."[35] With such crises it might not always be possible to maintain peaceable relations with Japan. Senator James Hamilton Lewis of Illinois had already pointed out what would happen in a war with Japan. "Do you think they will come to the Pacific coast to assail you?" he asked. "Your oriental foes would seize the Philippine Islands and say to you, 'Gentlemen of America, come and get them'."[36]

Obviously, so long as the islands remained under American control, the United States would be "in honor bound to retake them," if Japan should seize them. And this obligation would apply as well to a naval base only, which many were suggesting should be retained. The essential problem to be determined was one of policy. Brigadier General M. M. Macomb, Chief of the War College Division of the Army General Staff, had reported in a survey of American military policy in 1915 that a "decision to defend the Philippines against a foreign enemy is a matter of national and not of military policy."[37] It was so considered by Congress in debat-

[34] *Cong. Rec.*, LIII, January 11, 1916, p. 846; February 2, 1916, p. 1998.

[35] *Ibid.*, February 4, 1916, p. 2111. Senator Lawrence Y. Sherman of Illinois had introduced a resolution on January 28, 1916, in which the Senate declared its interest in the maintenance of the open door in China, and requested the President "to protest to Japan against its recent demands made upon China." The text of the resolution is printed in *Journal of the Senate of the United States of America*, 64th Cong., 1st sess., January 28, 1916, p. 130.

[36] *Cong. Rec.*, LIII, January 19, 1916, p. 1258.

[37] Report on a military policy for the United States, September 11, 1915, in *Annual Reports of the War Department*, 1915, I, 120.

ing the Philippine independence bill in 1916. Senator Porter J. McCumber of North Dakota asserted that the original request of the Roosevelt administration in 1907 for four battleships a year had been "based entirely upon the assumption that there was danger from the Asiatic side, not from the European side"; therefore, if he voted for the naval program of President Wilson, he would "be governed more by the necessity of defending the Philippine Islands than by any other single factor."[38]

This was also the judgment of the House Committee on Insular Affairs. The committee noted the insistent demands for stronger national defenses, but declared that before the extent of any increase could be determined, "it is absolutely essential that those charged with responsibility for the country's safety shall know whether the Philippines are to be given independence or be held as a colony to be fortified and defended."[39] The conclusion was that eventually the United States should divest herself of this dangerous responsibility by fulfilling her pledge to grant the Filipinos independence. Thus, the preamble of the bill as finally approved on August 29, 1916, proclaimed that "it is, as it has always been, the purpose of the people of the United States to withdraw their sovereignty over the Philippine Islands and to recognize their independence as soon as a stable government can be established therein."[40] Congress had consented in the face of a war threat to do for the national defense what it had long refused to do on moral grounds.

While the United States was thus consolidating her position in the Pacific, Japan was taking similar measures. As early as March 15, 1915, Russia had raised the question of revising or supplementing her treaties with Japan in order to clarify Russia's rights in Manchuria and Mongolia as they might be affected by the Twenty-one Demands. At that time, Japanese Ambassador Ichiro Motono had asserted in St. Petersburg that his government would not agree to this, at least "before the projected restoration of a closer political coöperation between Russia and Japan." The Japanese Govern-

[38] *Cong. Rec.*, LIII, January 26, 1916, p. 1564.

[39] *House Reports* (Ser. 6904), 64th Cong., 1st sess., No. 499, April 6, 1916, p. 16.

[40] For the text of the act, see *U. S. Statutes at Large,* XXXIX (1917), 545–556. By coincidence, the act which bore such a close relationship to the national defense was signed on the same day on which the President approved the great naval construction act of 1916.

ment, according to Baron Motono, would be placed in a very difficult position at home if it granted concessions to Russia which it did not claim for itself, because public opinion in Japan was still wrought up over California's denial to Japanese subjects of the right to own land in that state.[41]

But with the completion of the negotiations with China, a change came over the Japanese. The public turned on England and blamed her for the forced withdrawal of the "requests" in Group V. A member of the Japanese Diet, writing in *Yamato* on June 30, 1915, expressed the general feeling in Japan when he said: "International relations are constantly changing. For no state is there a perpetual enemy or friend. It chooses as a friend that state which it must stand by in order to safeguard its own position. Therefore, after the war, Japan will have to take an unexpected course." In reporting these views to Foreign Minister Sazonoff, the Russian Ambassador in Tokyo asserted that Russia, by contrast, was now the universal favorite of the newspapers; and there were increasing demands for an alliance with Russia. Japan feared German vengeance after the war; and the consensus seemed to be that "Russia will help us [the Japanese] to drive the Germans out of the Far East and to establish there a firm and lasting peace."[42]

The negotiations between Russia and Japan continued through the remaining months of 1915, involving such subjects as the guarding of Eastern Siberia by Japanese troops and the furnishing of munitions to Russia by Japan, the latter to receive compensation in Manchuria, Northern Sakhalin, and elsewhere. News of the projected alliance became public in April, 1916, but was promptly denied by the Japanese Foreign Office.[43] When the United States instituted inquiries in St. Petersburg, Sazonoff admitted on April 24, 1916, that an agreement was contemplated; but he denied that it was "yet in existence or in any way reduced to terms . . ."[44] Ru-

[41] *Die Internationalen Beziehungen,* Series 2, II:1, 345, 346. (Sazonoff to Malevsky-Malevich and Krupensky, March 15, 1915.) The Russian Government had referred to the Japanese demand in Group II to grant to Japanese subjects freedom of residence, travel, and occupation in South Manchuria and Eastern Inner Mongolia, inferring that Russian subjects should have similar rights in North Manchuria and the Russian sphere in Mongolia.

[42] *Ibid.,* III:1, 207, 208. (Malevsky-Malevich to Sazonoff, July 2, 1915.) See also *Foreign Relations,* 1916, pp. 441, 442. (Guthrie to Lansing, July 18, 1916.)

[43] *Foreign Relations,* 1916, pp. 429, 430. (Guthrie to Lansing, April 7, 1916.)

[44] *Ibid.,* p. 430. (Fred M. Dearing, American Chargé d'Affaires in St. Petersburg, to Lansing, April 24, 1916.) For evidence that the agreements had been "reduced to terms" as early as March 18, 1916, see the texts of the treaties,

mors were also rife in Chinese circles that Russia had agreed to hand over virtual control of the Far East to Japan in return for the munitions which she so badly needed.[45]

In these circumstances the House Committee on Naval Affairs, after lengthy hearings, submitted a naval construction program to the House on May 24, 1916. The recommendations proved disappointing to those who agreed with the President on the need for naval expansion. No dreadnaughts were included; but there were five battle cruisers, four scout cruisers, ten destroyers, three ocean-going submarines, seventeen coast submarines, and three auxiliaries. This was only a one-year program based, apparently, upon the committee's fear of the speedy battle cruisers possessed by other naval powers, notably Japan.[46] The minority of the committee dissented and declared that the program was "not the product, in any degree, of expert naval opinion and disregards every plan suggested by naval authorities for the development of the Navy." They urged the authorization of two dreadnaughts and six battle cruisers to restore the American fleet to second place among the navies of the world in the shortest possible time.[47] But the minority succeeded in making only one change—an increase in the number of submarines authorized from twenty to fifty. After a perfunctory debate of two days, the House passed the bill on June 2, 1916.

Meanwhile, the battle of Jutland on May 31, 1916, demonstrated that the battleship was still the only vessel which could stand in the battle line and take the punishment meted out by the opposing fleet. The battle cruiser's consequent loss of favor undoubtedly had its effect in the Senate. The Senate Committee on Naval Affairs, in its report of June 30, 1916, accepted the recommendations of the General Board with one important exception: the five-year program was transformed into one of three years, because "the Navy must always be our first line of defense and we have two great coasts to defend."[48] Senator Lodge defended the change by saying

---

both public and secret, in *Mezhdunarodnye otnosheniia v epokhu imperializma*, Series 3, X, 417–422. The public treaty as printed here was the same almost word for word as that which was finally ratified. The secret treaty contemplated a military alliance between Russia and Japan against any third power which should threaten the "vital interests" of either of the two allies in China.

[45] *The New York Times*, April 14, 1916, p. 5.

[46] *House Reports* (Ser. 6905), 64th Cong., 1st sess., No. 743, May 24, 1916, pp. 4, 5.

[47] *Ibid.*, No. 743:2, May 25, 1916, pp. 1–5 *passim*.

[48] *Sen. Reports* (Ser. 6899), 64th Cong., 1st sess., No. 575, June 30, 1916, pp. 4, 5.

that the program of the General Board was too small for five years if the Navy really were to be made adequate.[49] Thus the General Board, after years of struggling with an unyielding Congress, now had the exhilarating experience of hearing the greatest program it had ever presented to Congress called "too small" by a Senate Committee on Naval Affairs.

Before the Senate debate on the bill could begin, however, the State Department learned of the signing on July 3, 1916, of the new treaty between Japan and Russia.[50] The treaty, like those of 1907 and 1910, was ostensibly for maintaining "a constant peace" in the Far East; but whereas the earlier treaties contained the declaration that the two powers would observe the principle of equal opportunity and the independence and territorial integrity of China, the new treaty merely provided that neither power would participate in any agreement directed against the other, and each agreed to come to the aid of the other whenever the territorial rights or "special interests" of the other power should be threatened. The open door and the independence and integrity of China were not mentioned, and this the State Department quickly noticed. Inquiries concerning this important omission were soon sent to Tokyo and St. Petersburg;[51] but, as was to be expected, both powers earnestly denied that any threat to American interests was implied by this change in the treaty's wording.[52]

But more serious were reports from the Far East of Russian concessions to Japan in the secret treaty so extensive as to indicate that Russia was no longer in a position to check the Japanese. From St. Petersburg, Ambassador Francis reported that Russia was "forced to [the] execution of [the] treaty now which it preferred to defer until [the] war [was] terminated but Japan insisted on [the] immediate necessity [of] consummation."[53] Russia's desperate need for munitions and Japan's fear of a resurgent Germany

[49] *Cong. Rec.*, LIII, July 13, 1916, pp. 10926, 10927.

[50] *Foreign Relations*, 1916, pp. 431, 432. (David R. Francis, American Ambassador in St. Petersburg, to Lansing, July 7, 1916.)

[51] *Ibid.*, pp. 442, 443. (Lansing to Guthrie, August 16, 1916.) *Ibid.*, pp. 443, 444. (Lansing to Francis, August 16, 1916.)

[52] *Ibid.*, p. 444. (Guthrie to Lansing, August 21, 1916.) *Ibid.*, p. 445. (Francis to Lansing, August 23, 1916.)

[53] *Ibid.*, p. 436. (Francis to Lansing, July 14, 1916.) In view of the compulsion under which the Russian Government entered into this agreement, it is interesting to note that it was one of the last acts of Serge Sazonoff as Foreign Minister. He resigned on July 22, 1916.

had combined to force the agreement; but the advantage lay almost wholly with Japan. This is evident from the impression made by the treaty in the Far East. In a dispatch from Peking, Minister Reinsch informed Lansing that the "Russo-Japanese convention is interpreted in Chinese circles as a temporary yielding of Russia to Japanese pretensions and in that sense unfavorable to China."[54] From such interpretations, it was generally concluded that with the elimination of Germany and the weakening of Russia, the balance of power in the Far East had been destroyed. It was even felt that Japan was using the occasion to impress upon Great Britain Japan's independence of the Anglo-Japanese Alliance.[55] So Theodore Roosevelt's prediction of 1905 that the Japanese would "take advantage of our various national jealousies, and beat us in turn" appeared about to be realized.[56]

In these circumstances, the Senate began debate on the three-year naval construction program approved by its Committee on Naval Affairs. Senator Claude A. Swanson of Virginia, acting chairman of the committee, in the principal speech supporting the bill, asserted that the committee "believed that the necessity for an increase of the Navy was so immediate and urgent that we could not afford to wait longer than three years for the completion of the program."[57] Senator Swanson, later to be Secretary of the Navy, stated emphatically: "I deeply feel that the fate of this Republic, the preservation of our institutions and the maintenance of our well-defined foreign policies are dependent upon the strength and success of our Navy. America and her Navy, for weal or for woe, are united in indissoluble wedlock." No nation, according to the Senator, could live in isolation. This had been demonstrated by the widespread distress occasioned in the United States by the European war. The United States needed a navy adequate to protect her world-wide interests. "Are we foolish enough to believe that this Nation, which, with its vast wealth and unsurpassed possibilities—the object of envy and jealousy of other Nations—can be safe if we permit ourselves to become a fourth or fifth rate naval

[54] *Ibid.*, p. 437. (Reinsch to Lansing, July 17, 1916.)
[55] *Ibid.*, p. 442. (Guthrie to Lansing, July 18, 1916.) There was considerable friction between the British and Japanese in China, according to Guthrie; and this had been increased by "the position of the British colonies in regard to Japanese immigration."
[56] See above, p. 45.
[57] *Cong. Rec.*, LIII, July 13, 1916, p. 10924.

power?" asked the Senator; and then, "Have we not an aggressive eastern neighbor who looks with covetous eyes upon our Philippine possessions?" Other points of attack mentioned were American commerce, the Panama Canal, and the Monroe Doctrine. But the United States had no need to fear Great Britain, because she maintained no standing army; hence, the real need was a navy second only to that of the British. Senator Swanson concluded:

> . . . If we remain less than this, our vast foreign commercial interests, inseparable from our prosperity, will be jeopardized. Our Philippine possessions will be the prey of superior naval power. Our foreign policies and intercourse will necessarily become timid and vacillating. The great affairs of the world affecting our interests will be regulated without consultation with us. We will then become suppliants, pleading for rights instead of boldly and courageously demanding them. It will mean the surrender of our great prestige. It will mean a distinct loss to the world of the great power possessed by this Nation for peace, justice, and liberty.[58]

Republican leaders in the Senate joined with the majority in making naval preparedness a nonpartisan question. Senator Lodge remarked that should the Senate bill be passed, "as it ought, it will be of more value to our peace than all the diplomatic notes that can ever be written."[59] Republican Senator William E. Borah of Idaho also agreed with Senator Swanson. He said:

> . . . Would we submit to the views of a foreign power with reference to those matters which we deem to be vital to the existence of our Government and to the preservation of our civilization? We would not, and it is cheaper and wiser to settle grave questions in the atmosphere of security. The premier of Japan a short time ago said that the only way that diplomacy could become effective was when it was backed up by sufficient force. When he thus spoke he was not, I take it, making a threat but uttering a most practical precept of international action. *I would not like to sit down with the masterful men of that great nation to deal with matters of vital concern and have them feel that there was no force behind our diplomacy. I am too anxious to retain their respect.*[60]

Senator Borah then pointed out some of the main causes of wars, foremost among which was commerce with its fierce rivalries. The intermingling of races also aroused antagonisms, and the Senator referred to the altercations with Japan on this question. Although settled temporarily, he said ". . . he is a complacent soul, indeed, who does not scent danger in this close rub of irreconcilable nationalities." He then cited as a good example of unpreparedness the

[58] *Ibid.* The text of Senator Swanson's speech occupies pp. 10922–10926.
[59] *Ibid.*, p. 10926.
[60] *Cong. Rec.*, LIII, July 17, 1916, p. 11171. Italics mine.

plight of Great Britain before the World War. In 1900 Lord Salisbury had foreseen the danger of war with Germany over their commercial rivalry and had urged England to prepare; but his advice went unheeded. British leaders had pursued a "wait and see" policy, and the war had suddenly descended upon them. The United States, too, was being told calmly in the Senate debate that she was at peace, "that there is less danger of war now than at any time during the last 50 years." But Senator Borah, a fighter and a realist, had little faith in such a peace; and he stated his reasons frankly and cogently:

> ... Yes; we are at peace; we have not sought war, and we do not propose to seek war. But look about us. We have had some 200 of our citizens drowned at sea and from 500 to a thousand assassinated and murdered on land. We have had millions of property seized at sea and billions of property destroyed on land. We have seen the open door, supposedly well guarded by our treaties and by our honor, closed in the Orient, and we now watch the process while the door which has been closed is being bolted. No; we have not offended, but we have suffered incalculable loss in honor and in property. Weakness is an invitation to aggression, weakness is an invitation to war. As a people and as a Nation, we can not escape our responsibility.[61]

On July 21, 1916, the Senate demonstrated that it would not shirk its responsibility. By a vote of 71 to 8, it passed the greatest naval construction bill in the history of the United States. The House, too, had changed its views and soon accepted the Senate's program. Thus, on August 29, 1916, President Wilson signed the two measures which rounded out the national strategy of the United States in the Pacific—the Philippine Government Act and the Naval Appropriation Act of 1916.[62] American aims and policies were now quite clear. The Philippines were to be relinquished because they had proved to be a military hostage to an aggressively militaristic neighbor; but, in the spirit of Theodore Roosevelt, the United States let it be known that she would withdraw in her own good time and would not be forced by any nation.[63] A definite withdrawal date was not specified; and in the building up of the Navy, not only were the Philippines to be defended, but the other interests of the United States in the Far East as well.

[61] *Ibid.*, p. 11174.

[62] The text of the Naval Appropriation Act is in *U. S. Statutes at Large*, XXXIX (1917), 556–619. The new construction program will be found on pp. 616, 617.

[63] See above, p. 62.

The events which followed the passage of the Naval Appropriation Act of 1916 merely lend point to America's determination to build up her naval strength. Japan and Russia in attempting to prevent the consummation of an American loan to the Chinese Government made clear the cleavage in the consortium as a result of the war and Japan's activities in the Far East.[64] This division, appearing in connection with the relations of the German group to the consortium, had led Sir Edward Grey to suggest to the Russian Government as early as April 11, 1916, that the United States should be invited to enter the reconstituted consortium.[65] The British Government was obviously attempting to gain the support of the United States in heading off the advance of Japan and Russia in the Far East. Thus, by the end of 1916, negotiations were under way which were to result in the reëntry of an American group into the consortium with the blessing of the Wilson administration—the same administration whose earlier disapproval had caused the withdrawal of the American group.[66]

Moreover, Japan's renewal of demands similar to those in the original Group V as a result of clashes between Chinese and Japanese troops at Cheng-chiatun in Inner Mongolia,[67] added to the growing concern in the United States. The elevation of Field Marshal Count Masakata Terauchi to the premiership in Japan and the appointment of Viscount Ichiro Motono, formerly ambassador in St. Petersburg, as foreign minister were also portentous. But the United States Government, through the Secretary of the Navy, asserted that "this country is now determined to provide and maintain a first line of defense adequate to its needs."[68] Congress supported Secretary Daniels by authorizing the construction of the ships of the second year's program as scheduled: three dreadnaughts, one battle cruiser, three scout cruisers, fifteen destroyers, and eighteen submarines.[69]

The President was likewise deeply concerned at the possibility

[64] *Foreign Relations*, 1916, pp. 147 ff.

[65] *Mezhdunarodnye otnosheniia v epokhu imperializma*, Series 3, X, 609, 610. (Grey to Benckendorff, April 11, 1916.)

[66] For the pertinent documents on the new consortium, see *The Consortium*, Pamphlet No. 40, Division of International Law, Carnegie Endowment for International Peace (Washington: 1921).

[67] *The New York Times*, September 6, 1916, p. 1.

[68] Report of the Secretary of the Navy, December 1, 1916, in *Annual Reports of the Navy Department*, 1916, p. 4.

[69] *U. S. Statutes at Large*, XXXIX (1917), 1191. The act of March 4, 1917.

of war in the Pacific. While Walter Hines Page, Colonel Edward M. House, and others could see only the war in Europe, President Wilson, possessed of more information as well as keener insight, saw a greater and more lasting peril in Asia. At the cabinet meeting on February 2, 1917, at which the decision was made to sever relations with Germany, the President made a remarkable statement, according to Secretary of Agriculture David F. Houston, who reported the scene as follows:

> As we sat down, the President asked what we thought should be done. "Shall I break off diplomatic relations with Germany?" He immediately followed this question with a somewhat startling statement. He would say frankly that, if he felt that, in order to keep the white race or part of it strong to meet the yellow race—Japan, for instance, in alliance with Russia, dominating China—it was wise to do nothing, he would do nothing, and would submit to anything and any imputation of weakness or cowardice. This was a novel and unexpected angle.
>
> Several of us immediately began to speak. . . . Baker [Newton D. Baker, Secretary of War] was much impressed with the President's long look ahead, as was Daniels. . . .[70]

Thus, the end of a long road had been reached. The enemy of the future was Japan, and the responsible leaders of the United States knew it. The naval policy of the United States had at last taken account of the Pacific situation, and the Navy had finally come into its own as a vital force in the national strategy.

[70] Houston, *Eight Years with Wilson's Cabinet, 1913–1920,* I, 229.

CHAPTER VII

JAPAN, THE PROBABLE ENEMY

In these three things—production, with the necessity of exchanging products, shipping, whereby the exchange is carried on, and colonies, which facilitate and enlarge the operations of shipping and tend to protect it by multiplying points of safety—is to be found the key to much of the history, as well as of the policy, of nations bordering upon the sea.—ALFRED THAYER MAHAN.

THE PROMOTION of the welfare and material progress of a nation in modern industrial society involves not only the development of the nation's internal resources, but also vital relationships with the other powers of the world. Decisive in the history of the United States were the years from 1897 to 1917; for during those years, the United States abandoned her traditional isolation to enter into the fierce competition of world enterprise. Inevitably, the United States became involved in the international politics of the Pacific and of the Far East. The maintenance of the balance of power in those regions, inextricably connected with the open-door policy because of America's dependence upon diplomacy alone to achieve her aims, became a cardinal factor in the foreign policy of the United States. But those twenty years witnessed the gradual weakening of the Far Eastern balance of power and its total collapse with the outbreak of the World War. Thus, the United States was forced more and more to back up her diplomacy with force until the end was reached in 1916 with the realization that force had become the only effective diplomacy in the Far East. How the United States was drawn into the Far Eastern balance of power and how she eventually became its only effective supporter have been related, and the evidence presented tells its own story.

The territorial expansion of the United States in the Pacific area came partly as a result of the great expansion of American industry. American industrialists were seeking new outlets, especially for the products of the heavy industries—structural steel and rails, railway equipment, and machinery of all kinds—and naturally turned toward the Pacific, the one great undeveloped area in the world. Both of these phenomena meant radical changes in American policy. Abandoning territorial isolation for an Asiatic empire, the United States assumed obligations not only to protect the

Filipino people, but also to uphold her own honor and prestige in a far more vulnerable position. The industrial and commercial development of the United States ended the old idea of national self-sufficiency in the home market in favor of production for export. As Richard Olney stated it: "Nothing will satisfy us in the future but free access to foreign markets—especially to those markets in the East now for the first time beginning to fully open themselves to the Western nations."[1]

Through the use of astute diplomacy, the United States at first was successful in protecting her newly acquired interests in the Far East. The Hay policies of the open door and the integrity of China were enunciated and were outwardly accepted by the other interested powers. But these policies were only partially successful, and then only because of the balance of power which had been established in the Far East by the Anglo-Japanese Alliance of 1902. When the defeat of Russia in 1904–1905 upset the balance of power and led to a virtual quadruple alliance of Great Britain, France, Russia, and Japan, the United States Government was confronted with entirely new problems. Some of these arose out of the new alignment of the powers in the Far East and some out of Japan's new role as a world power.

Without sufficient naval power to speak with authority, the United States further sacrificed her tradition by adopting a policy of international coöperation with the four powers in order to act as a check upon them. This step plunged the United States even more deeply into Far Eastern politics and she was confronted by an uncompromising group of powers. America's efforts to maintain her Asiatic policies in this way failed largely because the consortium was perverted by Japan and Russia, supported by France, into an instrument for the oppression of the Chinese Government. These machinations at first forced the United States into closer accord with Germany, with whom she had amicably composed all outstanding differences. Later on, the government felt grave doubts about the purposes of Japan and Russia and this led eventually to a new orientation of policies in the Pacific by the Wilson administration.

Meanwhile, Japan, emerging from the Russo-Japanese War with a veteran army and a victorious navy, was prepared to assert her

[1] "Growth of Our Foreign Policy," *The Atlantic Monthly*, LXXXV (March, 1900), 299.

rights wherever they might be challenged. She immediately became embroiled over the question of the admission of her nationals into the United States and their treatment after they were once there. These issues produced two great crises in American-Japanese relations in 1907 and in 1913, both of which caused the United States to pause and take stock of her defenses in the Pacific. The problem of Japanese immigration was still an acute one at the end of the period. On February 5, 1917, Congress passed, over the veto of President Wilson, the Burnett Immigration Act, which contained a provision that "no alien now in any way excluded from, or prevented from entering, the United States shall be admitted to the United States."[2] Since the Japanese laborer was "prevented" from entering the United States by the "gentlemen's agreement," this provision in effect enacted that agreement into law. Such was the contention of the Japanese Government in its vigorous protests, but the argument in Congress was that the provision was merely for the protection of the United States should the Japanese Government ever decide unilaterally to abrogate the "gentlemen's agreement."[3]

The continued growth of American industry and commerce, therefore, with the inevitable necessity of finding open markets in which American farm and factory products could be sold, meant further and more intensive rivalry with Japan. In 1910 President Taft, speaking of the increase in American trade, had asserted that "our State Department could not vindicate its existence or justify a policy which in any way withheld a fostering, protecting, and stimulating hand in the development and extension of that trade."[4] He referred later to this attitude of government toward business as "a broad and a modern view";[5] but it remained for his successor to translate this view into actuality under the irresistible influence of a great war.

The World War was the decisive factor in the development of the new American policies in the Pacific. An inevitable result was a new attitude toward the possession of overseas territories as vulnerable points subject to attack by aggressive powers. As Japa-

[2] *U. S. Statutes at Large*, XXXIX (1917), 876.

[3] *Cong. Rec.*, LIV, February 5, 1917, pp. 2617–2629 *passim*.

[4] In a speech at Pittsburgh, May 2, 1910. See *The New York Times*, May 3, 1910, p. 2.

[5] In his annual message to Congress, December 3, 1912, in *Messages and Papers*, XVIII, 8170.

nese policy unfolded in the Far East after the Russo-Japanese War, the United States had virtually abandoned hope of fighting more than a delaying action in defense of the Philippine Islands. The correlative had been the development of naval facilities ashore at Pearl Harbor, Panama, San Francisco, and Alaska. The fact that Japan continued to encroach upon the rights of other nations in the Far East after the outbreak of the war and the further fact that, in spite of the acute shortage of steel, Japan managed during the war to increase her already powerful navy,[6] prompted the United States to reconsider her policy toward the Philippine Islands.

The collapse of regular ocean transportation schedules as a result of the war proved to be the turning point in the long struggle to reëstablish and to develop an adequate American merchant marine. The withdrawal of foreign vessels from trans-Atlantic and trans-Pacific routes proved that the United States could not afford to entrust the transportation of her products to the vessels of other nations. The dire results demonstrated also that the nation could no longer wait on the development of shipping lines by private capital. That was a government job in the national interest, and the government would have to operate its own vessels until the service could safely be entrusted to private enterprise.[7] The rare opportunity afforded by the war for commercial expansion made immediately necessary other measures, some of which had already been contemplated. Among these were the relaxing of the anti-trust laws to permit certain combinations in foreign trade, and the relaxing of the restrictions on banks in financing foreign accounts. Here, too, the government acted to make it possible for American merchants and manufacturers to compete in foreign markets on a more equitable basis. More than that, the government set up new

[6] "Japanese Naval Expansion," *The Engineer* (London), CXXV (March 8, 1918), 206. Japan had added to her fleet during the war three battleships and three battle cruisers and had projected a new construction program which would eventually produce three squadrons of eight battleships and eight battle cruisers each, or a total of forty-eight capital ships. Such a huge program led the writer to remark: "The publication of the new building programme . . . suggests that the Japanese Government intends to adopt a vigorous policy of naval development as soon as conditions again become normal. In the Far East, at all events, the idea of universal disarmament at the conclusion of this war does not appear to find favour."

[7] For a discussion of the merchant marine problem, see my article, "World War I and Our Merchant Navy: A Warning for the Future," *United States Naval Institute Proceedings,* LXXI (August, 1945), 919–929.

instrumentalities of its own and adapted existing ones to promote foreign trade information, to develop foreign markets for American producers, and to protect the producer or merchant against unfair competition or discrimination.

The war had also provided Japan with an opportunity, which she turned to her own advantage. But with Japan, it was not alone a question of expanding her commerce, but also her political influence. The Russo-Japanese War had already indicated what the Japanese could do when they were at war. President Roosevelt had exclaimed in admiration:

> What wonderful people the Japanese are! They are quite as remarkable industrially as in warfare. In a dozen years the English, Americans and Germans, who now dread one another as rivals in the trade of the Pacific, will have each to dread the Japanese more than they do any other nation. In the middle of this war they have actually steadily increased their exports to China, and are proceeding in the establishment of new lines of steamers in new points of Japanese trade expansion throughout the Pacific.[8]

In 1914, Japan had an even greater opportunity, for her only serious competitor was the United States. Thus, the rivalry over trade and shipping in the Pacific was certain to produce friction.

But more serious was the transformation of the strategic situation in the Pacific. The Japanese had driven the Germans out of Tsingtao and were attempting to monopolize the trade and development enterprises throughout Shantung Province. The former German islands in the Pacific were in the possession of Japan, and she raised no hopes that they would ever be returned. The Japanese Government had driven a hard bargain with a now helpless Russia in the alliance of July 3, 1916, which made Japan all but master of the Far East. None save the United States could say to her "thus far, and no farther." The flouting of the treaty rights of the United States in China, the disregard for her pledge to respect the administrative independence and the territorial integrity of China, and the insolent demands that her nationals should be admitted freely into the United States all attest to Japan's newly found feeling of unrestricted freedom of action.

It was this rise of Japan to supreme and unchecked power in the Far East which led President Wilson to say to Secretary of State

[8] Gwynn, *The Letters and Friendships of Sir Cecil Spring Rice: A Record,* I, 472. (Roosevelt to Spring-Rice, June 16, 1905.)

Lansing on January 31, 1917, after the German Government had announced resumption of unrestricted submarine warfare, that

> . . . he had been more and more impressed with the idea that "white civilization" and its domination over the world rested largely on our ability to keep this country intact, as we would have to build up the nations ravaged by the war. He said that as this idea had grown upon him he had come to the feeling that he was willing to go to any lengths rather than to have the nation actually involved in the conflict.[9]

When Lansing pointed out that if the United States failed to act, "our voice in the future would be treated with contempt by both the Allies and Germany," Wilson replied "that he was not sure of that; that, if he believed it was for the good of the world for the United States to keep out of the war in the present circumstances, he would be willing to bear all the criticism and abuse which would surely follow our failure to break with Germany . . ."[10]

For some years, Japan had been considered the "probable enemy" whom the United States must prepare to fight. In 1916, the differences between the United States and Japan were fundamental and permanent; those with Germany were temporary and the direct products of the war and of Germany's struggle to survive. It was inevitable, therefore, that the United States, when the failure of her diplomacy in the Far East had become obvious in the spring of 1915, should finally look to her naval defenses. Every element of the national strategy, as it had developed, had brought the United States into conflict with Japan. There remained for development the one element of the national strategy to which recourse could be had when all other means of resolution had failed—the Navy. President Roosevelt had seen the need for it; President Taft had seen it; President Wilson had seen it; and in 1916, Congress saw it.

That the Naval Construction Act of 1916 was directed against Japan, there can be little doubt. The attitude of the President and of Congress show this clearly. The Japanese themselves were convinced that the new fleet could have been authorized for no other purpose than to defeat "Japanese pretensions in the Pacific and Far East."[11] Less well known, however, is the fact that as late as December, 1917, the Allies were entreating the United States to

[9] [Robert Lansing], *War Memoirs of Robert Lansing, Secretary of State* (Indianapolis: Bobbs-Merrill, 1935), p. 212.
[10] *Ibid.*, p. 213.
[11] *Ibid.*, p. 285.

stop work on her great capital ships and to send them cruisers and destroyers to protect their supply lines against German submarines. If the United States would consent to do this, the Allied Governments offered to protect the United States by engaging "singly and severally to assist each other against any maritime attack for a period of four years after the conclusion of the present war."[12] To assist the United States "against any maritime attack" by whom? There could be only one answer. Japan alone was capable of attacking the United States. And to defend herself against Japan, the United States needed battleships, the masters of the sea. Truly, then, "America and her Navy, for weal or for woe . . . [were] united in indissoluble wedlock." The future place of the United States in the Pacific and the peace and happiness of her people rested squarely upon the power of the great ships of her fleet.

> Guard them well, admirals and captains, hardy tars and tall marines; guard them well and guide them true.—WINSTON CHURCHILL.

---

[12] Dugdale, *Arthur James Balfour, First Earl of Balfour*, II, 209.

APPENDIXES

APPENDIX I

Secretaries of the Navy, 1881 to 1921

William H. Hunt	March 7, 1881–April 16, 1882
William E. Chandler	April 17, 1882–March 6, 1885
William C. Whitney	March 7, 1885–March 5, 1889
Benjamin F. Tracy	March 6, 1889–March 6, 1893
Hilary A. Herbert	March 7, 1893–March 5, 1897
John D. Long	March 6, 1897–April 30, 1902
William H. Moody	May 1, 1902–June 30, 1904
Paul Morton	July 1, 1904–June 30, 1905
Charles J. Bonaparte	July 1, 1905–December 16, 1906
Victor H. Metcalf	December 17, 1906–November 30, 1908
Truman H. Newberry	December 1, 1908–March 5, 1909
George von L. Meyer	March 6, 1909–March 4, 1913
Josephus Daniels	March 5, 1913–March 4, 1921

APPENDIX II

Construction of Naval Vessels Recommended and Authorized

Recommended by the General Board	Recommended by the Secretary of the Navy	Authorized by Congress
1903	(Secretary Moody)	(Act of 1904)
2 battleships	1 battleship	1 battleship
1 armored cruiser	1 armored cruiser	2 armored cruisers
3 protected cruisers	3 protected cruisers	......
4 scout cruisers	2–4 scout cruisers	3 scout cruisers
3 destroyers	......	......
......	2 submarines	4 submarines
2 fuel ships	2 fuel ships	2 fuel ships
......	2 hospital ships	......
1904	(Secretary Morton)	(Act of 1905)
3 battleships	3 battleships	2 battleships
6 destroyers	6 destroyers (if practicable)	......
5 scout cruisers	......	......
6 torpedo boats	......	......
2 fuel ships	......	......
1 gunboat	......	......
2 river gunboats	......	......
2 Philippine gunboats	......	......
$850,000 for submarines	......	......
1905	(Secretary Bonaparte)	(Act of 1906)
3 battleships	2 battleships	1 battleship
1 gunboat	1 gunboat	......
2 river gunboats	2 river gunboats	......
3 scout cruisers	2 scout cruisers	......
4 destroyers	4 destroyers	3 destroyers
4 submarines	2 submarines	8 submarines
4 torpedo boats	......	......
2 small gunboats	......	......
1906	(Secretary Bonaparte)	(Act of 1907)
2 battleships	1 battleship, and, with hesitation, 2	1 battleship
1 gunboat	2 gunboats	......
2 river gunboats	3 river gunboats	......
4 destroyers	4 destroyers	2 destroyers
4 ships' torpedo boats	4 ships' torpedo boats	......
2 scout cruisers	......	......
2 small gunboats	......	......
1 ammunition ship	......	......

Recommended by the General Board	Recommended by the Secretary of the Navy	Authorized by Congress
1907	(Secretary Metcalf)	(Act of 1908)
4 battleships	4 battleships	2 battleships
4 scout cruisers	4 scout cruisers	......
10 destroyers	10 destroyers	10 destroyers
4 submarines	4 submarines	8 submarines
2 fuel ships	4 fuel ships	2 fuel ships
1 ammunition ship	1 ammunition ship	......
1 repair ship	1 repair ship	......
2 mine-laying ships (conversion of 2 cruisers on list)	2 mine-laying ships (conversion of 2 cruisers on list)	......
4 ships' motor torpedo boats	......	Purchase of 3 new fuel ships
1908	(Secretary Metcalf)	(Act of 1909)
4 battleships	4 battleships	2 battleships
4 scout cruisers	4 scout cruisers	......
10 destroyers	10 destroyers	5 destroyers
4 submarines	4 submarines	4 submarines
3 fuel ships	3 fuel ships	1 fuel ship
1 ammunition ship	1 ammunition ship	......
1 repair ship	1 repair ship	......
2 mine-laying ships (conversion of 2 cruisers on list)	2 mine-laying ships (conversion of 2 cruisers on list)	1 destroyer whose vitals are below the water line
1909	(Secretary Meyer)	(Act of 1910)
4 battleships	2 battleships	2 battleships
10 destroyers	......	6 destroyers
4 scout cruisers	......	......
1 repair ship	1 repair ship	......
1 fuel ship (oil tank)	......	2 fuel ships
......	......	4 submarines
1 ammunition ship	......	......

Recommended by the General Board	Recommended by the Secretary of the Navy	Authorized by Congress
1910	(Secretary Meyer)	(Act of 1911)
4 battleships	2 battleships	2 battleships
1 gunboat	1 gunboat	1 gunboat
2 river gunboats	1 river gunboat	1 river gunboat
......	2 submarines	4 submarines
4 fuel ships	1 fuel ship	2 fuel ships
2 tugs	2 tugs	2 tugs
3 submarine tenders	1 submarine tender	1 submarine tender
16 destroyers	......	8 destroyers
1 repair ship	......	......
4 scout cruisers	......	......
2 destroyer tenders	......	......
1 mine layer	......	......
2 transports	......	......
1 hospital ship	......	......
1911	(Secretary Meyer)	(Act of 1912)
4 battleships	2 battleships	1 battleship
4 fuel ships	2 fuel ships	2 fuel ships
16 destroyers	......	6 destroyers
2 destroyer tenders	......	1 destroyer tender
5 submarines	......	8 submarines
2 submarine tenders	......	1 submarine tender
1 repair ship	......	......
4 scout cruisers	......	......
1 ammunition ship	......	......
1 mine layer	......	......
2 transports	......	......
1912	(Secretary Meyer)	(Act of 1913)
4 battleships	3 battleships	1 battleship
2 battle cruisers	2 battle cruisers	......
2 gunboats	2 gunboats	......
16 destroyers	16 destroyers	6 destroyers
6 submarines	6 submarines	4 submarines
......	1 fuel ship (conditionally)	......
1 ammunition ship	1 ammunition ship	......
2 transports	2 transports	1 transport
2 tugs	2 tugs	......
1 submarine tender	1 submarine tender	......
1 destroyer tender	1 destroyer tender	......
1 supply ship	1 supply ship	1 supply ship
1 submarine testing dock	1 submarine testing dock	......

Recommended by the General Board	Recommended by the Secretary of the Navy	Authorized by Congress
1913	(Secretary Daniels)	(Act of 1914)
4 battleships	3 battleships	3 battleships
16 destroyers	8 destroyers	6 destroyers
8 submarines	3 submarines	8 or more submarines
1 destroyer tender	......	......
2 fuel ships (oilers)	......	1 submarine testing dock
2 gunboats	......	......
1 transport	......	......
1 supply ship	......	......
1 hospital ship	......	......
1914	(Secretary Daniels)	(Act of 1915)
4 battleships	2 battleships	2 battleships
16 destroyers	6 destroyers	6 destroyers
16 coast submarines	8 submarines or more,	2 seagoing submarines
3 fleet submarines	1 to be of seagoing	
4 scout cruisers	type and	16 coast defense sub-
4 gunboats	7 or more of coast	marines
2 oil fuel ships	defense type	1 oil fuel ship
1 destroyer tender	1 gunboat	......
1 submarine tender	1 oiler	......
1 Navy transport	......	......
1 hospital ship	......	......
1 supply ship	......	......

BIBLIOGRAPHY

NOTE: In any study of policies in the history of the United States, the Congress of the United States, as the policy-making authority under the Constitution, can be expected to play a major role. Therefore, the publications of Congress—its proceedings and debates, the reports of its various committees, and the materials contained in the various series of documents from time to time ordered published—become the principal source for any study of policies. The *Congressional Record* is perhaps the most valuable single source available, not alone for the important expressions of opinion which it contains, but also for the materials which are inserted by members of both branches in the course of the debates. In listing the various Congressional documents and reports in the bibliography, the practice has been followed of giving only so much of the title of each as will indicate the nature of the contents.

The publications of the other branches of the government also have a large share in providing information for such a study as this. A vast accumulation of data may be found in the publications of the Department of Commerce, much of it bearing directly upon the relations of the United States with other commercial nations. The Department of State quite naturally provides through its published diplomatic correspondence an invaluable source on international relations. This series is supplemented very largely through the period 1897 to 1917 by the published diplomatic correspondence of the European powers, of which full use has been made. There are, in addition, a large number of unofficial collections of correspondence and documents which further supplement the official publications. The same may also be said of the large number of collections of private letters, memoirs, and biographies, all of which contain more or less of the correspondence of important figures not elsewhere published.

It is obviously impossible to give anything approaching a complete list of secondary books and articles on the many subjects touched upon in this work. It is not even maintained that my selection comprises all the best works on any given subject. The most that can be said is that on every subject representative and, in nearly every instance, competent writings have been included. In addition to the use of the subject matter of these works, full use has also been made of the many excellent bibliographies and footnote references which they contain. Without such leads, research would become infinitely more difficult and far less complete. For all such contributions to this work not specifically acknowledged elsewhere, I hope that the inclusion of the book or article in the bibliography will be accepted as a sufficient acknowledgment of my indebtedness for the aid received.

BIBLIOGRAPHIES, GUIDES, AND OTHER AIDS TO RESEARCH

BEMIS, SAMUEL FLAGG, and GRIFFIN, GRACE GARDNER. *Guide to the Diplomatic History of the United States, 1775–1921* (Washington, Government Printing Office, 1935). 979 pp.

BRITISH MUSEUM. *Subject Index of the Modern Works Added to the Library of the British Museum in the Years 1881–1900*, ed. George K. Fortescue (3 vols.; London, 1902–1903). Supplements issued periodically.

BROWN, GEORGE DOBBIN. *An Essay towards a Bibliography of the Published Writings and Addresses of Woodrow Wilson, 1910–1917* (Princeton, 1917). 52 pp.

BUELL, RAYMOND LESLIE. *Problems of the Pacific, a Brief Bibliography,* World Peace Foundation Pamphlets, VIII, No. 1 (Boston, 1925). 34 pp.

CHANNING, EDWARD; HART, ALBERT B.; *and* TURNER, FREDERICK J. *Guide to the Study and Reading of American History* (rev. ed.; Boston, 1912). 650 pp.

COULTER, EDITH M., and GERSTENFELD, MELANIE. *Historical Bibliographies* (Berkeley, University of California Press, 1935). 206 pp.

FRANK, JOHN C. *American Interoceanic Canals: A List of References in the New York Public Library* (New York, 1916). 90 pp.

HASSE, ADELAIDE R. *Index to United States Documents Relating to Foreign Affairs, 1828–1861* (3 vols.; Washington, 1921).

KERNER, ROBERT J. *Northeastern Asia: A Selected Bibliography,* Contributions to the Bibliography of the Relations of China, Russia, and Japan.... (2 vols.; Berkeley, University of California Press, 1939).

LANGER, WILLIAM L., and ARMSTRONG, HAMILTON FISH. *Foreign Affairs Bibliography: A Selected and Annotated List of Books on International Relations, 1919–1932* (New York, Council on Foreign Relations, 1933). 551 pp.

MILLER, DOROTHY P., comp. *Japanese-American Relations: A List of Works in the New York Public Library* (New York, 1921). 67 pp.

PINSON, KOPPEL S. *A Bibliographical Introduction to Nationalism* (New York, Columbia University Press, 1935). 71 pp.

RAGATZ, LOWELL J. *A Bibliography of Articles, Descriptive, Historical, and Scientific, on Colonies and Other Dependent Territories, Appearing in American Geographical and Kindred Journals through 1934* (2 vols.; London, Arthur Thomas, 1935).

———. *A List of Books and Articles on Colonial History and Overseas Expansion Published in the United States 1900–1930* (Ann Arbor, Mich., Edwards Bros., 1939). 45 pp.

SCHMECKEBIER, LAURENCE F. *Government Publications and Their Use* (Washington, Brookings Institution, 1936). 446 pp.

TEMPERLEY, HAROLD, and PENSON, LILLIAN M. *A Century of Diplomatic Blue Books, 1814–1914,* lists edited, with historical introductions (Cambridge, Cambridge University Press, 1938). 600 pp.

UNITED STATES. LIBRARY OF CONGRESS. *Index to the Federal Statutes, 1874–1931; General and Permanent Law Contained in the Revised Statutes of 1874 and Volumes 18–46 of the Statutes at Large,* Revision of the Scott and Beaman Index Analysis of the Federal Statutes, by Walter H. McClenon and Wilfred C. Gilbert (Washington, Government Printing Office, 1933). 1432 pp.

———. *List of Books and Articles in Periodicals Relating to Interoceanic Canal and Railway Routes,* comp. Hugh A. Morrison, Jr. (Washington, 1900). 174 pp.

———. *A List of Books* [with references to periodicals] *on the Philippine Islands in the Library of Congress,* comp. A. P. C. Griffin (Washington, 1903). 397 pp.

———. *List of Books Relating to Hawaii* [including references to collected works and periodicals], comp. A. P. C. Griffin (Washington, 1898). 26 pp.

———. *List of Books* [with references to periodicals] *Relating to the Theory of Colonization, Government of Dependencies, Protectorates, and Related Topics,* comp. A. P. C. Griffin (2d ed.; Washington, 1900). 156 pp.

———. *A List of Books* [with references to periodicals] *on Samoa and Guam,* comp. A. P. C. Griffin (Washington, 1901). 54 pp.

———. SUPERINTENDENT OF DOCUMENTS. *Catalogue of the Public Documents, of . . . Congress . . . and of Other Departments of the Government of the United States* (22 vols.; Washington, 1896–1937).

———. *Check List of United States Public Documents, 1789–1909* (2 vols.; Washington, 1911–).

———. *Comprehensive Index to the Publications of the United States Government, 1881–1893,* comp. John G. Ames (2 vols.; Washington, 1905).

———. *Index to the Reports and Documents of the 54th Congress, 1st Session—72d Congress, 2d Session, December 2, 1895–March 4, 1933* (43 vols.; Washington, 1897–1933).

OFFICIAL PRINTED SOURCES

CALIFORNIA. LEGISLATURE. *The Statutes of California and Amendments to the Codes,* Thirty-fifth sess., 1903.

———. *The Statutes of California and Amendments to the Codes,* Fortieth sess., 1913.

———. LEGISLATURE. SENATE. *The Journal of the Senate,* Thirty-ninth sess., 1911.

———. *The Journal of the Senate.* Fortieth sess., 1913.

FRANCE. MINISTÉRE DES AFFAIRES ETRANGÈRES. *Documents diplomatiques français, 1871–1914* ([3 series, 28 vols., incompl.] Ser. 3, 11 vols.; Paris, Imprimerie Nationale, 1929–1939).

GERMANY. AUSWÄRTIGE AMT. *Die grosse Politik der europäischen Kabinette, 1871–1914: Sammlung der diplomatischen Akten des Auswärtigen Amtes,* eds. Johannes Lepsius, Albrecht M. Bertholdy, Friedrich Thimme (40 vols.; Berlin, Deutsche Verlagsgesellschaft für Politik u. Geschichte, 1922–1926).

———. KAISERLICHE STATISTISCHE AMT. *Statistik des deutschen Reichs,* "Auswärtiger Handel" (Berlin) Annual.

———. REICHSTAG. *Stenographische Berichte über die Verhandlungen des Reichstags,* XI. Legislaturperiode. II. Session. 1905–1906.

GREAT BRITAIN. FOREIGN OFFICE. *British Documents on the Origins of the War, 1898–1914,* eds. G. P. Gooch and Harold Temperley (11 vols. [in 13]; London, H.M. Stationery Office, 1926–1938).

———. *British and Foreign State Papers* (London, H.M. Stationery Office). Annual vols.

———. *Collected Diplomatic Documents Relating to the Outbreak of the European War* (London, H.M. Stationery Office, 1915). 561 pp.

———. PARLIAMENT. *Parliamentary Debates: Official Report.*

———. *Parliamentary Papers.* 1902, CXXX, [Cmd. 905], "Correspondence Respecting the Treaty Signed at Washington, Nov. 18, 1901 . . ." January, 1902.

———. 1904, CX, [Cmd. 1936], "Correspondence Respecting the Russian Occupation of Manchuria and Newchwang," February, 1904. China, No. 2 (1904).

———. 1911, CIII, [Cmd. 5556], "Treaty of Commerce and Navigation Between Great Britain and Japan, Signed at London, April 3, 1911." Japan, No. 1 (1911).

———. 1911, CIII, [Cmd. 5735], "Agreement Between the United Kingdom and Japan." Signed at London, July 13, 1911. Treaty Series. 1911. No. 18.

———. 1911, CIII, [Cmd. 5805], "Treaty of Arbitration Between the United Kingdom and the United States of America." signed at Washington, August 3, 1911. United States, No. 2 (1911).

———. 1912–1913, CXXI, [Cmd. 6148], "Correspondence Respecting the Affairs of China." May, 1912. China, No. 1 (1912).

———. 1912–1913, CXII, [Cmd. 6446], "Correspondence Respecting Chinese Loan Negotiations." October, 1912. China, No. 2 (1912).

———. 1912–1913, CXXII, [Cmd. 6447], "Further Correspondence Respecting the Affairs of China." November, 1912. China, No. 3 (1912).

———. 1914, CI, [Cmd. 7054], "Further Correspondence Respecting the Affairs of China." August, 1913. China, No. 3 (1913).

———. 1914, CI, [Cmd. 7356], "Further Correspondence Respecting the Affairs of China." April, 1914. China, No. 1 (1914).

———. 1916, XV, [Cmd. 8181], "British Trade after the War." January 28, 1916.

———. 1916, XV, [Cmd. 8275], "British Trade after the War, (2)." June 14, 1916.

———. 1916, XV, [Cmd. 8346], "Report to the Board of Trade by the Committee Appointed to Investigate the Question of Financial Facilities for Trade." August 31, 1916.

———. 1916, XXXIV, [Cmd. 8271], "Recommendations of the Economic Conference of the Allies Held at Paris on June 14, 15, 16, and 17, 1916." June 21, 1916.

———. 1917–1918, X, [Cmd. 8462], "Final Report of the Royal Commission on the Natural Resources, Trade, and Legislation of Certain Portions of His Majesty's Dominions." February 21, 1917.

———. 1917–1918, XVIII, [Cmd. 8815], "Report to the Board of Trade by the Advisory Committee on Commercial Intelligence . . ." October 31, 1917.

———. 1918, XIII, [Cmd. 9032], "Committee on Commercial and Industrial Policy—Interim Report on Certain Essential Industries." March 16, 1917.

———. 1918, XIII, [Cmd. 9033], "Committee on Commercial and Industrial Policy—Interim Report on the Importation of Goods from the Present Enemy Countries after the War." November 9, 1916.

———. 1918, XIII, [Cmd. 9034], "Committee on Commercial and Industrial Policy—Interim Report on . . . the Conservation of the Resources of the Empire During the Transitional Period After the War." December 14, 1916.

———. 1918, XIII, [Cmd. 9035], "Final Report of the Committee on Commercial and Industrial Policy after the War." December 3, 1917.

———. 1921, XLII, [Cmd. 1214], "Correspondence Respecting the New Financial Consortium in China." Miscellaneous, No. 9 (1921).

———. 1921, XIV, [Cmd. 1474], "Conference of Prime Ministers and Representatives of the United Kingdom, the Dominions, and India, Held in June, July, and August, 1921 [London]. Summary of Proceedings and Documents." August, 1921.

———. 1935–1936, XXVII, [Cmd. 5137], "Memorandum on the London Naval Conference, December 9, 1935, to March 25, 1936." Miscellaneous, No. 2 (1936).

———. 1936–1937, XXVIII, [Cmd. 5561], "Treaty . . . for the Limitation of Naval Armament . . . London, March 25, 1936." Text in French and English. Treaty Series, No. 36 (1937).

RUSSIA. (U.S.S.R.). KOMISSIIA PO IZDANIIU DOKUMENTOV EPOKHI IMPERIALIZMA. *Mezhdunarodnye otnosheniia v epokhu imperializma: dokumenty iz arkhivov tsarskogo i vremennogo pravitel'stv.* 1878–1917 gg. (Predsedatel'stvom-M.N. Pokrovskogo) (17 vols. in 3 series; Moskva-Leningrad: Gosudarstennoe Sotsial'no-Ekonomicheskoe Izdatel'stvo . . . 1931–1940). Incomplete.

———. *Die Internationalen Beziehungen im Zeitalter des Imperialismus: Dokumente aus den Archiven der Zarischen und der Provisorischen Regierung, 1878–1917*, herausgegeben von der Kommission . . . unter dem Vorsitz von M. N. Pokrowski. Deutsche Ausgabe herausgegeben von Otto Hoetzsch (3 series, 10 vols. in 13; Berlin, Verlag von Reimar Hobbing, 1931–1941) Incomplete.

UNITED STATES. CONGRESS. *The Congressional Globe* (46 vols. in 109; Washington, Globe Press, 1834–1873).

———. *Congressional Record, Proceedings and Debates.*

———. *U. S. Statutes at Large.*

———. SENATE. *Journal of the Executive Proceedings of the Senate of the United States* (32 vols. in 35; Washington, 1829–1909).

———. *Journal of the Senate of the United States of America* (Vols. by sessions, Washington).

———. *Senate Executive Documents.* [Ser. 1885], 46th Cong., 2d sess., No. 112, ". . . Proposed Interoceanic Canal Between the Atlantic and Pacific Oceans." March 9, 1880.

———. [Ser. 3062], 52d Cong., 2d sess., No. 76, "Annexation Treaty with the Hawaiian Islands of February 14, 1893." February 15, 1893.

———. [Ser. 3062], 52d Cong., 2d sess., No. 77, "Correspondence Respecting Relations Between the United States and the Hawaiian Islands from September, 1820, to January, 1893." February 17, 1893.

———. [Ser. 3160], 53d Cong., 2d sess., No. 13, "The Hawaiian Question." December 20, 1893.

———. [Ser. 3160], 53d Cong., 2d sess., No. 46, ". . . Additional Dispatches, and Exhibits Thereto, Relating to Hawaii." February 20, 1894.

———. [Ser. 3163], 53d Cong., 2d sess., No. 93, ". . . Report from the Secretary of State Relative to the Samoan Islands . . ." May 9, 1894.

———. [Ser. 3280], 53d Cong., 3d sess., No. 97, ". . . Report from the Secretary of State, with Copies of Correspondence, Touching Samoan Affairs." February 26, 1895.

———. *Senate Documents.* [Ser. 2698], 51st Cong., 1st sess., No. 81, "A General Act . . . Signed at Berlin on the 14th Day of June, 1889 . . . in Regard to the . . . Samoan Islands." January 7, 1890.

———. [Ser. 3600], 55th Cong., 2d sess., No. 188, "Views of Commodore George W. Melville, Chief Engineer of the Navy, as to . . . the Strategic Value of Hawaii . . ." March 14, 1898.

———. [Ser. 3731], 55th Cong., 3d sess., No. 60, "Promotion of Commerce and Increase of Foreign Trade . . ." January 12, 1899.

———. [Ser. 3732], 55th Cong., 3d sess., No. 62, Part 2, "A Treaty of Peace Between the United States and Spain, Signed at the City of Paris on December 10, 1898." January 13, 1899.

———. [Ser. 3848], 56th Cong., 1st sess., No. 51, ". . . Report Made by Hon. Bartlett Tripp, the Member of the Samoan Commission on Behalf of the United States of America." December 20, 1899.

———. [Ser. 3853], 56th Cong., 1st sess., No. 161, "Correspondence and Other Papers Relating to the Proposed Interoceanic Canal . . ." February 8, 1900.

———. [Ser. 3853], 56th Cong., 1st sess., No. 237, "Correspondence in Relation to an Interoceanic Canal Between the Atlantic and Pacific Oceans . . ." March 21, 1900.

———. [Ser. 4039], 56th Cong., 2d sess., No. 148, "Papers Relating to the Treaty with Spain." February 27, 1901.

———. [Ser. 4047–4054], 56th Cong., 2d sess., No. 231, "Compilation of Reports of Committee on Foreign Relations, United States Senate, 1789–1901." (8 vols.; Washington, 1901).

———. [Ser. 4587], 58th Cong., 2d sess., No. 51, "Correspondence Concerning the . . . Canal Across the Isthmus of Panama." December 19, 1903.

———. [Ser. 4588], 58th Cong., 2d sess., No. 95, "Relations of the United States with Colombia and the Republic of Panama." January 18, 1904.

———. [Ser. 4589], 58th Cong., 2d sess., No. 143, "Use By the United States of a Military Force in the Internal Affairs of Colombia . . ." February 3, 1904.

———. [Ser. 4913], 59th Cong., 1st sess., No. 248, "Coast Defences of the United States and the Insular Possessions." March 5, 1906. Report of the Taft Board.

———. [Ser. 4921], 59th Cong., 1st sess., No. 142, "Compilation of the Acts of Congress and Treaties Relating to Alaska from March 30, 1867 to March 3, 1905." January 10, 1906.

———. [Ser. 5070], 59th Cong., 2d sess., No. 147, "Japanese in the City of San Francisco, California." December 18, 1906.

———. [Ser. 5073], 59th Cong., 2d sess., No. 365, "Report of the Delegates of the United States to the Third International Conference of the American States, held at Rio de Janeiro, Brazil, July 21, to August 26, 1906." March 1, 1907.

———. [Ser. 5241], 60th Cong., 1st sess., No. 225, "Development of the American Ocean Mail Service and American Commerce." February 6, 1908.

———. [Ser. 5407], 60th Cong., 2d sess., No. 542, "Correspondence in Regard to the Relations of the United States with Colombia and Panama." December 8, 1908.

———. [Ser. 5658], 61st Cong., 2d sess., No. 425, "American Merchant Marine." March 14, 1910.

———. [Ser. 6177], 62d Cong., 2d sess., No. 640, "Land at Magdalena Bay." May 1, 1912.

———. [Ser. 6177], 62d Cong., 2d sess., No. 694, "Lands on Magdalena Bay." May 23, 1912.

———. [Ser. 6536], 63d Cong., 1st sess., No. 193, "World Peace Under American Leadership," a sermon by T. M. C. Birmingham, of Beatrice, Nebraska. July 23, 1913.

———. [Ser. 6582], 63d Cong., 2d sess., No. 474, "Diplomatic History of the Panama Canal." April 29, 1914.

———. [Ser. 6593], 63d Cong., 2d sess., No. 440, "Addresses before the Southern Commercial Congress . . . October 27–29, 1913." At Mobile, Alabama

———. [Ser. 6593], 63d Cong., 2d sess., No. 449, "The Relation of the Federal Government to Industrial Combinations." March 16, 1914.

———. [Ser. 6593], 63d Cong., 2d sess., No. 451, "Regulation and Restriction of Immigration." March 19, 1914.

———. [Ser. 6783], 63d Cong., 3d sess., No. 673, Part 1, "Increased Ocean Transportation Rates." December 29, 1914.

———. [Ser. 6783], 63d Cong., 3d sess., No. 713, "The Shipping Bill." January 11, 1915.

———. [Ser. 6783], 63d Cong., 3d sess., No. 714, "Report of the Latin-American Trade Committee." January 19, 1915.

———. [Ser. 6783], 63d Cong., 3d sess., No. 715, "Merchant Marine." January 22, 1915.

———. [Ser. 6951], 64th Cong., 1st sess., No. 4, "A Naval Auxiliary Merchant Marine." December 7, 1915.

———. [Ser. 6951], 64th Cong., 1st sess., No. 10, "What Congress Has Done to Build Up an American Mercantile Marine." December 10, 1915.

———. [Ser. 6951], 64th Cong., 1st sess., No. 26, "Experimental Tests of Matanuska Coal for Naval Ships." December 17, 1915.

———. [Ser. 6951], 64th Cong., 1st sess., No. 228, "Modification of the Seamen's Act." December 13, 1915.

———. [Ser. 6951], 64th Cong., 1st sess., No. 231, "Naval Policy with Present Requirements." January 5, 1916.

———. [Ser. 6951], 64th Cong., 1st sess., No. 242, "The Government of the Philippine Islands." January 12, 1916.

———. [Ser. 6951], 64th Cong., 1st sess., No. 251, "The Atlantic Fleet in 1915." January 25, 1916.

———. [Ser. 6951], 64th Cong., 1st sess., No. 263, "National Defense." January 28, 1916.

———. [Ser. 6951], 64th Cong., 1st sess., No. 311, "Preparedness for National Defense." February 7, 1916.

———. [Ser. 6951], 64th Cong., 1st sess., No. 323, "Preparations for Peace." February 14, 1916.

———. [Ser. 6952], 64th Cong., 1st sess., No. 342, "Occupation of Korea." February 23, 1916.

———. [Ser. 6952], 64th Cong., 1st sess., No. 344. "The Industrial and Strategical Importance of Our Naval Stations." By Rear Admiral John R. Edwards, U.S.N. (Ret.). March 18, 1916.

———. [Ser. 6952], 64th Cong., 1st sess., No. 387, "Naval Strength on the Pacific Coast." April 4, 1916.

———. [Ser. 6952], 64th Cong., 1st sess., No. 413, ". . . Communication from Rear Admiral Bradley A. Fiske, Relative to Bringing the Navy to a State of Preparedness . . ." April 21, 1916.

———. [Ser. 6952], 64th Cong., 1st sess., No. 426, "Coöperation in American Export Trade." May 3, 1916.

———. [Ser. 6952], 64th Cong., 1st sess., No. 430, "Government Control of Minerals on the Public Lands." January 26, 1916.

———. [Ser. 6952], 64th Cong., 1st sess., No. 432, "Labor Conditions in Hawaii." April 17, 1916.

———. [Ser. 6953], 64th Cong., 1st sess., No. 459, "Coöperation and Efficiency in Developing Our Foreign Trade." June 3, 1916.

———. [Ser. 6953], 64th Cong., 1st sess., No. 460, "Responding to the New Call of Duty." June 3, 1916.

———. [Ser. 6953], 64th Cong., 1st sess., No. 477, "Business Activity in the United States and in Leading Foreign Countries." June 29, 1916.

———. [Ser. 6953], 64th Cong., 1st sess., No. 490, "Trade Agreements Abroad." July 8, 1916. Text of Allied Agreement.

———. [Ser. 6953], 64th Cong., 1st sess., No. 491, "Trade Agreements Abroad." July 10, 1916.

———. [Ser. 6953], 64th Cong., 1st sess., No. 528, "Naval Appropriation Bill." August 11, 1916. Conference Report.

———. [Ser. 6953], 64th Cong., 1st sess., No. 543, "Speech of Notification [Sen. Ollie M. James, Kentucky] and Speech of Acceptance [President Woodrow Wilson]." September 2, 1916.

———. [Ser. 7121], 64th Cong., 2d sess., No. 741, "Annual Report of the Alaskan Engineering Commission. March 2, 1917.

———. [Ser. 7126], 64th Cong., 2d sess., No. 698, "Importance of Our South American Trade." December 21, 1916.

———. [Ser. 7126], 64th Cong., 2d sess., No. 712, "Limitation on Size of Battleships." February 16, 1917.

———. [Ser. 7264], 65th Cong., 1st sess., No. 41, "Merchant Vessel Construction in American Shipyards." June 2, 1917.

———. [Ser. 7329], 65th Cong., 2d sess., No. 210, "The Shipping Situation." March 28, 1918.

———. [Ser. 7329], 65th Cong., 2d sess., No. 218, "International Parliamentary Conference on Commerce." April 22, 1918.

———. [Ser. 7329], 65th Cong., 2d sess., No. 228, "American Sea Power and the Seamen's Act." April 16, 1918.

———. [Ser. 7330], 65th Cong., 2d sess., No. 268, "Development of the Naval Strength." July 13, 1918.

———. [Ser. 7469], 65th Cong., 3d sess., No. 335, "The Problem of British Shipping." January 13, 1919.

———. [Ser. 7605], 66th Cong., 1st sess., No. 106, "Hearings before the Committee on Foreign Relations United States Senate . . . on the Treaty of Peace with Germany . . ." [1919].

———. [Ser. 7606], 66th Cong., 1st sess., No. 120, "Addresses Delivered by President Wilson on his Western Tour, September 4 to September 25, 1919." October 7, 1919.

———. [Ser. 7608], 66th Cong., 1st sess., No. 41, "League of Nations—Letters of the Hon. Elihu Root . . ." June 23, 1919.

———. [Ser. 7608], 66th Cong., 1st sess., No. 76, "Treaty of Peace with Germany." August 20, 1919.

———. [Ser. 7609], 66th Cong., 1st sess., No. 60, "American Troops in Siberia." July 25, 1919.

———. [Ser. 9801], 73d Cong., 2d sess., No. 161, "Direct Aid to American Vessels in Foreign Trade." March 22, 1934.

———. [Ser. 10009], 74th Cong., 2d sess., No. 232, "The Constitution of the United States of America (Annotated)." (Washington, 1938).

———. [Ser. 10097], 75th Cong., 1st sess., No. 35, "The United States Navy: Information Relative to Organization, Personnel, Fleet, and Shore Establishments of the United States Navy." March 11, 1937.

———. *Senate Reports.* APPROPRIATIONS, COMMITTEE ON. [Ser. 6899], 64th Cong., 1st sess., No. 538, "Fortifications Appropriations." June 26, 1916.

———. [Ser. 9879], 74th Cong., 1st sess., 1935, No. 598, "Navy Department and Naval Service Appropriation Bill, Fiscal Year, 1936." May 9, 1935.

———. COMMERCE, COMMITTEE ON. [Ser. 4755], 58th Cong., 3d sess., No. 2949, "Development of the American Merchant Marine and American Commerce." January 12, 1905.

———. [Ser. 4904], 59th Cong., 1st sess., No. 10, "Development of the American Merchant Marine and American Commerce." December 15, 1905.

———. [Ser. 4904], 59th Cong., 1st sess., No. 10, Part 2, "Development of the American Merchant Marine and American Commerce—Views of the Minority." January 9, 1906.

———. [Ser. 5218], 60th Cong., 1st sess., No. 168, "Ocean Mail Service Between United States and Foreign Ports." February 3, 1908.

———. [Ser. 6762], 63d Cong., 3d sess., No. 841, "Promotion of Foreign Commerce of the United States by Providing Adequate Shipping Facilities." December 16, 1914.

———. [Ser. 6762], 63d Cong., 3d sess., No. 841, Part 2, "Promotion of Foreign Commerce of the United States by Providing Adequate Shipping Facilities." January 4, 1915.

———. [Ser. 6899], 64th Cong., 1st sess., No. 689, "Creating a Shipping Board, a Naval Auxiliary, a Merchant Marine . . ." July 19, 1916.

———. [Ser. 7249], 65th Cong., 1st sess., No. 23, "To Authorize the President in Time of War to Give Direction to Exports from the United States . . ." April 19, 1917.

———. [Ser. 7304], 65th Cong., 2d sess., No. 535, "Authority to the President to Prescribe Charter Rates and Freight Rates and to Requisition Vessels . . ." July 1, 1918.

———. [Ser. 7304], 65th Cong., 2d sess., No. 536, "Increasing the Powers of the United States Shipping Board." July 1, 1918.

———. [Ser. 9988], 74th Cong., 2d sess., No. 1807, "Preliminary Examination of Matanuska River, Alaska." April 9, 1936.

———. FOREIGN RELATIONS, COMMITTEE ON. [Ser. 2173], 48th Cong., 1st sess., No. 76, "Termination of the Reciprocity Convention of June 3, 1875, with Hawaii." January 24, 1884.

———. [Ser. 3180], 53d Cong., 2d sess., No. 277, "Investigation of Irregularities in the Diplomatic or Other Intercourse Between the United States and Hawaii . . ." February 26, 1894.

———. [Ser. 3622], 55th Cong., 2d sess., No. 681, "Annexation of Hawaii." March 16, 1898.

———. [Ser. 6552], 63d Cong., 2d sess., No. 437, "Enforcement of Certain Demands Against Victoriano Huerta." April 21, 1914.

———. INDIAN AFFAIRS, COMMITTEE ON. [Ser. 7249], 65th Cong., 1st sess., No. 166, "Metalliferous Minerals on Indian Reservations." October 5, 1917.

———. INTEROCEANIC CANALS, COMMITTEE ON. [Ser. 3895], 56th Cong., 1st sess., No. 1649, "Clayton-Bulwer Treaty." June 4, 1900.

———. [Ser. 6553], 63d Cong., 2d sess., No. 719, "Admission of Foreign-Built Ships to American Registry." August 4, 1914.

———. INTERSTATE COMMERCE, COMMITTEE ON. [Ser. 7106], 64th Cong., 2d sess., No. 1056, "Export Trade." February 15, 1917.

———. [Ser. 7249], 65th Cong., 1st sess., No. 9, "Export Trade." April 16, 1917.

———. [Ser. 7249], 65th Cong., 1st sess., No. 109, "Export Trade." August 20, 1917.

———. MERCHANT MARINE, JOINT COMMISSION ON THE. [Ser. 4757, 4758, 4759], 58th Cong., 3d sess., No. 2755, "Development of the American Merchant Marine and American Commerce." January 4, 1905.

———. [Ser. 4904], 59th Cong., 1st sess., No. 1, "Development of the American Merchant Marine and American Commerce." December 6, 1905.

———. MUNITIONS INDUSTRY, SPECIAL COMMITTEE ON INVESTIGATION OF THE. [Ser. 9881], 74th Cong., 1st sess., No. 944, "Munitions Industry, Naval Shipbuilding." June 24, 1935.

———. NAVAL AFFAIRS, COMMITTEE ON. [Ser. 6552], 63d Cong., 2d sess., No. 163, "Dry Docks at Hunter's Point, San Francisco, California." January 21, 1914.

———. [Ser. 6553], 63d Cong., 2d sess., No. 505, "Naval Appropriation Bill." May 12, 1914.

———. [Ser. 6553], 63d Cong., 2d sess., No. 718, "United States Navy Mail Lines Between United States and South America." August 3, 1914.

———. [Ser. 6762], 63d Cong., 3d sess., No. 1021, "Naval Appropriation Bill." February 22, 1915.

———. [Ser. 6897], 64th Cong., 1st sess., No. 216, "Puget Sound Navy Yard." March 3, 1916.

———. [Ser. 6899], 64th Cong., 1st sess., No. 575, "Naval Appropriation Bill." June 30, 1916.

———. [Ser. 7106], 64th Cong., 2d sess., No. 1101, "Naval Appropriation Bill." February 21, 1917.

———. [Ser. 7249], 65th Cong., 1st sess., No. 19, "Requisition of Ships, . . ." April 18, 1917.

———. [Ser. 7304], 65th Cong., 2d sess., No. 448, "Naval Appropriation Bill for the Year Ending June 30, 1919." May 21, 1918.

———. [Ser. 7452], 65th Cong., 3d sess., No. 777, "Naval Appropriation Bill." February 27, 1919.

———. [Ser. 7590], 66th Cong., 1st sess., No. 32, "Naval Appropriation Bill." June 23, 1919.

———. [Ser. 9878], 71st Cong., 1st sess., No. 425, "To Regulate the Strength and Distribution of the Line of the Navy . . ." April 5, 1935.

———. PHILIPPINES, COMMITTEE ON THE. [Ser. 6762], 63d Cong., 3d sess., No. 942, "Future Political Status of the People of the Philippine Islands." February 2, 1915.

———. [Ser. 6897], 64th Cong., 1st sess., No. 18, "Future Political Status of the Philippine Islands." December 17, 1915.

———. PUBLIC LANDS, COMMITTEE ON. [Ser. 6553], 63d Cong., 2d sess., No. 790, "Leasing of Coal Lands in Alaska." September 16, 1914.

———. TERRITORIES, COMMITTEE ON. [Ser. 6510], 63d Cong., 1st sess., No. 65, "Construction of Railroads in Alaska." June 17, 1913.

———. HOUSE OF REPRESENTATIVES. *Journal of the House of Representatives of the United States* (Washington). Vols. by sessions.

———. *House Executive Documents.* [Ser. 893], 34th Cong., 3d sess., No. 1, "Message from the President of the United States to the Two Houses of Congress . . . [With Accompanying Documents]." December, 1856.

———. [Ser. 1339], 40th Cong., 2d sess., No. 177, "Correspondence in Relation to Russian America." February 19, 1868.

———. [Ser. 1691], 44th Cong., 1st sess., No. 161, "A. B. Steinberger." May 2, 1876.

———. [Ser. 2560], 50th Cong., 1st sess., No. 238, "American Rights in Samoa." April 2, 1888.

———. [Ser. 3224], 53d Cong., 2d sess., No. 47, "President's Message Relating to the Hawaiian Islands." December 18, 1893.

———. [Ser. 3224], 53d Cong., 2d sess., No. 48, ". . . Instructions Given to Mr. Albert S. Willis, the Representative of the United States Now in the Hawaiian Islands . . ." December 18, 1893.

———. [Ser. 3224], 53d Cong., 2d sess., No. 140, "United States Naval Force in Hawaiian Islands." March 10, 1894.

———. [Ser. 3224], 53d Cong., 2d sess., No. 256, "Dispatches from the United States Minister at Honolulu." July 31, 1894.

———. *House Documents.* [Ser. 4565], 58th Cong., 1st sess., No. 8, "Correspondence . . . Relating to the Recent Revolution on the Isthmus of Panama." November 16, 1903.

———. [Ser. 4565], 58th Cong., 1st sess., No. 8, Part 2, "Revolution on the Isthmus of Panama." [Additional Correspondence.] November 27, 1903.

———. [Ser. 4984], 59th Cong., 1st sess., No. 56, "Development of the American Merchant Marine." December 6, 1905.

———. [Ser. 4988], 59th Cong., 1st sess., No. 564, "Development of the American Merchant Marine and American Commerce." February 24, 1906.

———. [Ser. 4990], 59th Cong., 1st sess., No. 876, "Discriminating Tonnage Taxes . . ." June 6, 1906.

———. [Ser. 4990], 59th Cong., 1st sess., No. 895, "Views of the Minority. . ." [On Tonnage Taxes]. June 16, 1906.

———. [Ser. 5835], 61st Cong., 2d sess., No. 490, ". . . Estimate of Appropriation for Naval Station, Pearl Harbor, Hawaii." January 7, 1910.

———. [Ser. 6323], 62d Cong., 2d sess., No. 735, "Immigration of Aliens into Hawaii." May 6, 1912.

———. [Ser. 6323], 62d Cong., 2d sess., No. 758, "Speech of Hon. Wm. C. Redfield on 'The Progress of Japanese Industry'." May 15, 1912.

———. [Ser. 6323], 62d Cong., 2d sess., No. 875, "Cost of Occupation of the Philippine Islands." July 19, 1912.

———. [Ser. 6323], 62d Cong., 2d sess., No. 914, "Panama Canal . . . Joint Resolution Relative to the Hay-Pauncefote Treaty." August 19, 1912.

———. [Ser. 6484], 62d Cong., 3d sess., No. 1346, "Railway Routes in Alaska . . ." February 6, 1913.

———. [Ser. 6600], 63d Cong., 2d sess., No. 398, " . . . Estimates of Appropriations . . . Fiscal Year Ending June 30, 1915." December 1, 1913.

———. [Ser. 6751], 63d Cong., 2d sess., No. 805, "Report . . . on Steamship Agreements and Affiliations in the American Foreign and Domestic Trade . . ." Prepared by S. S. Huebner (Washington, 1914).

———. [Ser. 6755], 63d Cong., 2d sess., No. 876, "Report on Coal in Alaska for Use in United States Navy." April 3, 1914.

———. [Ser. 6888], 63d Cong., 3d sess., No. 1492, "Answers to Questions Propounded in House Resolution No. 698." January 16, 1915.

———. [Ser. 7098], 64th Cong., 1st sess., No. 389, "Report on Building of Four Warships, Based on War in Europe." December 14, 1915.

———. [Ser. 7098], 64th Cong., 1st sess., No. 803, "Addresses of President Wilson, January 27–February 3, 1916 [On National Defense]." February 3, 1916.

———. [Ser. 7101], 64th Cong., 1st sess., No. 424, "Deficiency Appropriation for Alaskan Railroad." December 17, 1915.

———. [Ser. 7102], 64th Cong., 1st sess., No. 813, ". . . Fortifications in Insular Possessions." March 1, 1916.

———. [Ser. 7158], 64th Cong., 2d sess., No. 1946, "Report of the Navy Yard Commission." [Helm Board.]

———. [Ser. 7239], 64th Cong., 2d sess., No. 2111, "The Problems of Neutrality When the World Is at War . . ." by Simeon D. Fess. March 3, 1917 (Washington, 1917).

———. [Ser. 7240], 64th Cong., 2d sess., No. 1485, "Annual Report of the Federal Trade Commission . . . 1916." (Washington, 1916.)

———. [Ser. 7240], 64th Cong., 2d sess., No. 1788, "International High Commission." December 20, 1916.

———. [Ser. 7240], 64th Cong., 2d sess., No. 2112, "Ocean Shipping . . ." (2d ed., rev., Washington). March, 1917.

———. [Ser. 7300], 65th Cong., 1st sess., No. 119, "International Parliamentary Conference on Commerce at Rome." May 5, 1917.

———. [Ser. 7300], 65th Cong., 1st sess., No. 265, "Estimate of Appropriation—Railroads in Alaska." July 14, 1917.

———. [Ser. 7300], 65th Cong., 1st sess., No. 326, "Invitation to the Congress to Take Part in Interallied Parliament." August 7, 1917.

———. [Ser. 7443], 65th Cong., 2d sess., No. 394, "First Annual Report of the Shipping Board." January 30–October 31, 1917.

———. [Ser. 7443], 65th Cong., 2d sess, No. 587, "Report of the Board of Ordnance and Fortification . . . 1917." December 6, 1917.

———. [Ser. 10031], 74th Cong., 2d sess., No. 400, "Compilation of Documents Relating to the Inauguration of the Government of the Commonwealth of the Philippines." January 27, 1936.

———. *House Reports*, AGRICULTURE, COMMITTEE ON. [Ser. 6905], 64th Cong., 1st sess., No. 772, "Mineral Resources of Certain National Forests." May 26, 1916.

———. APPROPRIATIONS, COMMITTEE ON. [Ser. 6766], 63d Cong., 3d sess., No. 1416, "Fortifications Appropriation Bill." February 18, 1915.

———. [Ser. 6904], 64th Cong., 1st sess., No. 498, "Fortifications Appropriation Bill." April 6, 1916.

———. [Ser. 9887], 74th Cong., 1st sess., No. 746, "Navy Department and Naval Service Appropriation Bill." April 23, 1935.

———. BANKING AND CURRENCY, COMMITTEE ON. [Ser. 6904], 64th Cong., 1st sess., No. 447, "Federal Reserve Act." March 28, 1916.

———. CONFERENCE, COMMITTEE OF. [Ser. 6558], 63d Cong., 2d sess., No. 341, "Construction of Railroads in Alaska." March 5, 1914.

———. [Ser. 6560], 63d Cong., 2d sess., No. 1178, "Leasing of Coal Lands in Alaska." October 6, 1914.

———. [Ser. 6766], 63d Cong., 3d sess., No. 1500, "Naval Appropriation Bill—Conference Report." March 3, 1915.

———. [Ser. 6905], 64th Cong., 1st sess., No. 1155, "Naval Appropriation Bill." August 18, 1916.

———. [Ser. 7110], 64th Cong., 2d sess., No. 1633, "Naval Appropriation Bill." March 3, 1917.

———. [Ser. 7307], 65th Cong., 2d sess., No. 468, "To Promote Export Trade." April 5, 1918.

———. [Ser. 7308], 65th Cong., 2d sess., No. 663, "Naval Appropriation Bill." June 15, 1918.

———. [Ser. 9888], 74th Cong., 1st sess., No. 1262, "Navy Department Appropriation Bill, 1936." June 19, 1935.

———. FOREIGN AFFAIRS, COMMITTEE ON. [Ser. 3269], 53d Cong., 2d sess., No. 243, "Intervention of United States Government in Affairs of Foreign Friendly Governments." December 21, 1893.

———. [Ser. 3721], 55th Cong., 2d sess., No. 1355, "Annexation of Hawaii." May 17, 1898.

———. [Ser. 6559], 63d Cong., 2d sess., No. 560, "Enforcing Certain Demands Made Upon Victoriano Huerta, of Mexico." April 20, 1914.

———. INDIAN AFFAIRS, COMMITTEE ON. [Ser. 6904], 64th Cong., 1st sess., No. 533, "Metalliferous Minerals on Indian Reservations." April 12, 1916.

———. [Ser. 7308], 65th Cong., 2d sess., No. 730, "Metalliferous Minerals on Indian Reservations." July 1, 1918.

———. INSULAR AFFAIRS, COMMITTEE ON. [Ser. 6131], 62d Cong., 2d sess., No. 606, "Independent Government for the Philippines." April 26, 1912.

———. [Ser. 6560], 63d Cong., 2d sess., No. 1115, "Political Status of the People of the Philippine Islands." August 26, 1914.

———. [Ser. 6560], 63d Cong., 2d sess., No. 1115, Part 2, "Government of the Philippines—Views of the Minority." August 31, 1914.

———. [Ser. 6904], 64th Cong., 1st sess., No. 499, "Political Status of the Philippine Islands." April 6, 1916.

———. [Ser. 6904], 64th Cong., 1st sess., No. 499, Part 2, Political Status of the Philippine Islands." Views of the Minority. April 12, 1916.

———. INTERSTATE AND FOREIGN COMMERCE, COMMITTEE ON. [Ser. 7252], 65th Cong., 1st sess., No. 32, "Economical Distribution of Exports from the United States in Time of War." April 27, 1917.

———. JUDICIARY, COMMITTEE ON THE. [Ser. 6905], 64th Cong., 1st sess., No. 1118, "Promotion of Export Trade . . ." August 15, 1916.

———. [Ser. 7252], 65th Cong., 1st sess., No. 50, "Promotion of Export Trade." May 11, 1917.

———. [Ser. 7308], 65th Cong., 2d sess., No. 777, "Authorizing the President to Prohibit Exports to the Philippine Islands." September 12, 1918.

———. MERCHANT MARINE AND FISHERIES, COMMITTEE ON THE. [Ser. 5591], 61st Cong., 2d sess., No. 502, "American Merchant Marine in Foreign Trade and the National Defense." February 21, 1910.

———. [Ser. 6560], 63d Cong., 2d sess., No. 1149, "Government Ownership and Operation of Merchant Vessels in the Foreign Trade of the United States." September 8, 1914.

———. [Ser. 6560], 63d Cong., 2d sess., No. 1149, Part 2, "Government Ownership and Operation of Merchant Vessels in the Foreign Trade of the United States." "Minority Views." September 15, 1914.

———. [Ser. 6904], 64th Cong., 1st sess., No. 659, "Creating a Shipping Board, a Naval Auxiliary, a Merchant Marine . . ." May 9, 1916.

———. [Ser. 7252], 65th Cong., 1st sess., No. 162, "Admitting Foreign Shipping to the Coastwise Trade." September 24, 1917.

———. [Ser. 7308], 65th Cong., 2d sess., No. 568, "Increasing the Powers of the United States Shipping Board." May 15, 1918.

———. [Ser. 7308], 65th Cong., 2d sess., No. 569, "Empowering President to Regulate Ocean Freight Rates and to Requisition Vessels." May 15, 1918.

———. NAVAL AFFAIRS, COMMITTEE ON. [Ser. 5226], 60th Cong., 1st sess., No. 1385, "Establishment of a Naval Base at Pearl Harbor, in the Hawaiian Islands." April 4, 1908.

———. [Ser. 5226], 60th Cong., 1st sess., No. 1398, "Naval Appropriation Bill . . . 1909." April 8, 1908. Part 2, April 8, 1908. "Views of the Minority."

———. [Ser. 6131], 62d Cong., 2d sess., No. 584, "Council of National Defense." April 22, 1912.

———. [Ser. 6558], 63d Cong., 2d sess., No. 314, "Naval Appropriation Bill, 1915." February 28, 1914. Includes Minority Views.

———. [Ser. 6766], 63d Cong., 3d sess., No. 1287, "Naval Appropriation Bill . . . 1916." January 16, 1915.

———. [Ser. 6766], 63d Cong., 3d sess., No. 1344, "Creation of the Office of Chief of Naval Operations." February 2, 1915.

———. [Ser. 6766], 63d Cong., 3d sess., No. 1423, "National Advisory Committee for Aeronautics." February 19, 1915.

———. [Ser. 6905], 64th Cong., 1st sess., No. 743, "Naval Appropriation Bill." May 24, 1916.

———. [Ser. 6905], 64th Cong., 1st sess., No. 743, Part 2, "Naval Appropriation Bill—Views of the Minority." May 25, 1916.

———. [Ser. 6905], 64th Cong., 1st sess., No. 1049, "Naval Appropriation Bill with Senate Amendments." July 27, 1916.

———. [Ser. 7110], 64th Cong., 2d sess., No. 1392, "Naval Appropriation Bill." January 30, 1917.

———. [Ser. 7307], 65th Cong., 2d sess., No. 393, "Naval Appropriation Bill . . . 1919." March 19, 1918.

———. [Ser. 7454], 65th Cong., 3d sess., No. 1024, "Naval Appropriation Bill, 1920." February 1, 1919.

———. [Ser. 7592], 66th Cong., 1st sess., No. 35, "Naval Appropriation Bill." June 12, 1919.

———. [Ser. 9775], 73d Cong., 2d sess., No. 338, "To Establish the Composition of the United States Navy." January 24, 1934.

———. [Ser. 9886], 74th Cong., 1st sess., No. 211, "To Regulate the Strength and Distribution of the Line of the Navy . . ." February 22, 1935.

———. [Ser. 10233], 75th Cong., 3d sess., No. 1899, "To Establish the Composition of the United States Navy, to Authorize the Construction of Certain Naval Vessels, and for Other Purposes." March 4, 1938.

———. [Ser. 10233], 75th Cong., 3d sess., No. 1899, Part 2, "To Establish the Composition of the United States Navy, to Authorize the Construction of Certain Naval Vessels, and for Other Purposes." March 7, 1938.

———. POST OFFICE AND POST ROADS, COMMITTEE ON THE. [Ser. 5384], 60th Cong., 2d sess., No. 2261, "Ocean Mail Service Between United States and Foreign Ports." February 23, 1909.

———. PUBLIC LANDS, COMMITTEE ON THE. [Ser. 6558], 63d Cong., 2d sess., No. 352, "Leasing of Coal Lands in Alaska." March 9, 1914.

———. TERRITORIES, COMMITTEE ON THE. [Ser. 6513], 63d Cong., 1st sess., No. 92, "Construction of Railroads in Alaska." November 26, 1913.

———. [Ser. 6558], 63d Cong., 2d sess., No. 204, "Construction of Railroads in Alaska." January 31, 1914.

UNITED STATES. AGRICULTURE, DEPARTMENT OF. *Yearbook of the United States Department of Agriculture.* (Washington.)

———. SECTION OF FOREIGN MARKETS, Bulletin No. 14, *Trade of the Philippine Islands,* by Frank H. Hitchcock (Washington, 1898). 160 pp.

———. Bulletin No. 18, *Our Trade with Japan, China, and Hongkong, 1889–1899,* by Frank H. Hitchcock (Washington, 1900). 168 pp.

———. Bulletin No. 23, *Our Foreign Trade in Agricultural Products, 1891–1900,* by Frank H. Hitchcock (Washington, 1900). 61 pp.

———. COMMERCE AND LABOR, DEPARTMENT OF. *Reports of the Department of Commerce and Labor* (Washington, Government Printing Office, 1904–1912). Annual.

———. COMMERCE, DEPARTMENT OF. *Reports of the Department of Commerce* (Washington, Government Printing Office, 1913–). Annual.

———. BUREAU OF FOREIGN AND DOMESTIC COMMERCE. *Foreign Commerce and Navigation of the United States* (Washington, Government Printing Office, 1911–). Annual.

———. *Monthly Summary of the Foreign Commerce of the United States* (Washington, 1912–). Seminannual.

———. *Statistical Abstract of the United States* (Washington, Government Printing Office). Annual.

———. MISCELLANEOUS SERIES. No. 11, *American Manufactures in Foreign Markets* (Washington, 1913). 177 pp.

———. No. 14, *Annual Review of the Foreign Commerce of the United States, 1913*, by O. P. Austin (Washington, 1914). 37 pp.

———. No. 18, *Statements on the Latin-American Trade Situation* (Washington, 1914). 39 pp.

———. No. 35, *Export Trade Suggestions* (Washington, 1916). 141 pp.

———. No. 44, *Trans-Pacific Shipping*, by Julean Arnold and M. D. Kirjassoff (Washington, 1916). 30 pp.

———. SPECIAL AGENTS SERIES. No. 67, *Commerce and Industries of Alaska, Hawaii, Porto Rico, and the Philippine Islands*, by A. G. Robinson (Washington, 1913). 116 pp.

———. No. 86, *Cotton Goods in Japan and Their Competition on the Manchurian Market*, by W. A. Graham Clark (Washington, 1914). 282 pp.

———. No. 107, *Cotton Goods in China*, by Ralph M. Odell (Washington, 1916). 242 pp.

———. No. 119, *Government Aid to Merchant Shipping*, by Grosvenor M. Jones (rev. ed., Washington, 1925). 470 pp.

———. No. 156, *Railway Materials, Equipment and Supplies in Australia and New Zealand*, by Frank Rhea (Washington, 1918). 164 pp.

———. No. 158, *Textile Markets of Bolivia, Ecuador, and Peru*, by W. A. Tucker (Washington, 1918). 106 pp.

———. No. 160, *Construction Materials and Machinery in Colombia*, by W. W. Ewing (Washington, 1918). 75 pp.

———. No. 164, *Textile Market of Chile*, by W. A. Tucker (Washington, 1918). 52 pp.

———. No. 166, *Agricultural Implements and Machinery in Australia and New Zealand*, by Juan Homs (Washington, 1918). 195 pp.

———. No. 169, *Investments in Latin America and the British West Indies*, by Frederic M. Halsey (Washington, 1918). 544 pp.

———. No. 170, *Motor Vehicles in Japan, China and Hawaii*, by Tom O. Jones (Washington, 1918). 75 pp.

———. No. 172, *Electrical Goods in China, Japan, and Vladivostok*, by R. A. Lundquist (Washington, 1918). September 21, 1918. 197 pp.

———. No. 173, *Shoe and Leather Trade, China and Japan*, by C. E. Bosworth (Washington, 1918). 37 pp.

———. No. 175, *Construction Materials and Machinery in Chile, Peru, and Ecuador* (Washington, 1919). 205 pp.

———. No. 180, *Far Eastern Markets for Railway Materials, Equipment, and Supplies*, by Frank Rhea (Washington, 1919). 339 pp.

———. No. 193, *British Industrial Reconstruction and Commercial Policies*, by Fred W. Powell (Washington, 1920). 88 pp.

———. No. 215, *Asiatic Markets for Industrial Machinery*, by Walter H. Rastall (Washington, 1922). 332 pp.

———. No. 218, *Netherlands East Indies and British Malaya: A Commercial and Industrial Handbook,* by John Q. Fowler (Washington, 1923). 411 pp.
———. TRADE INFORMATION BULLETIN. No. 385, *Foreign Combinations to Control Prices of Raw Materials,* statements by Herbert Hoover, Secretary, and other officers of Department of Commerce (Washington, Government Printing Office, 1926). 34 pp.
———. No. 603, *British Colonial Office Reports on the Rubber Situation,* comp. E. G. Holt (Washington, Government Printing Office, 1929). 35 pp.
———. No. 612, *The Production of Iron and Steel in Japan,* by J. H. Ehlers (Washington, Government Printing Office, 1929). 46 pp.
———. No. 644, *British Trade in Rubber and Rubber Products,* by Robert B. Macatee, American Consul, London (Washington, 1929). 15 pp.
———. TRADE PROMOTION SERIES. No. 38, *China: A Commercial and Industrial Handbook,* by Julean Arnold and others (Washington, Government Printing Office, 1926). 818 pp.
———. No. 129, *Shipping and Shipbuilding Subsidies,* by Jesse E. Saugstad (Washington, Government Printing Office, 1932). 611 pp.
———. No. 181, *Rubber Statistics, 1900–1937, Production, Absorption, Stocks, and Prices,* by P. W. Barker (Washington, Government Printing Office, 1938). 55 pp.
———. No. 197, *Rubber Industry of the United States, 1839–1939,* by P. W. Barker (Washington, Government Printing Office, 1939). 42 pp.
———. FEDERAL TRADE COMMISSION. *Report on Coöperation in American Export Trade* (2 vols.; Washington, 1916).
———. INTERIOR, DEPARTMENT OF THE. *Reports of the Department of the Interior . . .* (2 vols. in 4; Washington, 1908). Annual.
———. BUREAU OF MINES. *Mineral Raw Materials, Survey of Commerce and Sources in Major Industrial Countries* (New York, McGraw-Hill, 1937). 342 pp.
———. GEOLOGICAL SURVEY. *Mineral Resources of the United States* (Washington). Annual.
———. Bulletin 666, *Our Mineral Supplies,* by H. D. McCaskey and E. F. Burchard (Washington, Government Printing Office, 1919). 278 pp.
———. LABOR, DEPARTMENT OF. *Reports of the Department of Labor* (Washington). Annual.
———. NAVY, DEPARTMENT OF. *Annual Reports of the Navy Department* (Washington).
———. *Official Records of the Union and Confederate Navies in the War of the Rebellion* (Series I, 27 vols.; Series II, 3 vols.; Washington, Government Printing Office, 1894–1922).
———. HYDROGRAPHIC OFFICE. H. O. No. 117, *Table of Distances between Ports via the Shortest Navigable Routes* (Washington, Government Printing Office, 1936). 424 pp.
———. PRESIDENT. *A Compilation of the Messages and Papers of the Presidents, 1789–1917,* ed. James D. Richardson (20 vols.; New York, Bureau of National Literature, 1917).
———. *Executive Orders of the President of the United States.*

———. State, Department of. *A Digest of International Law As Embodied . . . Especially in Documents . . . Issued by Presidents and Secretaries of State of the United States,* by John Bassett Moore (8 vols.; Washington, 1906).

———. *List of Treaties Submitted to the Senate, 1789–1931, Which Have Not Gone Into Force* (Washington, Government Printing Office, 1932). 25 pp.

———. *Memorandum on the Monroe Doctrine,* prepared by J. Reuben Clark (Washington, Government Printing Office, 1930). December 17, 1928. 238 pp.

———. *Papers Relating to Foreign Affairs Accompanying the Annual Message of the President* (Washington, 1862–1869). For the years 1861–1868. Sometimes cited as *Diplomatic Correspondence of the United States.*

———. *Papers Relating to the Foreign Relations of the United States* (Washington). Annual with supplements for 1915, 1916, 1917, 1918.

———. *Papers Relating to the Foreign Relations of the United States,* "The Lansing Papers, 1914–1920" (2 vols.; Washington, Government Printing Office, 1939).

———. *The Policy of the United States toward Maritime Commerce in War,* prepared by Carlton Savage (2 vols.; Washington, Government Printing Office, 1934–1936).

———. *Treaties, Conventions, International Acts, Protocols, and Agreements between the United States of America and other Powers, 1776–1909,* comp. William M. Malloy (4 vols.; Washington, Government Printing Office, 1910–1938).

———. Treasury, Department of. *Proceedings of the First Pan American Financial Conference . . . May 24 to 29, 1915* (Washington, 1915). 744 pp.

———. Bureau of Statistics. *The Foreign Commerce and Navigation of the United States* (Washington). Annual to 1910.

———. *Monthly Summary of Commerce and Finance of the United States* (Washington). Annual to 1912.

———. War, Department of. *Annual Reports of the War Department for the Fiscal Year 1915* (Washington). Formerly entitled *Annual Reports of the Secretary of War.*

Unofficial Printed Sources

Carnegie Endowment for International Peace. Division of International Law. *The Consortium: The Official Text of the Four-Power Agreement for a Loan to China and Relevant Documents.* Pamphlet No. 40 (Washington, 1921). 76 pp.

———. *The Hague Conventions and Declarations of 1899 and 1907, Accompanied by Tables of Signatures, Ratifications and Adhesions of the Various Powers and Texts of Reservations,* ed. James Brown Scott (2d ed., New York, 1915). 303 pp.

———. *Instructions to the American Delegates to the Hague Peace Conferences and Their Official Reports,* ed. James Brown Scott (New York, 1916). 138 pp.

———. *Outbreak of the World War,* German documents collected by Karl Kautsky; eds. Count Max Montgelas and Professor Walter Schücking, translated, Division of International Law (New York, Oxford University Press, 1924). 688 pp.

———. *The Proceedings of the Hague Peace Conferences, Translation of the Official Texts,* prepared under the direction of James Brown Scott (5 vols.; New York, Oxford University Press, 1920–1921).

———. *The Sino-Japanese Negotiations of 1915: Japanese and Chinese Documents and Chinese Official Statement.* Pamphlet No. 45 (Washington, 1921). 76 pp.

Clyde, Paul Hibbert, comp. *United States Policy toward China: Diplomatic and Public Documents, 1839–1939* (Durham, N. C., Duke University Press, 1940). 321 pp.

Cocks, F. Seymour, ed. *The Secret Treaties and Understandings,* Text of the Available Documents (London, Union of Democratic Control, 1918). 94 pp.

Die deutschen Dokumente zum Kriegsausbruch, collected by Karl Kautsky, eds. Count Max Montgelas and Professor Walter Schücking (4 vols.; Charlottenburg, 1919).

Germany. Auswärtige Amt. *Der diplomatische Schriftwechsel Iswolskis, 1911–1914, Aus den Geheimakten der russischen Staatsarchive,* ed. Friedrich Stieve (4 vols.; Berlin, Deutsche Verlagsgesellschaft für Politik u. Geschichte, 1924).

Laloy, Emile. *Les documents secrets des archives, du Ministère des Affaires Etrangères de Russie,* publiés par les Bolcheviks (Paris, 1919). 197 pp.

MacMurray, John V. A. *Treaties and Agreements with and Concerning China, 1894–1919* (2 vols.; Washington, 1921).

———. *Treaties and Agreements with and Concerning China, 1919–1929* (Washington, Carnegie Endowment, 1929). 282 pp.

Un livre noir, diplomatie d'avant-guerre d'après les documents des archives russes, novembre, 1910–juillet, 1914, ed. René Marchand (3 vols., in 6 parts; Paris, Librarie du Travail, 1922–1931). Izvolsky correspondence.

Siebert [Zibert], Benno A. de. *Entente Diplomacy and the World, Matrix of the History of Europe, 1909–1914* (New York, 1921). Translated by Siebert from originals, and edited, arranged, and annotated by George Abel Schreiner. 762 pp.

———. *Graf Benckendorffs diplomatischer Schriftwechsel,* ed. Count Benno von Siebert [Zibert] (3 vols.; Berlin, Walter de Gruyter, 1928).

Letters, Memoirs, and Biographies

Adler, Cyrus, *Jacob H. Schiff, His Life and Letters* (2 vols.; London, Heinemann, 1929).

Bailey, Thomas A. *Theodore Roosevelt and the Japanese-American Crises: An Account of the International Complications Arising from the Race Problem on the Pacific Coast* (Stanford University; Stanford University Press, 1934). 353 pp.

Baker, George E., ed. *The Works of William H. Seward* (5 vols.; Boston, 1853–1884).

Baker, Ray Stannard. *Woodrow Wilson: Life and Letters* (8 vols.; New York, Doubleday, Doran, 1927–1939).

Baker, Ray S., and Dodd, William E., eds. *The Public Papers of Woodrow Wilson* (6 vols.; authorized ed., New York, Harper, 1925–1927).

[Balfour, Arthur J.]. *Opinions and Argument from Speeches and Addresses of the Earl of Balfour, 1910–1927* (New York, Doubleday, Doran, 1928). 301 pp.

Bemis, Samuel F., ed. *American Secretaries of State and Their Diplomacy* (10 vols.; New York, A. A. Knopf, 1927–1929).

Bigelow, John, ed. *The Complete Works of Benjamin Franklin* (10 vols.; New York and London, 1887–1888).

Bishop, Joseph B. *Theodore Roosevelt and His Time, Shown in His Own Letters* (2 vols.; New York, Scribner's, 1920).

Bowers, Claude G. *Beveridge and the Progressive Era* (Boston, Houghton Mifflin, 1932). 610 pp.

[Coolidge, Calvin]. *Foundations of the Republic: Speeches and Addresses* (New York, Scribner's, 1926). 463 pp.

Cortissoz, Royal. *The Life of Whitelaw Reid* (2 vols.; New York, 1921).

Croly, Herbert. *Willard Straight* (New York, Macmillan, 1924). 569 pp.

Dennett, Tyler. *John Hay, from Poetry to Politics* (New York, Dodd Mead, 1933). 476 pp.

———. *Roosevelt and the Russo-Japanese War: A Critical Study of American Policy in Eastern Asia in 1902–5, Based Primarily upon the Private Papers of Theodore Roosevelt* (New York, Doubleday, Page, 1925). 357 pp.

Dennis, Alfred L. P. *Adventures in American Diplomacy, 1896–1906* (From unpublished documents) (New York, Dutton, 1928). 537 pp.

[Dewey, George]. *Autobiography of George Dewey, Admiral of the Navy* (New York, 1913). 337 pp.

Dodd, William E. *Woodrow Wilson and His Work* (new and rev. ed.; New York, Peter Smith, 1932). 454 pp.

[Dole, Sanford B.]. *Memoirs of the Hawaiian Revolution,* ed. Andrew Farrell (Honolulu, Advertiser Publishing Co., 1936). 188 pp.

Dugdale, Blanche E. C. *Arthur James Balfour, First Earl of Balfour* (2 vols.; London, Hutchinson, 1936).

Ford, Paul Leicester, ed. *The Writings of Thomas Jefferson* (10 vols.; New York, 1892–1899).

Gérard, Auguste. *Ma mission en Chine (1893–1897)* (Paris, 1918). 347 pp.

———. *Ma mission au Japon* (1907–1914) Paris, 1919. 412 pp.

Gleaves, Rear Admiral Albert. *Life and Letters of Rear Admiral Stephen B. Luce, U. S. Navy, Founder of the Naval War College* (New York, 1925). 381 pp.

Grey, Sir Edward, Viscount of Fallodon. *Twenty-five Years, 1892–1916* (2 vols.; London, Hodder and Stoughton, 1925).

Gwynn, Stephen, ed. *The Letters and Friendships of Sir Cecil Spring Rice: A Record* (2 vols.; Boston, Houghton Mifflin, 1929).

Hibben, Paxton. *The Peerless Leader, William Jennings Bryan* (New York, Farrar and Rinehart, 1929). 446 pp.

[Hoar, George F.]. *Autobiography of Seventy Years* (2 vols.; New York, 1903).

[Hohenlohe, Prince von]. *Denkwürdigkeiten des Fürsten Chlodwig zu Hohenlohe-Schillingsfürst* (2 vols.; Stuttgart, Deutsche Verlags-Anstalt, 1906).

HOUSTON, DAVID F. *Eight Years with Wilson's Cabinet, 1913 to 1920, with a Personal Estimate of the President* (2 vols.; New York, Doubleday, Page, 1926).

HOWE, GEORGE F. *Chester A. Arthur: A Quarter-Century of Machine Politics* (New York, Dodd Mead, 1934). 307 pp.

HOWE, M. A. DE WOLFE. *George von Lengerke Meyer, His Life and Public Services* (New York, 1920). 556 pp.

ISHII, VISCOUNT KIKUJIRO. *Diplomatic Commentaries*, ed. William R. Langdon (Baltimore, Johns Hopkins Press, 1936). 351 pp.

JAMES, HENRY. *Richard Olney and His Public Service* (Boston, Houghton Mifflin, 1923). 335 pp.

JESSUP, PHILIP C. *Elihu Root* (2 vols.; New York, Dodd Mead, 1938).

JOHNSON, ALLEN, *et. al.*, eds. *Dictionary of American Biography*, under auspices of the American Council of Learned Societies (20 vols. and index; New York, Scribner's, 1928–1936).

KENNAN, GEORGE. *E. H. Harriman, a Biography* (2 vols.; Boston, Houghton Mifflin, 1922).

LAMONT, THOMAS W. *Henry P. Davison, the Record of a Useful Life* (New York, Harper, 1933). 373 pp.

LANE, ANNE W., and WALL, LOUISE H., eds. *The Letters of Franklin K. Lane, Personal and Political* (Boston, Houghton Mifflin, 1922). 473 pp.

LANSING, ROBERT. *The Peace Negotiations, a Personal Narrative* (Boston, 1921). 321 pp.

———. *War Memoirs of Robert Lansing, Secretary of State* (Indianapolis, Bobbs-Merrill, 1935). 383 pp.

LAWRENCE, DAVID. *The True Story of Woodrow Wilson* (New York, Doran, 1924). 368 pp.

LEE, SIR SIDNEY. *King Edward VII: A Biography* (2 vols.; London, Macmillan, 1925–1927).

LLOYD GEORGE, DAVID. *Memoirs of the Peace Conference* (2 vols.; New Haven, Yale University Press, 1939).

———. *War Memoirs of David Lloyd George* (6 vols.; Boston, Little, Brown, 1933–1937).

MCADOO, WILLIAM G. *Crowded Years: The Reminiscences of William G. McAdoo* (Boston, Houghton Mifflin, 1931). 542 pp.

MCELROY, ROBERT. *Grover Cleveland: The Man and the Statesman* (2 vols.; New York, Harper, 1933).

[MCKINLEY, WILLIAM]. *Speeches and Addresses of William McKinley from March 1, 1897 to May 30, 1900* (New York, 1900). 388 pp.

MEIGS, WILLIAM M. *The Life of Charles Jared Ingersoll*, by his grandson (2d ed.; Philadelphia, 1900). 351 pp.

MILLER, DAVID HUNTER. *My Diary at the Conference of Paris with Documents* (21 vols.; New York, 1924).

MOTT, T. BENTLEY. *Myron T. Herrick; Friend of France: An Autobiographical Biography* (New York, Doubleday, Doran, 1930). 399 pp.

MULLER, KARL A. VON. *Fürst Chlodwig zu Hohenlohe-Schillingsfürst, Denkwürdigkeiten der Reichskanzlerzeit* (Stuttgart, Deutsche Verlags-Anstalt, 1931). 637 pp.

NEVINS, ALLAN. *Grover Cleveland: A Study in Courage* (New York, Dodd Mead, 1932). 832 pp.

———. *Henry White: Thirty Years of American Diplomacy* (New York, Harper, 1930). 518 pp.

NEWTON, THOMAS W. L., *Lord Lansdowne: A Biography* (London, Macmillan, 1929). 536 pp.

OLCOTT, CHARLES S. *The Life of William McKinley* (2 vols.; Boston, Houghton Mifflin, 1916).

POOLEY, A. M., ed. *The Secret Memoirs of Count Tadasu Hayashi G.C.V.O.* (New York, 1915). 331 pp.

PRINGLE, HENRY F. *The Life and Times of William Howard Taft* (2 vols.; New York, Farrar and Rinehart, 1939).

———. *Theodore Roosevelt, a Biography* (New York, Harcourt, Brace, 1931). 627 pp.

PULESTON, W. D. *The Life and Work of Captain Alfred Thayer Mahan, U.S.N.* (New Haven, Yale University Press, 1939). 380 pp.

REDFIELD, WILLIAM C. *With Congress and Cabinet* (New York, Doubleday, Page, 1924). 307 pp.

REID, WHITELAW. *Problems of Expansion as Considered in Papers and Addresses* (New York, 1900). 294 pp.

ROBINSON, WILLIAM A. *Thomas B. Reed, Parliamentarian* (New York, Dodd Mead, 1930). 423 pp.

[ROOSEVELT, THEODORE]. *Selections from the Correspondence of Theodore Roosevelt and Henry Cabot Lodge, 1884–1918,* ed. H. C. Lodge (2 vols.; New York, Scribner's, 1925).

———. *Theodore Roosevelt, an Autobiography* (New York, 1913). 647 pp.

ROSEN, BARON ROMAN R. *Forty Years of Diplomacy* (2 vols.; London, 1922).

SAITO, HIROSI. *Japan's Policies and Purposes: Selections from Recent Addresses and Writings* (Boston, Marshall Jones Co., 1935). 231 pp.

SEWARD, FREDERICK W. *Reminiscences of a War-Time Statesman and Diplomat, 1830–1915* (New York, 1916). 489 pp.

SEYMOUR, CHARLES. *The Intimate Papers of Colonel House* (4 vols; Boston, Houghton Mifflin, 1926–1928).

STEPHEN, LESLIE, *et al.*, eds. *Dictionary of National Biography* (66 vols., and supplements; London, Smith, Elder, 1885–1937).

[SUMNER, CHARLES]. *The Works of Charles Sumner* (15 vols.; Boston, 1875–1883).

THAYER, WILLIAM ROSCOE. *The Life and Letters of John Hay* (2 vols.; Boston, Houghton Mifflin, 1915).

[THURSTON, LORRIN A.]. *Memoirs of the Hawaiian Revolution,* ed. Andrew Farrell (Honolulu, Advertiser Publishing Co., 1936). 664 pp.

[WHITE, ANDREW D.]. *Autobiography of Andrew Dickson White* (2 vols.; New York, 1914).

Secondary Works

Acworth, Captain Bernard, R. N., *The Navy and the Next War, a Vindication of Sea Power* (London, Eyre and Spottiswoode, 1934). 305 pp.

Andrews, Clarence L. *The Story of Alaska* (Caldwell, Idaho; Caxton Printers, 1938). 303 pp.

Angell, Norman. *America and the New World State, a Plea for American Leadership in International Organization* (New York, 1915). 305 pp.

———. *This Have and Have-Not Business, Political Fantasy and Economic Fact* (London, Hamish Hamilton, 1936). 206 pp.

Bain, H. Foster. *Ores and Industry in the Far East; the Influence of Key Mineral Resources on the Development of Oriental Civilization* (New York, Council on Foreign Relations, 1933). 288 pp.

Baker, Ray Stannard. *Woodrow Wilson and World Settlement, Written from His Unpublished and Personal Material* (3 vols.; New York, Doubleday, Page, 1922–).

Barber, Joseph, Jr. *Hawaii: Restless Rampart* (Indianapolis and New York, Bobbs-Merrill, 1941). 285 pp.

Bau [Pao], Mingchien J. *The Open Door Doctrine in Relation to China* (New York, Macmillan, 1923). 245 pp.

Benson, William S. *The Merchant Marine* (New York, Macmillan, 1924). 183 pp.

Bienstock, Gregory. *The Struggle for the Pacific* (New York, Macmillan, 1937). 299 pp.

Bishop, Joseph Bucklin. *The Panama Gateway* (New York, 1913). 459 pp.

Blount, James H. *The American Occupation of the Philippines, 1898–1912* (New York, 1913). 664 pp.

Brown, J. Coggin. *India's Mineral Wealth: A Guide to the Occurrences and Economics of the Useful Minerals of the Indian Empire* (London, Oxford University Press, 1936). 335 pp.

Bywater, Hector C. *Sea Power in the Pacific, a Study of the American-Japanese Naval Problem* (Boston, 1921). 334 pp.

———. *A Searchlight on the Navy* (London, Constable and Co., 1934). 308 pp.

Callahan, James M. *The Alaska Purchase and Americo-Canadian Relations,* in West Virginia University Studies in American History, Series I, Nos. 2–3 (Morgantown, W. Va., February and March, 1908). 44 pp.

———. *An Introduction to American Expansion Policy,* in West Virginia University Studies in American History, Series I, No. 4 [?] (Morgantown, W. Va., April, 1908). 36 pp.

———. *Russo-American Relations during the American Civil War,* in West Virginia University Studies in American History, Series I, No. 1 (Morgantown, W. Va., January, 1908). 18 pp.

Carnegie Endowment for International Peace. Division of Economics and History. *The Balance Sheets of Imperialism; Facts and Figures on Colonies,* (New York, Columbia University Press, 1936). 136 pp.

Castle, William R., Jr. *Hawaii Past and Present* (New York, 1913). 242 pp.

Causton, E. E. N., *Militarism and Foreign Policy in Japan* (London, Allen and Unwin, 1936). 207 pp.

CHAPUT, ROLLAND A. *Disarmament in British Foreign Policy* (London, Allen and Unwin, 1935). 432 pp.

CHURCHILL, WINSTON S. *The World Crisis* (4 vols.; London, Thornton Butterworth, 1923–1927).

CLAUSEWITZ, GENERAL CARL VON. *On War,* translated by J. J. Graham from the 3d German edition (3 vols. in 1; London, 1873).

CLOSE, UPTON [Josef Washington Hall]. *Challenge: Behind the Face of Japan* (New York, Farrar and Rinehart, 1934). 409 pp.

CLYDE, PAUL H. *Japan's Pacific Mandate* (New York, Macmillan, 1935). 244 pp.

CORBETT, JULIAN S. *Some Principles of Maritime Strategy* (London, 1911). 317 pp.

CRECRAFT, EARL WILLIS. *Freedom of the Seas* (New York, D. Appleton-Century, 1935). 304 pp.

CRESWELL, JOHN. *Naval Warfare, an Introductory Study* (London, Sampson Low, Marston, 1936). 304 pp.

CULBERTSON, WILLIAM S. *Commercial Policy in War Time and After, a Study of the Application of Democratic Ideas to International Commercial Relations,* in series *Problems of War and of Reconstruction,* ed. Francis G. Wickware (New York, 1919). 479 pp.

DARRIEUS, GABRIEL. *War on the Sea, Strategy and Tactics,* translated from the French by Philip R. Alger (Annapolis, 1908). 322 pp.

DAS, TARAKNATH. *Foreign Policy in the Far East* (New York, Longmans, Green, 1936). 292 pp.

DAVIS, GEORGE T. *A Navy Second to None, the Development of Modern American Naval Policy* (New York, Harcourt, Brace, 1940). 508 pp.

DENLINGER, SUTHERLAND, and GARY, CHARLES B. *War in the Pacific: A Study of Navies, People, and Battle Problems* (New York, 1936). 338 pp.

DENNIS, ALFRED L. P. *The Anglo-Japanese Alliance,* in University of California Publications, Bureau of International Relations, I, No. 1 (Berkeley, University of California Press, 1923). 111 pp.

———. *The Foreign Policies of Soviet Russia* (New York, Dutton, 1924). 500 pp.

DUBOSCQ, ANDRÉ. *Le problème du Pacifique* (Paris, Librairie Delagrave, 1927). 126 pp.

DULLES, FOSTER RHEA. *Forty Years of American-Japanese Relations* (New York, D. Appleton-Century, 1937). 289 pp.

ELIOT, GEORGE FIELDING. *The Ramparts We Watch: A Study of the Problems of American National Defense* (New York, Reynal and Hitchcock, 1938). 370 pp.

EMENY, BROOKS. *The Strategy of Raw Materials* (New York, Macmillan, 1934). 202 pp.

ENGELY, GIOVANNI. *The Politics of Naval Disarmament,* translated from Italian by H. V. Rhodes (London, Williams and Norgate, 1932). 301 pp.

EVANS, ULICK R. *Metals and Metallic Compounds* (4 vols.; New York, Longmans, Green, 1923).

FARR, VICTOR J. *The Annexation of Russian America to the United States* (Washington, W. F. Roberts, 1937). 142 pp.

FAY, SIDNEY B. *The Origins of the World War* (2d ed. rev.; 2 vols. in 1; New York, Macmillan, 1939).

FIELD, FREDERICK V. *American Participation in the China Consortiums* (Chicago, University of Chicago Press, 1931). 198 pp.

———. *Economic Handbook of the Pacific Area* (New York, Doubleday, Doran Co., 1934). 649 pp.

FISKE, BRADLEY A. *The Navy as a Fighting Machine* (New York, 1916). 411 pp.

FORBES, W. CAMERON. *The Philippine Islands* (2 vols.; Boston, Houghton Mifflin, 1928).

FOSTER, JOHN W. *American Diplomacy in the Orient* (Boston, 1903). 498 pp.

FOX, FRANK. *Problems of the Pacific* (Boston, n.d.). 294 pp.

FRANKE, OTTO. *Die Grossmächte in Ostasien von 1894 bis 1914: Ein Beitrag zur Vorgeschichte des Krieges* (Braunschweig, Georg Westermann, 1923). 407 pp.

FRASER, HERBERT F. *Foreign Trade and World Politics* (New York, A. A. Knopf, 1926). 346 pp.

FRIEDJUNG, HEINRICH. *Das Zeitalter des Imperialismus, 1884–1914* (3 vols.; Berlin, 1922).

FUJISAWA, RIKITARO. *The Recent Aims and Political Development of Japan* (New Haven, Yale University Press, 1923). 222 pp.

FULLER, J. F. C. *The Foundations of the Science of War* (London, Hutchinson, 1926). 335 pp.

GOLOVIN, [GENERAL] N. *The Problem of the Pacific in the Twentieth Century,* aided by Admiral A. D. Bubnov; translated by C. Nabokoff (London, Gyldendal, 1922). 256 pp.

VON DER GOLTZ, COLMAR. *The Conduct of War, a Brief Study of Its Most Important Principles and Forms,* translated by Lieutenant Joseph T. Dickman, U.S.A. (Kansas City, 1896). 217 pp.

———. *The Nation in Arms, a Treatise on Modern Military Systems and the Conduct of War,* translated by Philip A. Ashworth (new ed.; London, 1906). 475 pp.

GOOCH, GEORGE P. *History of Modern Europe, 1878–1919* (New York, Henry Holt, 1923). 728 pp.

GRISWOLD, A. WHITNEY. *The Far Eastern Policy of the United States* (New York, Harcourt, Brace, 1938). 530 pp.

HARRIS, NORMAN D. *Europe and the East* (Boston, Houghton Mifflin, 1926). 677 pp.

HENDERSON, JOHN B., JR. *American Diplomatic Questions* (New York, 1901). 529 pp.

HINDMARSH, ALBERT E. *The Basis of Japanese Foreign Policy* (Cambridge, Mass., Harvard University Press, 1936). 250 pp.

HOFFMAN, KARL. *Flottenabrüstung Kriegsächtung und Revision* (Berlin, Verlag Arbeitsausschuss Deutscher Verbände, 1932). 103 pp.

HOLLAND, SIR THOMAS H. *The Mineral Sanction as an Aid to International Security* (London, Oliver and Boyd, 1935). 95 pp.

HOLT, W. STULL. *Treaties Defeated by the Senate, a Study of the Struggle between President and Senate over the Conduct of Foreign Relations* (Baltimore, Johns Hopkins Press, 1933). 328 pp.

HORNBECK, STANLEY K. *Contemporary Politics in the Far East* (New York, 1919). 462 pp.

HOWE, HENRY MARION. *Iron, Steel, and Other Alloys* (2d ed.; Cambridge, Mass., 1906). 495 pp.

HURLEY, EDWARD N. *Plan for the Operation of the New American Merchant Marine* (Washington, 1919). 16 pp.

ICHIHASHI, YAMATO. *The Washington Conference and After* (Stanford University, Stanford University Press, 1928). 443 pp.

INUI, KUJO SUE. *The Unsolved Problem of the Pacific* (Tokyo, Japan Times, 1926). 619 pp.

ISHIMARU, TŌTA. *Japan Must Fight Britain,* translated by G. V. Rayment, R.N. (New York, The Telegraph Press, 1936). 329 pp.

JAMES, WILLIAM. *Memories and Studies* (New York and London, 1911). 411 pp.

JOHNSTON, R. M. *Arms and the Race, The Foundations of Army Reform* (New York, 1915). 219 pp.

KAWAI, TATSUO. *The Goal of Japanese Expansion,* translated from the Japanese (Tokyo, Hokuseido Press, 1938). 120 pp.

KENNAN, GEORGE. *E. H. Harriman's Far Eastern Plans* (New York, 1917). 48 pp.

KNOX, DUDLEY W. *The Eclipse of American Sea Power* (New York, American Army and Navy Journal, 1922). 140 pp.

KORFF, BARON SERGEI A. *Russia's Foreign Relations during the Last Half Century* (New York, Macmillan, 1922). 227 pp.

KRANOLD, HERMAN. *The International Distribution of Raw Materials* (London, George Routledge, 1938). 269 pp.

LA FARGUE, THOMAS EDWARD. *China and the World War,* in Hoover War Library Publications, No. 12 (Stanford University, Stanford University Press, 1937). 278 pp.

LATANÉ, JOHN H. *From Isolation to Leadership, a Review of American Foreign Policy* (New York, 1918). 215 pp.

LAWRENCE, JAMES COOPER. *The World's Struggle with Rubber* (New York and London, Harper, 1931). 151 pp.

LEA, HOMER. *The Valor of Ignorance* (New York, 1909). 344 pp.

LEITH, C. K. *World Minerals and World Politics: A Factual Study of Minerals in Their Political and International Relations* (New York, McGraw-Hill, 1931). 213 pp.

LEWIS, CLEONA. *America's Stake in Foreign Investment* (Washington, Brookings Institution, 1938). 710 pp.

LONG, JOHN D. *The New American Navy* (2 vols.; New York, 1903).

MCCAIN, WILLIAM D. *The United States and the Republic of Panama* (Durham, N. C., Duke University Press, 1937). 278 pp.

MCCORMICK, FREDERICK. *The Menace of Japan* (Boston, 1917). 372 pp.

MACKENZIE, NORMAN, ed. *The Legal Status of Aliens in Pacific Countries, an International Survey of Law and Practice Concerning Immigration, Naturalization and Deportation of Aliens and Their Legal Rights and Disabilities* (London, Oxford University Press, 1937). 374 pp.

MAHAN, ALFRED T. *The Influence of Sea Power upon the French Revolution and Empire, 1793–1812* (2 vols.; Boston, 1892).

———. *The Influence of Sea Power upon History, 1660–1783* (Boston, 1890). 557 pp.

———. *The Interest of America in International Conditions* (Boston, 1910). 212 pp.

———. *The Interest of America in Sea Power, Present and Future* (London, 1898). 314 pp.

———. *Lessons of the War with Spain, and Other Articles* (Boston, 1899). 320 pp.

———. *Mahan on Naval Warfare; Selections from the Writings of Rear Admiral Alfred T. Mahan*, ed. Allan Westcott (Boston, 1918). 372 pp.

———. *Naval Strategy, Compared and Contrasted with the Principles and Practice of Military Operations on Land* (Boston, 1911). 475 pp.

———. *The Problem of Asia and Its Effect upon International Policies* (London, 1900). 233 pp.

———. *Retrospect and Prospect: Studies in International Relations, Naval and Political* (Boston, 1902). 309 pp.

———. *Sea Power in Its Relations to the War of 1812* (2 vols.; Boston, 1905).

MARDER, ARTHUR J. *The Anatomy of British Sea Power, a History of British Naval Policy in the Pre-Dreadnaught Era, 1880–1905* (New York, A. A. Knopf, 1940). 580 pp.

MILLARD, THOMAS F. *China: Where It Is Today and Why* (New York, Harcourt, Brace, 1928). 350 pp.

———. *Conflict of Policies in Asia* (New York, Century, 1924). 507 pp.

———. *Democracy and the Eastern Question, the Problem of the Far East as Demonstrated by the Great War, and Its Relation to the United States of America* (New York, 1919). 446 pp.

MILLIS, WALTER. *The Future of Sea Power in the Pacific* (New York, World Peace Foundation, 1935). "World Affairs Pamphlets No. 9." 51 pp.

MINER, DWIGHT C. *The Fight for the Panama Route, the Story of the Spooner Act and the Hay-Herran Treaty* (New York, Columbia University Press, 1940). 469 pp.

MITSUBISHI ECONOMIC RESEARCH BUREAU, TOKYO. *Japanese Trade and Industry, Present and Future* (London, Macmillan, 1936). 663 pp.

MOGI, SOBEI, and REDMAN, H. V. *The Problem of the Far East* (London, Gollancz, 1935). 348 pp.

MONG, G. *La position juridique du Japon en Mandchourie* (Paris, A. Pedone, 1933). 263 pp.

MOON, PARKER T. *Imperialism and World Politics* (New York, Macmillan, 1930). 583 pp.

MORLEY, FELIX. *Our Far Eastern Assignment* (New York, Doubleday, Page, 1926). 199 pp.

MOULTON, HAROLD G. *Japan: An Economic and Financial Appraisal* (Washington, Brookings Institution, 1931). 645 pp.

NORTON, HENRY KITTREDGE. *The Far Eastern Republic of Siberia* (London, Allen and Unwin, 1923). 316 pp.

NOTTER, HARLEY. *The Origins of the Foreign Policy of Woodrow Wilson* (Baltimore, Johns Hopkins Press, 1937). 695 pp.

ORCHARD, JOHN E. *Japan's Economic Position; the Progress of Industrialization* (New York, Whittlesey House, 1930). 504 pp.

PARK, NO-YONG. *Retreat of the West; the White Man's Adventure in Eastern Asia* (Boston, Hale, Cushman, and Flint, 1937). 336 pp.

PASVOLSKY, LEO. *Russia in the Far East* (New York, Macmillan, 1922). 181 pp.

PAULLIN, CHARLES O. *Diplomatic Negotiations of American Naval Officers, 1778–1883* (Baltimore, 1912). 380 pp.

PEFFER, NATHANIEL. *Must We Fight in Asia?* (New York, Harper, 1935). 244 pp.

POQLEY, ANDREW M. *Japan's Foreign Policies* (London, 1920). 202 pp.

POTTER, PITMAN B. *The Freedom of the Seas in History, Law, and Politics* (London, Longmans, Green, 1924). 299 pp.

PRATT, JULIUS W. *Expansionists of 1898, the Acquisition of Hawaii and the Spanish Islands,* The Albert Shaw Lectures on Diplomatic History, 1936 (Baltimore, Johns Hopkins Press, 1936). 393 pp.

PRICE, ERNEST B. *The Russo-Japanese Treaties of 1907–1916 Concerning Manchuria and Mongolia* (Baltimore, Johns Hopkins Press, 1933).

RAM, V. SHIVA. *Comparative Colonial Policy with Special Reference to the American Colonial Policy* (Calcutta, Longmans, Green, 1926). 297 pp.

REDFIELD, WILLIAM COX. *Dependent America* (Boston, Houghton Mifflin, 1926). 278 pp.

REID, WHITELAW. *American and English Studies* (2 vols.; New York, 1913).

REINSCH, PAUL S. *An American Diplomat in China* (New York, Doubleday, Page, 1922). 396 pp.

REMER, CHARLES F., and PALMER, WILLIAM B. *A Study of Chinese Boycotts with Special Reference to Their Economic Effectiveness* (Baltimore, Johns Hopkins Press, 1933). 306 pp.

RHODES, JAMES F. *The McKinley and Roosevelt Administrations, 1897–1909* (New York, Macmillan, 1922). 418 pp.

RICHMOND, VICE-ADMIRAL SIR HERBERT W. *National Policy and Naval Strength, and Other Essays* (London, Longmans, Green, 1928). 356 pp.

———. [Admiral]. *Sea Power in the Modern World* (New York, Reynal and Hitchcock, 1934). 323 pp.

ROBERTS, FREDERICK S., FIELD MARSHAL [EARL]. *Fallacies and Facts: An Answer to "Compulsory Service"* (London, 1911). 247 pp.

ROBERTS, STEPHEN H. *Population Problems of the Pacific* (London, Routledge, 1927). 411 pp.

ROHRBACH, PAUL. *German World Policies,* translated by Edmund von Mach from the author's *Der deutsche Gedanke in der Welt* (New York, 1915, [1912]). 243 pp.

ROOSEVELT, NICHOLAS. *The Restless Pacific* (New York, Scribner's, 1928). 291 pp.

RYDEN, GEORGE H. *The Foreign Policy of the United States in Relation to Samoa* (New Haven, Yale University Press, 1933). 634 pp.

SAROLEA, CHARLES. *The Anglo-German Problem* (London, 1912). 384 pp.

SEYMOUR, CHARLES. *American Diplomacy during the World War,* The Albert Shaw Lectures on Diplomatic History, 1933 (Baltimore, Johns Hopkins Press, 1934). 417 pp.

SMITH, DARRELL H. *The Panama Canal: Its History, Activities and Organization,* in Publications of the Institute for Government Research, No. 44 (Baltimore, Johns Hopkins Press, 1927). 413 pp.

SMITH, JOE PATTERSON. *The Republican Expansionists of the Early Reconstruction Era* (Chicago, Privately printed, 1933). 129 pp.

SMITH, WILFRED. *A Geographical Study of Coal and Iron in China* (London, University Press of Liverpool, 1926). 83 pp.

SOKOLSKY, GEORGE E. *The Tinder Box of Asia* (New York, Doubleday, Doran, 1933). 453 pp.

SOYESHIMA, MICHIMASA. *Oriental Interpretations of the Far Eastern Problems* (Chicago, Harris Foundation, 1925). 219 pp.

SPARGO, JOHN. *Russia as an American Problem* (New York and London, 1920). 444 pp.

SPROUT, HAROLD, and MARGARET. *The Rise of American Naval Power, 1776–1918* (Princeton, N. J., Princeton University Press, 1939). 398 pp.

———. *Toward a New Order of Sea Power, American Naval Policy and the World Scene, 1918–1922* (Princeton, N. J., Princeton University Press, 1940). 332 pp.

SPURR, JOSIAH E., ed. *Political and Commercial Geology and the World's Mineral Resources* (New York, 1920). 562 pp.

STALEY, EUGENE. *Raw Materials in Peace and War* (New York, Council on Foreign Relations, 1937). 326 pp.

STEWART, EDGAR I., JR. "American Foreign Policy Incident to the Russian-Japanese War, 1904–1905" (unpublished Ph.D. thesis, University of California, 1938). 323 numbered leaves.

STIEVE, FRIEDRICH. *Isvolsky and the World War, Based on the Documents Recently Published by the German Foreign Office,* translated by E. W. Dickes (London, Allen and Unwin, 1926). 254 pp.

STOUGHTON, BRADLEY. *The Metallurgy of Iron and Steel* (4th ed.; New York, McGraw-Hill, 1934). 559 pp.

SUYEMATSU, BARON KENCHO. *The Risen Sun* (New York, 1905). 355 pp.

TAKEUCHI, TATSUJI. *War and Diplomacy in the Japanese Empire* (New York, Doubleday, Doran, 1935). 505 pp.

TANSILL, CHARLES C. *America Goes to War* (Boston, Little, Brown, 1938). 731 pp.

TEMPERLEY, HAROLD W. V., ed. *A History of the Peace Conference* (6 vols.; London, Henry Frowde, 1920–1924).

THOMPSON, WARREN S. *Danger Spots in World Population* (New York, A. A. Knopf, 1930). 343 pp.

TOKUTOMI, IICHIRO. *Japanese-American Relations,* translated by Sukeshige Yanagiwara (New York, Macmillan, 1922). 207 pp.

TORGASHEFF, BORIS P. *The Mineral Industry of the Far East, Economic and Geological Report on the Mineral Resources and Mineral Industries of the Far Eastern Countries* (Shanghai, Chali Co., 1930). 510 pp.

TREVELYAN, GEORGE MACAULAY. *History of England* (London, Longmans Green, 1933). 723 pp.

TRYON, F. G., and ECKEL, E. C., eds. *Mineral Economics, Lectures under the Auspices of the Brookings Institution* (Washington, McGraw-Hill, 1932). 311 pp.

TYLER, ALICE F. *The Foreign Policy of James G. Blaine* (Minneapolis, University of Minnesota Press, 1927). 411 pp.

VAGTS, ALFRED. *Deutschland und die Vereinigten Staaten in der Weltpolitik* (2 vols.; New York, Macmillan, 1935).

VILLENEUVE-TRANS, R. DE. *A l'ambassade de Washington, October, 1917–April, 1919* (Paris, 1921). 287 pp.

WARE, EDITH E. *Business and Politics in the Far East* (New Haven, Yale University Press, 1932). 250 pp.

WEALE, B. L. PUTNAM [pseud. of BERTRAM LENOX SIMPSON]. *The Fight for the Republic in China* (New York, 1917). 490 pp.

WEINBERG, ALBERT K. *Manifest Destiny: A Study of Nationalist Expansionism in American History* (Baltimore, Johns Hopkins Press, 1935). 559 pp.

WHEELER-BENNETT, J. W. *Information on the Reduction of Armaments* (London, Allen and Unwin, 1925). 216 pp.

WILLARD, MYRA. *History of the White Australia Policy,* in University of Melbourne Publications, No. 1 (Melbourne, Melbourne University Press, 1923). 217 pp.

WILLIAMS, DANIEL R. *The United States and the Philippines* (New York, Doubleday, Page, 1924). 335 pp.

WILLIAMS, EDWARD T. *China Yesterday and Today* (rev. ed.; New York, Crowell, 1927). 664 pp.

WILLOUGHBY, WESTEL W. *Foreign Rights and Interests in China* (2 vols. rev. ed.; Baltimore, Johns Hopkins Press, 1927).

WOLF, HOWARD, and RALPH. *Rubber, a Story of Glory and Greed* (New York, Covici, Friede, 1936). 533 pp.

WOOD, GE-ZAY. *The Shantung Question: A Study in Diplomacy and World Politics* (New York, Fleming Revell, 1922). 372 pp.

WOOLF, LEONARD. *Economic Imperialism* (New York, 1920). 111 pp.

WORCESTER, DEAN C. *The Philippines Past and Present,* new edition in one volume with biographical sketch and four additional chapters by Ralston Hayden (New York, Macmillan, 1930). 862 pp.

WRISTON, HENRY S. *Executive Agents in American Foreign Relations,* The Albert Shaw Lectures on Diplomatic History, 1923 (Baltimore, Johns Hopkins University Press, 1929). 874 pp.

YAKHONTOFF, VICTOR A. *Eyes on Japan* (New York, Coward-McCann, 1936). 329 pp.

YAMASAKI, KAKUJIRO, and OGAWA, GOTARO. *The Effect of the World War upon the Commerce and Industry of Japan,* in *Economic and Social History of the World War,* ed. James T. Shotwell (New Haven, Yale University Press, 1929). 345 pp.

YANAIKARA, TADAO. *Pacific Islands under Japanese Mandate,* International Research Series, Institute of Pacific Relations (London and New York, Oxford University Press, 1940). 312 pp.

YOSHITOMI, M. *Les conflits nippo-americains sur l'immigration japonaise* (Grenoble, Aubert, 1926). 388 pp.

YOUNG, C. WALTER. *The International Legal Status of the Kwantung Leased Territory,* in the series Japan's Jurisdiction and International Legal Position in Manchuria (Baltimore, Johns Hopkins University Press, 1931). 249 pp.

———. *The International Relations of Manchuria: A Digest and Analysis of Treaties, Agreements, and Negotiations Concerning the Three Eastern Provinces of China* (Chicago, University of Chicago Press, 1929). 307 pp.

———. *Japanese Jurisdiction in the South Manchuria Railway Areas,* in the series Japan's Jurisdiction and International Legal Position in Manchuria (Baltimore, Johns Hopkins University Press, 1931). 332 pp.

———. *Japan's Special Position in Manchuria: Its Assertion, Legal Interpretation and Present Meaning,* in the series Japan's Jurisdiction and International Legal Position in Manchuria (Baltimore, Johns Hopkins University Press, 1931). 412 pp.

Periodicals

Aldridge, Francis. "The New Menace in the Far East," *The North American Review,* CCI (May, 1915), 714–718.

Bailey, Thomas A. "Dewey and the Germans at Manila Bay," *The American Historical Review,* XLV (October, 1939), 59–81.

———. "Japan's Protest Against the Annexation of Hawaii," *The Journal of Modern History,* III (March, 1931), 46–61.

———. "The United States and Hawaii During the Spanish-American War," *The American Historical Review,* XXXVI (April, 1931), 552–560.

———. "Why the United States Purchased Alaska," *The Pacific Historical Review,* III (March, 1934), 39–49.

Bain, H. Foster. "Singapore's Control of Key Mineral Resources," *Foreign Affairs: an American Quarterly Review,* VII (July, 1929), 666–669.

———. "World Mineral Production and Control," *Foreign Affairs: an American Quarterly Review,* XI (July, 1933), 707–710.

Bancroft, Frederic. "Seward's Ideas of Territorial Expansion," *The North American Review,* CLXVII (July, 1898), 79–89.

Barker, J. Ellis. "Coal, Iron—And the Domination of the World," *The Nineteenth Century and After,* LXXXIII (April, 1918), 698–714.

Benson, William S. "Our New Merchant Marine," *United States Naval Institute Proceedings,* LII (October, 1926), 1941–1950.

Beveridge, Albert J. "The Development of a Colonial Policy for the United States," *The Annals of the American Academy of Political and Social Science,* XXX (July, 1907) 3–15.

Blane, William. "The Japanese in China," *The Nineteenth Century and After,* LXXVII (May, 1915), 1103–1118.

Brebner, J. Bartlet. "Canada, the Anglo-Japanese Alliance, and the Washington Conference," *Political Science Quarterly,* L (March, 1935), 45–58.

Brooks, Albert H. "The Development of Alaska by Government Railroads," *The Quarterly Journal of Economics,* XXVIII (May, 1914), 586–596.

Bryce, James. "The Policy of Annexation for America," *The Forum,* XXIV (December, 1897), 385–395.

Buell, Raymond L. "The Development of the Anti-Japanese Agitation in the United States," *Political Science Quarterly,* XXXVII (December, 1922), 605–638.

———. "The Development of Anti-Japanese Agitation in the United States, II," *Political Science Quarterly,* XXXVIII (March, 1923), 57–81.

BUTLER, HAMILTON. "A New Deal in the Pacific," *The North American Review,* CCXXXV (June, 1933), 485–497.

CAMERON, MERIBETH E. "American Recognition Policy Toward the Republic of China, 1912–1913," *The Pacific Historical Review,* II (June, 1933), 214–230.

CARR-SAUNDERS, A. M. "Fallacies About Overpopulation," *Foreign Affairs: an American Quarterly Review, IX* (July, 1931), 646–656.

CHAMBERLAIN, SIR AUSTEN. "The Permanent Bases of British Foreign Policy," *Foreign Affairs: an American Quarterly Review,* IX (July, 1931), 535–546.

CHAMBERLIN, WILLIAM H. "Aims of the Japanese Army and Navy," *Foreign Affairs: an American Quarterly Review,* XV (October, 1936), 112–123.

———. "Naval Bases in the Pacific," *Foreign Affairs: an American Quarterly Review,* XV (April, 1937), 484–494.

CHILD, RICHARD W. "Japan, the Peace, and the Destiny of Asia," *The World's Work,* XXXVIII (July, 1919), 313–329.

CLINARD, OUTTEN J. "World War I and Our Merchant Navy: A Warning for the Future," *United States Naval Institute Proceedings,* LXXI (August, 1945), 919–929.

CLYDE, PAUL H. "An Episode in American-Japanese Relations: The Manchurian Freight-Rate Controversy, 1914–1916," *The Far Eastern Review,* XXVI (August, 1930), 410–412; (September, 1930), 480–483.

———. "Railway Politics and the Open Door in China, 1916–1917," *The American Journal of International Law,* XXV (October, 1931), 642–657.

COLCORD, LINCOLN. "Seamanship and the Merchant Marine," *The North American Review,* CCIII (January, 1916), 25–34.

COMPTON-RICKETT, JOSEPH. "Commercial Supremacy After the War," *The Contemporary Review,* CIX (May, 1916), 545–555.

CULBERTSON, WILLIAM S. "Raw Materials and Foodstuffs in the Commercial Policies of Nations," *The Annals of the American Academy of Political and Social Science,* CXII (March, 1924), 1–298.

CURTI, MERLE. "Bryan and World Peace," *Smith College Studies in History,* XVI (April–July, 1931), 107–262.

DAVIS, JOHN W. "The Permanent Bases of American Foreign Policy," *Foreign Affairs: an American Quarterly Review,* X (October, 1931), 1–12.

DAVIS, MALCOLM W. "Railway Strategy in Manchuria," *Foreign Affairs: an American Quarterly Review,* IV (April, 1926), 499–502.

DAWSON, WILLIAM H. "The Future of the German Colonies: The Case for Conditional Return," *The Contemporary Review,* CXII (September, 1917), 256–263.

DELBRÜCK, HANS. "Germany's Terms," *The Atlantic Monthly,* CXV (April, 1915), 525–535.

———. "The Price of a German-English Entente," *The Contemporary Review,* XCIX (February, 1911), 129–138.

———. "Ueber die Ziele unserer Kolonialpolitik," *Preussische Jahrbücher,* CXLVII (March, 1912), 503–513.

DENNETT, TYLER. "President Roosevelt's Secret Pact With Japan," *Current History: a Monthly Magazine,* XXI (October, 1924), 15–21.

DEWAVRIN, MAURICE. "Les Etats-Unis d'Amérique et le conflit Européen: le mouvement économique," *Revue des sciences politiques,* XXXVI (October 15, 1916), 185–213.

———. "Le mouvement commercial pan-Américain aux Etats-Unis," *Revue politique et parlementaire,* LXXXIX (November, 1916), 206–219.

DIEDERICHS, VICE-ADMIRAL OTTO VON. "A Statement of Events in Manila, May–October, 1898," *Journal of the Royal United Service Institution,* LIX (November, 1914), 421–446.

DUBERN, EUGENE B. "Domaine et perspectives: d'union économique internationale," *Revue des sciences politiques,* XXXVI (October 15, 1916), 214–238.

———. "Les projet d'union économique entre les Allies dans l'hiver 1915–1916," *Revue des sciences politiques,* XXXV (June 15, 1916), 363–376.

DUNNING, WILLIAM A. "Paying for Alaska," *Political Science Quarterly,* XXVII (September, 1912), 385–398.

DYER, BRAINERD. "Confederate Naval and Privateering Activities in the Pacific," *The Pacific Historical Review,* III (December, 1934), 433–443.

D'EICHTHAL, EUGÈNE. "Alliances et guerre économiques: la conférence économique de Paris," *Revue des sciences politiques,* XXXVI (August 15, 1916), 30–46.

FARRAR, VICTOR J. "The Background of the Purchase of Alaska," *The Washington Historical Quarterly,* XIII (April, 1922), 93–104.

FAYLE, C. ERNEST. "The Supply of Raw Materials in Time of War," *Journal of the Royal United Service Institution.* LXXII (August, 1927), 541–555.

FELD, DR. WILHELM. "Ein neuer Kurs der amerikanischen Trustpolitik," *Jahrbücher für Nationalökonomie und Statistik,* CIX (August, 1917), 213–219.

FERGUSON, MAJOR K. B. "The Situation in the Pacific," *Journal of the Royal United Service Institution,* LXX (May, 1925), 288–304.

FISKE, BRADLEY A. "Naval Policy," *The North American Review,* CCIII (January, 1916), 63–74.

FROST, H. H. "Sea Power," *United States Naval Institute Proceedings,* LIII (October, 1927), 1102–1110.

GARDINER, WILLIAM H. "Functions of Naval Power," *United States Naval Institute Proceedings,* LV (October, 1929), 839–846.

———. "Naval Policy and Naval Power," *United States Naval Institute Proceedings,* LII (February, 1926), 229–248.

GARNER, JAMES W. "The Freedom of the Seas," *The American Journal of International Law,* XXIII (April, 1929), 363–370.

GÉRARD, AUGUSTE. "Les Etats Unis et l'Extrême-Orient," *Revue des deux mondes,* XLIII (February, 1918), 912–934.

———. "La situation politique et économique de l'Extrême-Orient après la guerre de 1914–1918," *Revue économique internationale,* III (August, 1920), 7–26.

GEROULD, JAMES THAYER. "Freedom of the Seas the Crux of Disarmament: An American Standpoint," *Current History,* XXIX (February, 1929), 727–732.

GOLDER, FRANK A. "The Purchase of Alaska," *The American Historical Review,* XXV (April, 1920), 411–425.

GRATTAN, C. HARTLEY. "Australia and the Pacific," *Foreign Affairs: an American Quarterly Review,* VII (October, 1928), 144–149.

GREELY, A. W. "The Economic Evolution of Alaska," *The National Geographic Magazine,* XX (July, 1909), 585–593.

GUYOT, YVES. "L'imperialisme économique," *Journal des économistes: revue des science économique et de la statistique,* XXXVII (March, 1913), 353–369.

———. "Les rapports économiques de la Chine et des étrangers," *Revue économique internationale,* III (August, 1920), 27–57.

HACKER, LOUIS M. "The Incendiary Mahan: A Biography," *Scribner's Magazine,* XCV (April, 1934), 263–268; 311–320.

HARRIS, FRANK S. M. "The Navy and the Diplomatic Frontier," *United States Naval Institute Proceedings,* LXII (April, 1936), 473–486.

HARRIS, JOHN H. "Colonial Dependencies: 'Possession' or 'Trusteeship?' " *The Contemporary Review,* CXIII (February, 1918), 207–212.

HAUSER, HENRI. "German Economic Methods and Their Defeat," *The Fortnightly Review,* CVI (July, 1916), 100–109.

HENSCHEN, SIGMUND. "What is Behind the Japanese Peril?" *The Forum,* LVI (July, 1916), 63–78.

HORNBECK, STANLEY K. "Has the United States a Chinese Policy?" *Foreign Affairs: an American Quarterly Review,* V (July, 1927), 617–632.

———. "Trade, Concessions, Investments, Conflict and Policy in the Far East," *Proceedings of the Academy of Political Science,* VII (July, 1917), [80–98] 604–622.

HOWE, FREDERIC C. "Dollar Diplomacy and Imperialism," *Proceedings of the Academy of Political Science,* VII (July, 1917), [73–79] 597–603.

HUEBNER, GROVER G. "Probable Effects of the War on the Foreign Trade of the United States," *Proceedings of the Academy of Political Science,* VI (October, 1915), 174–184.

HURD, ARCHIBALD. "America's New Naval Policy," *The Fortnightly Review,* CVI (November, 1916), 743–757.

———. "The United States and Sea Power: A Challenge," *The Fortnightly Review,* CXI (February, 1919), 175–189.

HYNDMAN, HENRY M. "The Awakening of Asia," *The Fortnightly Review,* CVI (October, 1916), 677–690.

ISHII, VISCOUNT KIKUJIRO, "The Permanent Bases of Japanese Foreign Policy," *Foreign Affairs: an American Quarterly Review,* XI (January, 1933), 220–229.

IYENAGA, T. "The New Chino-Japanese Treaties and Their Import," *The American Review of Reviews,* LII (September, 1915), 338–342.

JENKS, JEREMIAH W. "China, America's Silent Partner," *The World's Work,* XXXIII (December, 1916), 165–171.

JOHNSON, EMORY R. "The Isthmian Canal in Its Economic Aspects," *The Annals of the American Academy of Political and Social Science,* XIX (January, 1902), 1–23.

———. "Probable Changes in the Foreign Trade of the United States Resulting from the European War," *American Economic Review,* VI Supplement (March, 1916), 17–49.

JOHNSTON, CHARLES. "Russia and the War After the War," *The North American Review,* CCVII (March, 1918), 378–387.

KALAW, MAXIMO M. "Why the Filipinos Expect Independence," *Foreign Affairs: an American Quarterly Review,* X (January, 1932), 304–315.

KANEKO, BARON KENTARO. "Japan and the United States: A Proposed Economic Alliance," *International Quarterly,* VIII (December–March, 1903–1904), 399–404.

KAWAKAMI, KIYOSHI K. "England and Japan," *The Atlantic Monthly,* CXIX (February, 1917), 174–182.

———. "Japan and the United States, *The Atlantic Monthly,* CXIX (May, 1917), 671–681.

———. "Shall America Prepare Against Japan?" *The North American Review,* CCIII (May, 1916), 675–689.

KELSEY, CARL, ed. "Present-day Immigration with Special Reference to the Japanese," *The Annals of the American Academy of Political and Social Science,* XCIII (January, 1921), 1–232.

KERNER, ROBERT J. "America's Interest and Britain's Policy," *Pacific Affairs,* XI (September, 1938), 363–367.

KING, CLYDE L., ed. "America's Interests After the European War," *The Annals of the American Academy of Political and Social Science,* LXI (September, 1915), 1–323.

KNOWLSON, T. SHARPER. "Germany's Ruling Idea," *The Fortnightly Review,* CX (September, 1918), 344–353.

KNOX, DUDLEY W. "The Navy and the National Life," *United States Naval Institute Proceedings,* LX (June, 1934), 774–783.

———. "Our 'Stake' in Sea Power," *United States Naval Institute Proceedings,* LIII (October, 1927), 1087–1089.

KORFF, BARON SERGE A. "Russia in the Far East," *The American Journal of International Law,* XVII (April, 1923), 252–284.

LEIGH, JOHN GEORGE. "Gains and Losses in the Pacific," *The Fortnightly Review,* LXXIII (January, 1900), 45–58.

———. "The Powers and Samoa," *The Fortnightly Review,* LXXI (January, 1899), 54–73.

LEITH, C. K. "The Mineral Position of the Nations," *Foreign Affairs: an American Quarterly Review,* IX (October, 1930), 133–148.

———. "The Mineral Resources of the Far East," *Foreign Affairs: an American Quarterly Review,* IV (April, 1926), 433–442.

———. "The Political Control of Mineral Resources," *Foreign Affairs: an American Quarterly Review,* IV (October, 1925), 123 ff.

LEWIS, SIR WILLMOTT. "The Paramount Interests of Britain and America," *Foreign Affairs: an American Quarterly Review,* XIII (July, 1935), 574–582.

LEYLAND, JOHN. "The United States Navy in the Making," *The Nineteenth Century and After,* LXXX (October, 1916), 785–798.

LOCKEY, JOSEPH B. "A Neglected Aspect of Isthmian Diplomacy," *The American Historical Review,* XLI (January, 1936), 295–305.

MACHRAY, ROBERT. "Japan's Part in the War," *The Nineteenth Century and After,* LXXX (September, 1916), 531–542.

———. "The Sino-Japanese Military Convention," *The Fortnightly Review,* CX (August, 1918), 245–255.

MCPHERSON, HALLIE M., ed. "Documents: The Projected Purchase of Alaska, 1859–60," *The Pacific Historical Review,* III (March, 1934), 80–87.

———. "The Interest of William McKendree Gwin in the Purchase of Alaska, 1854–1861," *The Pacific Historical Review,* III (March, 1934), 28–38.

MAHAN, ALFRED T. "The True Significance of the Pacific Cruise," *Scientific American,* XCVII (December 7, 1907), 407, 412, 413.

MARRIOTT, J. A. R. "Mitteleuropa and the Meaning of the Paris Pact," *The Nineteenth Century and After,* LXXX (November, 1916), 1097–1112.

MILLARD, THOMAS F. "America in China," *The Forum,* XLIV (July, 1910), 67–89.

———. "The Japanese Menace," *The Century Magazine,* XCI (March, 1916), 673–682.

MITFORD, E. BRUCE. "Action and Reaction in the Far East," *The Fortnightly Review,* CV (January, 1916), 153–162.

MOORE, JOHN BASSETT. "The Peace Problem," *Columbia University Quarterly,* XVIII (June, 1916), 210–225.

MURRAY, GILBERT. "Great Britain's Sea Policy," *The Atlantic Monthly,* CXVIII (December, 1916), 732–745.

MUSSEY, HENRY RAYMOND. "Neglected Realities in the Far East," *Proceedings of the Academy of Political Science,* VII (July, 1917), [14–23], 538–547.

[Naval Expert, A]. "Selling out Alaska," *The Century Magazine,* XCIII (December, 1916), 241–248.

NOTZ, WILLIAM. "Export Trade Problems and an American Foreign Trade Policy," *The Journal of Political Economy,* XXVI (February, 1918), 105–124.

OKUMA, COUNT SHIGENOBU. "Japan's Policy in Korea," *The Forum,* XXXVII (April–June, 1906), 571–580.

OLNEY, RICHARD. "Growth of Our Foreign Policy," *The Atlantic Monthly,* LXXXV (March, 1900), 289–301.

———. "International Isolation of the United States," *The Atlantic Monthly,* LXXXI (May, 1898), 577–588.

ORCHARD, JOHN E. "Economic Consequences of Japan's Asiatic Policy," *Foreign Affairs: an American Quarterly Review,* XII (October, 1933), 71–85.

———. "Oriental Competition in World Trade," *Foreign Affairs: an American Quarterly Review,* XV (July, 1937), 707–719.

PATTERSON, E. M., ed. "America's Changing Investment Market," *The Annals of the American Academy of Political and Social Science,* LXVIII (November, 1916), 1–342.

———., ed. "American Policy in the Pacific," *The Annals of the American Academy of Political and Social Science,* CLXVIII (July, 1933), 1–274.

PIESSE, E. L. "Japan and Australia," *Foreign Affairs: an American Quarterly Review,* IV (April, 1926), 475–488.

PIGGOTT, SIR FRANCIS J. "China and the War," *The Nineteenth Century and After,* LXXVII (March, 1915), 531–559.

POLLEN, ARTHUR H. "The Needs of Our Navy, As Perceived by the Foremost British Expert," *The North American Review,* CCIII (March, 1916), 345–362.

PRATT, WILLIAM V. "The Broad Aspect of Our Pacific Problem," *United States Naval Institute Proceedings,* LIII (January, 1927), 1–12.

———. "Our Naval Policy," *United States Naval Institute Proceedings,* LVIII (July, 1932), 953–970.

PROCTOR, JOHN R. "Hawaii and the Changing Front of the World," *The Forum,* XXIV (September, 1897), 34–45.

RADEK, KARL. "The Bases of Soviet Foreign Policy," *Foreign Affairs: an American Quarterly Review,* XII (January, 1934), 193–206.

RAKOVSKY, CHRISTIAN. "The Foreign Policy of Soviet Russia," *Foreign Affairs: an American Quarterly Review,* IV (July, 1926), 574–584.

REA, GEORGE BRONSON. "Closing the Open Door," *The North American Review,* CCIII (May, 1916), 690–699.

ROBERTS, GEORGE E. "Property Rights and Trade Rivalries As Factors in International Complications," *Proceedings of the Academy of Political Science,* VII (July, 1917), [99–114] 623–638.

RODGERS, W. L. "The Navy As an Aid in Carrying Out Diplomatic Policies," *United States Naval Institute Proceedings,* LV (February, 1929), 99–104.

ROMULO, CARLOS P. "The Philippines Look at Japan," *Foreign Affairs: an American Quarterly Review,* XIV (April, 1936), 476–486.

ROOP, W. P. "The Naval Policy of the United States in the Pacific Area," *United States Naval Institute Proceedings,* XLIX (March, 1923), 409–426.

ROORBACH, G. B., ed. "The International Trade Situation," *The Annals of the American Academy of Political and Social Science,* XCIV (March, 1921), 1–226.

ROOSEVELT, THEODORE. "How the United States Acquired the Right to Dig the Panama Canal," [Editorial] *The Outlook,* XCIX (October 7, 1911), 314–318.

ROOT, ELIHU. "The Real Monroe Doctrine," *The American Journal of International Law,* VIII (July, 1914), 427–442.

———. "The Real Questions under the Japanese Treaty and the San Francisco School Board Resolution," *The American Journal of International Law,* I (July, 1907), 273–286.

SCOTT, F. R. "The Permanent Bases of Canadian Foreign Policy," *Foreign Affairs: an American Quarterly Review,* X (July, 1932), 617–631.

SFORZA, COUNT CARLO. "Imperialistic Russia in China," *Foreign Affairs: an American Quarterly Review,* VI (October, 1927), 67–74.

SHEPHERD, WILLIAM R. "Our Trade with South America and China," *Proceedings of the Academy of Political Science,* VI (October, 1915), 163–167.

SHIBUSAWA, BARON EIICHI. "America and Japan," *The Century Mazagine,* XCI (February, 1916), 541–544.

SHIGEOKA, KUNGORO. "What Japan Should Do for Korea," *The American Review of Reviews,* XXX (September, 1904), 349, 350.

SHIPPEE, LESTER B. "Germany and the Spanish-American War," *The American Historical Review,* XXX (July, 1925), 754–777.

SIEWERT, WULF. "Die Seemachtlage im Fernen Osten," *Zeitschrift für Geo-Politik,* XV (June, 1938), 428–438.

SMITH, THEODORE C. "Expansion after the Civil War, 1865–71," *Political Science Quarterly,* XVI (September, 1901), 412–436.

SPENALE, GEORGES. "La rivalité du Japon et des Etats-Unis dans le Pacifique," *Revue d'histoire des colonies,* XXIV (October, 1936), 213–266.

SPERBER, O. P. "Strategical and Economical Importance of the Panama Canal," *Overland Monthly,* LVII (April, 1911), 409–412.

SPURR, JOSIAH EDWARD. "Steel-making Minerals," *Foreign Affairs: an American Quarterly Review,* IV (July, 1926), 601–612.

STEED, WICKHAM. "British Policy in the Pacific," *The Nineteenth Century and After,* CXI (April, 1932), 396–409.

———. "Freedom of the Seas the Crux of Disarmament: A British Point of View," *Current History* XXIX (February, 1929), 721–727.

STIMSON, HENRY L. "Future Philippine Policy under the Jones Act," *Foreign Affairs: an American Quarterly Review,* V (April, 1927), 459–471.

STIRLING, YATES, JR. "Naval Preparedness in the Pacific Area," *United States Naval Institute Proceedings,* LX (May, 1934), 601–608.

STODDARD, T. LOTHROP. "The Economic Heresy of the Allies," *The Century Magazine,* XCIII (December, 1916), 260–265.

———. "The Japanese Question in California," *The Annals of the American Academy of Political and Social Science,* XCIII (January, 1921), 42–47.

STRAIGHT, WILLARD. "Governmental Policy and Trade Relations with the Far East," *Proceedings of the Academy of Political Science,* VI (October, 1915), 147–153.

SUTTON, CHARLES W. "The Relation of Government to Property and Enterprise in the Americas," *Proceedings of the Academy of Political Science,* VII (July, 1917), [310–321] 502–513.

TAUSSIG, F. W. "How to Promote Foreign Trade," *The Quarterly Journal of Economics,* XXXII (May, 1918), 417–445.

———. "Necessary Changes in Our Commercial Policy," *Foreign Affairs: an American Quarterly Review,* XI (April, 1933), 397–405.

THAYER, WILLIAM R., ed. and comp. "John Hay and the Panama Republic" [From the unpublished letters of John Hay], *Harper's Magazine,* CXXXI (July, 1915), 165–175.

THOMAS, EUGENE P. "Investment and Trade in China," *Proceedings of the Academy of Political Science,* VI (October, 1915), 154–162.

TOGO, M. "Japan and Ships," *The North American Review,* CCVII (March, 1918), 370–377.

VIALLATE, ACHILLE. "Les Etats-Unis d'amerique et le conflit Européen: consequences politiques," *Revue des sciences politiques,* XXXVI (December 15, 1916), 360–381.

VINER, JACOB. "National Monopolies of Raw Materials," *Foreign Affairs: an American Quarterly Review,* IV (July, 1926), 585–600.

WILSON, HUNTINGTON. "The Relation of Government to Foreign Investment," *The Annals of the American Academy of Political and Social Science,* LXVIII (November, 1916), 298–311.

YOUNG, GEORGE. "The Freedom of the Seas," *The New Europe,* X (January 16, 1919), 5–9.

Unsigned Articles

"American Naval Expansion," *The Engineer* [London], CXXII (August 11, 1916), 122–123.

"England and Germany," *Saturday Review of Politics,* LXXXIV (September 11, 1897), 278, 279.

"Japanese Naval Expansion," *The Engineer* [London], CXXV (March 8, 1918), 206.

"La conférence économique des Alliés," *L'économiste français,* XLIV (June 17, 1916), 827, 828.

"The Premier of Japan to the American People, A Message from Count Okuma," *The Independent,* LXXIX (August 31, 1914), 291.

Miscellaneous Periodicals

The China Year Book.

The Commercial and Financial Chronicle. Weekly.

Deutsche Wehr, die Zeitschrift für Wehrmacht und Wehrpolitik. Weekly.

The Economist, Weekly Commercial Times, Bankers Gazette, and Railway Monitor (London).

Export, Organ des Centralvereins für Handelsgeographie und Förderung Deutscher Interessen im Auslande. (Berlin). Weekly.

The Iron Age. Weekly.

The Japan Year Book.

The Literary Digest.

The Mineral Industry, Its Statistics, Technology, and Trade in the United States and Other Countries, ed. Richard P. Rothwell *et al.* (New York). Annual.

The Naval Annual (London, J. Griffin).

The New York Times.

The Statesman's Year Book.

The Times (London).

Transactions and Proceedings of the Japan Society, London.

INDEX

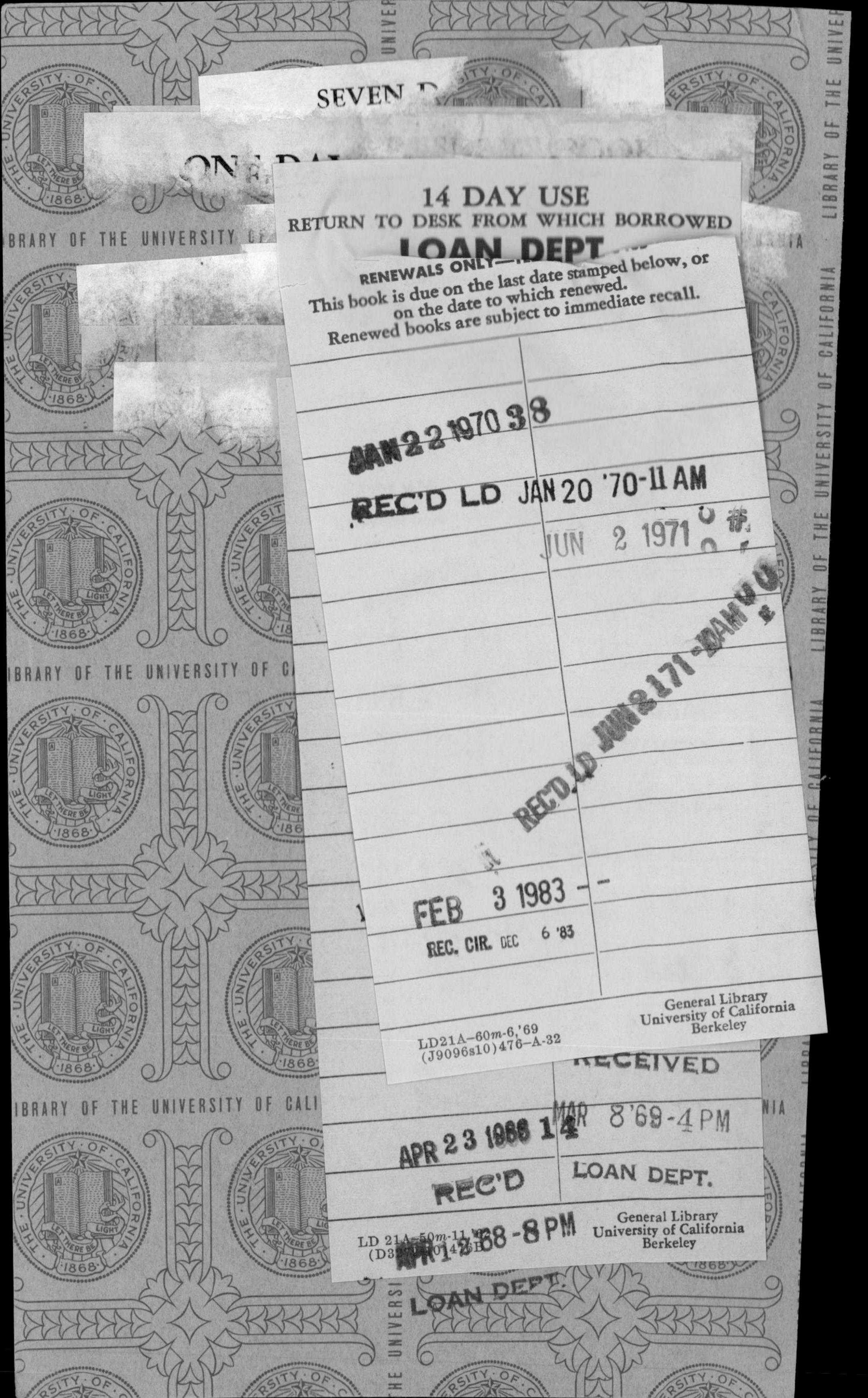

SEVEN D
ONE DAY
14 DAY USE
RETURN TO DESK FROM WHICH BORROWED
LOAN DEPT
RENEWALS ONLY
This book is due on the last date stamped below, or
on the date to which renewed.
Renewed books are subject to immediate recall.
JAN 22 1970 3 8
REC'D LD JAN 20 '70-11 AM
JUN 2 1971
REC'D LD JUN 2 1 71
FEB 3 1983
REC. CIR. DEC 6 '83
General Library
University of California
Berkeley
LD21A-60m-6,'69
(J9096s10)476-A-32
RECEIVED
MAR 8'69-4PM
APR 23 1968 14
LOAN DEPT.
REC'D
APR 12 '68 -8 PM
LD 21A-50m-11
General Library
University of California
Berkeley
LOAN DEPT.
LIBRARY OF THE UNIVERSITY OF CALIFORNIA
THE UNIVERSITY OF CALIFORNIA
LET THERE BE LIGHT
1868